Women & Depression

Other books by M. Sara Rosenthal

The Thyroid Sourcebook

The Gynecological Sourcebook

The Pregnancy Sourcebook

The Fertility Sourcebook

The Breastfeeding Sourcebook

The Breast Sourcebook

The Gastrointestinal Sourcebook

Managing Your Diabetes

Managing Diabetes for Women

The Type 2 Diabetic Woman

The Thyroid Sourcebook for Women

Fifty Ways to Prevent Colon Cancer

Women & Depression

A Sane Approach to Mood Disorders

M. Sara Rosenthal

Foreword by

Dr. Debra Lander

Assistant Professor of Psychiatry
University of Manitoba

LOWELL HOUSE

LOS ANGELES

NTC/Contemporary Publishing Group

Library of Congress Cataloging-in-Publication Data
Rosenthal, M. Sara.
      Women & depression: a sane approach to mood disorders / M. Sara Rosenthal.
          p. cm.
      Includes bibliographical references and index.
      ISBN 0-7373-0325-5
      1. Depression in women—Popluar works. I. Title: Women and depression. II. Title.

RC537.R6385 2000
616.58'27'0082—dc

00-035207
CIP

Excerpts from *An Unquiet Mind* by Kay Redfield Jamison. Copyright © 1995 by Kay Redfield Jamison. Reprinted by permission of Alfred A. Knopf, a Division of Random House, Inc.

"Mental Health Bill of Rights" reprinted with permission of the American Psychological Association. Copyright © 1997 by the American Psychological Association.

Requests for such permissions should be addressed to:

Lowell House
2020 Avenue of the Stars, Suite 300
Los Angeles, CA 90067

Published by Lowell House,
a division of NTC/Contemporary Publishing Group, Inc.
4255 West Touhy Avenue, Lincolnwood, Illinois 60646-1975 U.S.A.

Text design: Wendy Staroba Loreen

Printed and bound in the United States of America

International Standard Book Number: 0-7373-0325-5

00 01 02 03 04 DHD 18 17 16 15 14 13 12 11 10 9 8 7 6 5 4 3 2 1

For my mother, Naomi

Contents

FOREWORD xiii

ACKNOWLEDGMENTS xv

INTRODUCTION
What This Book Is About xix

CHAPTER 1
Are You Depressed or "Just Sad"? 1

Sadness 1
- Sadness versus depression
- Grieving versus depression

Depression 6
- Signs of depression
- Who gets depressed?
- Causes of depression
- When depression is a symptom of a physical ailment
- The genetic link
- Why we become depressed

CHAPTER 2

All Types of Depression   23

Unipolar Disorders: The Moody Blues   24

Bipolar Disorders: Feeling Groovy   28
  • The myth of mania
  • Signs of bipolar disorder
  • The crash
  • Types of bipolar disorders
  • Your mood cycle
  • Almost manic: cyclothymia

Treating Different Types of Depression: An Overview   38
  • Short-term treatment strategies
  • Long-term solutions
  • Family support

CHAPTER 3

**When Depression Is a Symptom of
a Physical Ailment**   43

Normal Stress and Fatigue   44
  • Sleep deprivation
  • Raising a family
  • Lifestyle factors

Chemical Reactions   48
  • Reproductive concerns

Abnormal Fatigue: Chronic Fatigue Syndrome   52
  • The symptoms of CFS
  • What your doctor should rule out
  • Fibromyalgia versus CFS
  • Causes of CFS
  • Treatments

Thyroid Disorders   59
  • Symptoms
  • Treatment

Seasonal Affective Disorder (SAD): Light-Deprived   61
  • Treating SAD

Bathroom Blues   63
  • Hazards of not being able to go to the bathroom
  • Irritable bowels?
  • Bladder problems

Stress Reduction   71
  • A little hedonism goes a long way

CHAPTER 4

**Body Image, Hormones, and
Cycle-Logical Issues**   75

Body Image   75
  • What it means to be thin
  • What it means to be fat
  • The act of getting fat: compulsive eating
  • Drug treatment for obesity
  • Depression, stress, and weight
  • Do you have a body-image problem?

Having the Time of Your Month   88
  • Who cares about premenstrual signs?
  • Do you have premenstrual "disorder"?
  • Tender breasts affect your mood
  • Treating premenstrual changes

Having a Hard Time After Having a Baby   99
  • Maternal blues
  • Postpartum depression (PPD)
  • Postpartum psychosis
  • Postpartum thyroiditis

Depression and Menopause   105
  • The menopause blues

CHAPTER 5

The History of Women and Psychotherapy   109

A Brief History of Women and "Madness"   111
  • The career psych patient
  • Asylum life
  • Women in male therapy

Feminism as a Cure?   118
  • The stigma of sexual abuse
  • Why are liberated women still depressed?

CHAPTER 6

Finding Someone to Talk to   123

In Search of a Good Therapist   123
  • Locating names
  • Looking for credentials
  • Going for a test drive

Styles of Therapy   134
  • Biologically informed psychotherapy
  • Cognitive-behavioral therapy
  • Feminist therapy
  • Interpersonal therapy
  • Psychoanalysis
  • Psychodynamic therapy

Getting the Most Out of Talking Heads   140
  • Repressed memories versus false memories
  • Talking versus drugs
  • When is therapy finished?
  • The rent-a-friend problem

Support Groups   144
- Where do you look for support?
- Understanding your mental health-care rights

CHAPTER 7

Women and Medication   155

Drugs for Depression   157
- Prozac
- SSRIs and hypomania
- Combination therapy

Drugs for Mania   163
- Lithium
- Other mood-stabilizing drugs
- A final word about mania

What to Ask About Your Drugs   167
- A dozen more questions
- A word about dosages
- Drug studies
- Informed consent and medication

Electroconvulsive Therapy (ECT)   173
- The early years of ECT
- Twenty-first century ECT
- Side effects

CHAPTER 8

Self-Healing Strategies   177

How Are You?   177
- Diet and depression
- Carbohydrates and moods
- Exercise and depression
- Common sense
- Herbs

The A–Z of Complementary Medicine   186
- Acupuncture
- Aromatherapy
- Ayurvedic medicine
- Chinese medicine
- Chiropractic medicine
- Environmental medicine
- Holistic medicine
- Homeopathy
- Iridology
- Massage therapy
- Mind/body medicine
- Naturopathy
- Reflexology

Are There Risks?   195

APPENDIX
Where to Go for More Information   197

GLOSSARY   237

BIBLIOGRAPHY   241

INDEX   247

Women & Depression

Foreword

Depression, mood swings, and other mood and anxiety disorders cause great suffering to millions of North Americans. Recently, the U.S. Surgeon General labeled suicide as a major public health problem, and mood disorders are clearly the most important factor related to completed suicides.

Women are particularly vulnerable to a variety of mood disorders. Certainly much has been written on the stressors common to so many women. When experiencing a major depressive episode or a manic episode, it is critical to treat the illness. One must then begin to develop strategies to cope with ongoing stress.

While a variety of effective treatments is available, remarkably, only a fraction of individuals seek treatment. Of those who do, some are so disappointed with the results that they do not continue the therapy.

Why is this? Most often it is because of a lack of knowledge. People assume they can talk themselves out of their depression; families assume that their loved one will "snap out of it." Perhaps it's a matter of medication side effects not being fully explained, and thus the person stops attending appointments and discontinues her medication. Sadly, she may be unaware that there are ways to minimize side effects or that alternate medications may be more easily tolerated.

The value of various psychotherapies to develop coping skills; to address negative thinking; and to develop healthier relationships, etc., may also have been overlooked.

Women & Depression provides valuable information for women (and men) who suffer from mood disorders. The book specifically discusses the distinction between sadness and depression; the nature and treatment of bipolar disorders; therapies, including medication and various psychotherapies; and the importance of ruling out underlying medical illness. Various alternative therapies, with less scientific evidence to support them, are also reviewed so that readers will be aware of other available approaches. This book will be a valuable tool in the education process.

Mood disorders often leave people feeling hopeless. Through education and the pursuit of effective treatment, hope can be restored.

DEBRA LANDER, M.D., F.R.C.P.C.

Acknowledgments

I wish to thank the following people, whose expertise and dedication helped to lay so much of the groundwork for this book:

Debra Lander, M.D., F.R.C.P.C., Assistant Professor of Psychiatry, University of Manitoba, served as medical adviser. Without her suggestions and contributions, this book would not have come to fruition. Mark Lander, M.D., F.R.C.P.C., Associate Professor of Psychiatry, University of Manitoba, and a member of the Mood Disorders Clinic, Health Sciences Centre, Winnipeg, Manitoba; and Sheila Lander, L.P.N./R.N., a psychiatric nurse practitioner, Health Sciences Centre, Winnipeg, Manitoba, spent an enormous amount of time reading through selected chapters and making valuable suggestions for content.

I'd also like to thank Donna Stewart, M.D., F.R.C.P.; Lillian Love Chair in Women's Health, University Health Network and University of Toronto; Judith Ross, Ph.D., Clinical Psychologist and Special Lecturer, Department of Psychology, University of Toronto; and Trudo Lemmens, Lic. Iur., LL.M. (bioethics), Assistant Professor, Faculty of Law, Department of Molecular Medicine and Microbiology and Department of Psychiatry, University of Toronto, and formerly bioethicist at the Centre for Addiction and Mental Health, for reading selected chapters and making important content suggestions. Robert S. Williams, B.A. (Hons.), B.S.W., M.F.A., M.S.W.,

Ph.D. (candidate), University of Toronto Joint Centre for Bioethics, spent a great deal of time explaining the politics and system of mental health to me, as well as made significant content suggestions. Clinical psychologists Sergio Rueda, M.Sc., and Eliana Cohen, M.Sc., Ph.D. (candidate), Department of Psychology, York University, went to great lengths to make sure the content was up-to-date and reflected what *actually* occurs in practice.

Other experts, ranging from social workers and counselors to feminist therapists, gave me dozens of hours of their time and expertise. Some preferred, for reasons of confidentiality, to remain as background experts. But without their suggestions, this book would not be as accurate or as balanced a work. I also wish to thank the women interviewed for this book: Your stories, struggles, and suggestions were greatly appreciated.

A number of past medical advisers on previous works helped me to shape the content for this work. And so I wish to thank the following people (listed alphabetically): Gillian Arsenault, M.D., C.C.F.P., I.B.L.C., F.R.C.P.; Pamela Craig, M.D., F.A.C.S., Ph.D.; Masood Khathamee, M.D., F.A.C.O.G.; Gary May, M.D., F.R.C.P.; James McSherry, M.B., Ch.B., F.C.F.P., F.R.C.G.P., F.A.A.F.P., F.A.B.M.P.; Suzanne Pratt, M.D., FA.C.O.G.; and Robert Volpe, M.D., F.R.C.P., F.A.C.P.

William Harvey, Ph.D., L.L.B., Director, University of Toronto Joint Centre for Bioethics, whose devotion to bioethics has inspired me, continues to support my work, and makes it possible for me to have the courage to question and challenge issues in health care and medical ethics. Irving Rootman, Ph.D., Director, University of Toronto Centre for Health Promotion, continues to encourage my interest in primary-prevention and health-promotion issues. Helen Lenskyj, Ph.D., Department of Sociology and Equity Studies, Ontario Institute for Studies in Education/University of Toronto; and Laura M. Purdy, Ph.D., Department of Philosophy, University of Toronto, and bioethicist, University of Toronto Joint Centre for

Bioethics have been central figures in my understanding the complexities of women's health issues and feminist bioethics.

Larissa Kostoff, my editorial consultant, worked hard to make this book happen. Finally, Hudson Perigo, my editor, made many wonderful and thoughtful suggestions to help make this book what it is.

Introduction

*W*hat This Book Is About

In the majority of cases, women suffering from depression have *unipolar depression,* a mood disorder characterized by one low mood. This is distinct from *bipolar depression,* a mood disorder in which there are two moods: one high and one low.

Most cases of unipolar depression are caused by life's circumstances, which is why mental health-care professionals often use the term *situational depression* to describe mild, moderate, or even severe unipolar depression in women. Examples of life events that can trigger depression include:

- illness
- loss of a loved one (the relationship may have ended or a loved one may have died)
- reproductive life change (childbirth, hysterectomy, or menopause)
- job loss or change
- moving

Situational depression can also mean that your unipolar depression has been triggered by the *absence* of change in your life, meaning that you are living in a state of continuous struggle, unhappiness, or stress in which no light appears at the end of the tunnel. Examples of continuous struggle include:

- chronic illness
- abusive relationships
- poverty and/or economic worries
- job stress
- body-image problems, such as feeling fat or unattractive

A third trigger for situational depression can be an absence of resolution regarding traumas and abuses you suffered as a child or younger woman. Examples of past traumas include:

- sexual abuse
- incest
- violence
- rape
- emotional abuse

The first thing this book will do is to help you verify whether you are, in fact, depressed. Chapter 1 details the symptoms of depression and clearly distinguishes these symptoms from the features of normal sadness and grief. Chapter 2 will help you to make sense of the medical jargon surrounding depression so you can understand what your mental health-care provider is talking about if you decide to seek treatment. Chapter 3 is also a "verifying" chapter in that it addresses women whose symptoms of depression are actually symptoms of an underlying chronic illness or condition, such as chronic fatigue syndrome, environmental or stress-related illnesses, thyroid disorders, or even simply a lack of sunlight (known as SAD, seasonal affective disorder).

If you're struggling with depression, this book can help you to understand how you got there by discussing women's situations in life and society at large. Many readers will identify immediately with the situations discussed, but others may see for the first time how one's culture can chip away at self-esteem. Examples of how this occurs involve imposition of unfair roles, as well as standards of beauty or ability that can make it hard for you to achieve your personal or professional goals. The purpose of such discussion is to assure you that you are not alone in your struggles with life and that many such struggles are not your fault. Instead, they may originate because you're a woman living in a nine-to-five culture that was initially structured for a white male who does not menstruate, get pregnant, breast-feed, or go through menopause. That fact alone makes it hard to get along in this world. But when you factor in other problems, life can get pretty difficult. Because almost all women are affected by body image and hormonal shifts, which can trigger depression, I devote chapter 4 to these issues.

Finally, this book discusses all the treatment options available to women struggling with depression, including all the forms of talk therapy (chapter 6), medication and herbs (chapter 7), self-healing strategies, and alternative systems of healing (chapter 8). I also outline your rights as a patient receiving help for depression.

I believe it's impossible to present a complete picture of the treatment for depression without providing you with some history on how women *used* to be diagnosed and treated for depression, which is the focus of chapter 5. Although such material has typically been excluded from other books on depression, I believe these past experiences in psychotherapy often led to more problems than solutions and helped to shape the woman-centered approaches to therapy seen today.

Many experts in the field of mental health were consulted for this book. In some cases, opinions on treatment were divided. Where there was consensus, I used the phrase *mental health experts* to convey general recommendations and opinions ranging from psychiatrists to social workers. Where there was controversy, I said so and outlined the differing opinions. In some cases, I even stated criticisms made about this text. I welcome your questions and comments and can be contacted in care of the publisher.

Overall, there are many messages in this book, but they are simple ones. Some of us just need a break. Some of us need validation. Some of us need to modify our lifestyles to reduce stress and incorporate other systems of healing, ranging from herbs to therapeutic massage. Some of us need medication. Some of us need talk therapy. Some of us need all of the above. If your emotional life is unhappy and a struggle, *Women & Depression* will help you to figure out *what* you need and *who* can help.

$\mathscr{A}$re You Depressed or "Just Sad"?

Everyone experiences sadness, bad days, and bad moods. Feeling sad is not the same as depression. So the first order of business is to define what normal sadness is and how that is distinct from depression. This chapter will define the symptoms of depression, explore possible situations that can trigger the condition, and offer reasons why some of us are more prone to depression than others. Many physicians use surveys on behavior (such as on page 2) as an aid to the diagnosis of depression.

If you're unclear as to whether you're "just sad" or depressed, remember: Even if you don't exhibit the obvious or classic symptoms of depression discussed in this chapter, thinking you may be depressed is a good enough reason to seek help.

SADNESS

What is sadness? *Sadness* can be defined as mental anguish or suffering in the absence of any physical pain, as in experiencing the death of a loved one or empathizing with a loved one who is ill. For

• • • • • • • • • •

Review the following symptoms. If you answer yes to four or more of the questions below, you may be suffering from depression.
For at least two weeks, have you . . .

- been feeling down, low, or blue almost every day?
- lost interest in things you once enjoyed?
- lost energy, felt physically tired or fatigued?
- had trouble concentrating or making decisions?
- felt agitated or restless, sluggish, or slowed down?
- thought about death or wanted to die, or felt life isn't worth living?
- worried, or felt guilty about things you have no control over or didn't do?
- had trouble sleeping, or been oversleeping?
- lost your appetite or had weight loss, or been overeating or had weight gain?

Source: Adapted from Russell Joffe, M.D., and Anthony Levitt, M.D., *Conquering Depression* (Hamilton: Empowering Press, 1998), pp. 34–35.

• • • • • • • • • •

example, a mother watching her child suffer is not herself feeling physical pain, but she still suffers and experiences sadness. When you are sad, you express your emotions by crying, talking, or thinking constantly about your sorrow. You find it difficult to sleep or concentrate, or you may be unable to eat. Sadness is characterized by sad *feelings*, which is the opposite of numbness—the main feature of depression.

The problem for so many people in affluent cultures is that sadness is not triggered by anything obvious. For example, sadness can develop when you realize your life is not improving. Stagnating, or "being in a rut," or finding your life is growing worse rather than better are conditions that lead to sadness and suffering. As human beings, once our basic needs (safety, food, shelter, love) are satisfied, we are driven toward self-actualization. But when our life circumstances stymie self-actualization or spiritual growth, we suffer—and feel sad. The longing for material possessions, money, or an intimate relationship is often just an expression of longing for self-realization. Later in life, many of us also begin to question our attachments to material possessions and power. We see the difference between real needs (e.g., love, friendship, respect) and artificial needs (e.g., money, power, or prestige).

When you are content with your life, an abrupt change in the status quo can also cause sadness and suffering, which threatens your identity or selfhood. The "threat" can be from an infinite variety of sources, of course, ranging from physical illness (such as breast cancer) to financial hardship.

Sadness Versus Depression

Sadness *lifts*, depression *persists*. That's how you can tell if you're just feeling sad or are actually depressed. Feelings of sadness and grief are common and normal in an infinite variety of circumstances. Again, the symptoms of sadness often mirror depression: You're crying; you can't sleep; you can't eat. But eventually, as time passes and you find yourself returning to your routine, the sadness lifts. You may still be sad or grieving, but you can also enjoy elements of your life and put your thoughts on the back burner. That's not to say that the problem disappears, but with the right support you will be able to cope. You may need to talk about your problem or life event to friends or family, but every day gets easier. You *can* get out of bed and appreciate *something* in life, whether it's a nice day, a funny movie, or a good dessert.

However, when you're depressed, *nothing* lifts. Life grows more difficult, is grayer and bleaker, until you begin to feel numb, and what you once found pleasurable no longer interests you. Your ability to function *decreases* with each passing day when you're depressed; your ability to function *increases* with each passing day when you're just sad about something. But the trigger—the event that has caused you to feel sad or depressed—is always real, understandable, and legitimate. Never forget that.

What is tricky about the "sadness versus depression" question is that what triggered your sadness can also trigger a depression. Again, when the symptoms *persist* rather than lift, you are not getting better, which means you may need some help. Instead of every day getting better, every day grows worse. When sadness lifts, you can actually relate to the song lyric: "I can see clearly now, the rain is gone." When depression persists, you are in that "dark cloud that has you blind." I don't mean to be glib, but sometimes songs really do say it best.

Grieving Versus Depression

One of the most common causes of sadness and suffering is grief. If you're grieving the loss of a loved one, and the inability to eat, sleep, or concentrate persists beyond three months, your grief may have developed into depression. Because women generally outlive their spouses, women tend to suffer from grief more often. About 10 percent of all people who suffer the loss of a loved one require treatment for depression. But certain people are more likely to become depressed after a loss: People with a history of depression, people who have lost a relationship of many years, and people who have lost a relationship that was unresolved (creating profound feelings of guilt and regret) are more likely to suffer from depression. When a depression is triggered by grief, there are likely feelings of self-worth that are connected to your loss, which the depression may be bringing to the surface.

It's important to remember that you can also grieve for the loss of someone who is still very much alive. When you experience the end of a relationship or friendship, feelings of grief over that loss are similar to the feelings of grief you experience when someone dies.

For many women, the loss of a pet can elicit profound feelings of grief. But because of embarrassment over the feelings we have for our pets, many of us are afraid to admit or express such grief. Pets are real companions that offer unconditional acceptance and love. They may serve as vessels for many emotions that are never "released" into relationships with our own species. And, unlike the loss of a human being, people are often guilt-ridden over putting their pets to sleep, which adds another dimension to their grieving.

Grief may have progressed to depression when:

- your grief persists longer than three months
- you feel like dying or are suicidal
- you experience hallucinations or delusions (e.g., you may see your loved one or believe he is still alive)
- you feel depressed every day and have experienced the symptoms of depression discussed on page 7 for more than a month
- you aren't caring for yourself (e.g., you're not eating or bathing).

In the film *Men Don't Leave,* Jessica Lange gives a faithful portrayal of a depression brought on by grief. Lange plays a homemaker who lacks the skills necessary for employment but who must suddenly provide for her two sons after her husband is killed in an accident. She goes through the normal stages of grieving and seems able to make significant changes in her life to respond to her new financial pressures and realities. She sells her house in a rural area and moves to an apartment in the nearby urban center. She finds a job with a catering company. She *seems* to be doing well, all things considered. But her life begins to fall apart when loneliness sets in, and the stresses of being a single parent overwhelm her. She drifts into a depression: She goes to bed for five consecutive days. In a particularly poignant scene, her son tries to wake her, asking her if she's still "tired." Barely able to get out of bed, Lange's character asks her son if he's hungry. When he replies "yes," she drags herself out of bed into a dirty, unkempt kitchen and serves him a peanut butter sandwich on a paper towel and gives him tap water to drink when she discovers there is no milk or juice in the house. The kitchen table is piled high with dirty laundry and dishes. The child sits at a clean "corner" of the table, quietly eating his sandwich while his mother heads back to bed. She awakens the next day out of what looks like a fitful sleep and stumbles into the kitchen to feed herself—cold spaghetti out of a can. What's so accurate about this portrayal is that the depression doesn't immediately follow the death of the husband; it takes several months to manifest. But it is still triggered by feelings of loss and grief.

DEPRESSION

Depression is distinct from sadness in that it is a point *beyond* it and is characterized by a numbness and inability to act. Depression is clinically known as a mood disorder. It's impossible to define what a normal mood is since we all have such complex personalities and exhibit different moods throughout a given week—or even a given day. But it's not impossible for *you* to define what your normal mood is. *You* know how you feel when you're functioning: You're eating, sleeping, interacting with friends and family, being productive, active, and generally interested in life's daily occurrences. Well, depression is when you feel you've *lost* the ability to function for a prolonged period of time. Or, if you're functioning at a reasonable level to the outside world, you've lost *interest* in participating in life.

Signs of Depression

One bad day or bad week (including "relief time," when you laugh or take pleasure in something) from time to time is not a sign that you're depressed. Feeling you've lost the ability to function *normally*, all day, every day, for a period of at least two weeks may be a sign that you're depressed. The symptoms of depression vary from person to person but can include some or all of the following:

* feelings of sadness and/or "empty mood"
* difficulty sleeping (usually waking up frequently in the middle of the night)
* loss of energy and feelings of fatigue and lethargy
* change in appetite (usually a loss of appetite)
* difficulty thinking, concentrating, or making decisions
* loss of interest in formerly pleasurable activities, including sex
* anxiety or panic attacks
* obsessing over negative experiences or thoughts
* feeling guilty, worthless, hopeless, or helpless
* feeling restless and irritable
* thinking about death or suicide

When you can't sleep

A depressed person's typical sleep pattern is to go to bed at the normal time, only to wake up around two in the morning and find that they can't fall back to sleep. Endless hours are spent watching infomercials or simply tossing and turning, usually obsessing over negative experiences or thoughts. Lack of sleep affects your ability to function and leads to increased irritability, loss of energy, and fatigue. Insomnia by itself is not a sign of depression, but when you look at depression as a package of symptoms, the inability to fall or stay asleep can aggravate all your other symptoms.

And in some cases, people who are depressed oversleep, requiring ten to twelve hours of sleep every night.

When you can't think clearly

Another debilitating feature of depression is finding that you simply can't concentrate or think clearly. You feel scattered, disorganized, and unable to prioritize. This usually hits hardest in the workplace or a center of learning and can severely impair your performance on the job. You may miss important deadlines and important meetings or find you can't focus when you *do* attend meetings. When you can't think clearly, you can be overwhelmed with feelings of help-lessness or hopelessness. *I can't even perform a simple task such as X anymore* may dominate your thoughts, while you become more dis-illusioned with your dwindling productivity.

Anhedonia: When nothing gives you pleasure

One of the most telling signs of depression is a loss of interest in ac-tivities that used to excite, enthuse, or give you pleasure. This is known as anhedonia, derived from the word *hedonism* (meaning the "philosophy of pleasure"). A hedonist is a person who indulges her every pleasure without considering (or caring about) the conse-quences. Anhedonia simply means "no pleasure."

Different people have different ways of expressing anhedonia. You might tell your friends that you have "no desire" to do X or Y; you can't "get motivated"; or X or Y just doesn't "hold your interest or attention." You may also notice that you no longer feel a sense of satisfaction from a job well done. For example, artists (photogra-phers, painters, writers, etc.) may find the passion has gone out of their work.

However, many of the other symptoms of depression hinge on this loss of pleasure. One of the reasons weight loss is so common in depression is because food and/or cooking no longer gives the de-pressed person pleasure. The sense of satisfaction we get from hav-ing a clean home or clean kitchen may also disappear. Therefore, tackling cleaning up the kitchen in order to prepare food may be too taxing, which contributes to a lack of interest in food.

Of course, weight gain is also common because a depressed per-son may not eat properly, filling up on snack foods, or high-calorie, low-nutrient foods because she's not motivated to prepare or eat

When You Feel Life Isn't Worth Living

About 40 percent of all people who suffer from depression have thoughts of suicide. You may have hoarded pills, bought a gun, prepared a will, or written a suicide letter. If you're thinking life isn't worth living or considering acting on your thoughts, doing just one of these things can help:

- Immediately call a friend, family member, therapist (if you have one), or family doctor (if you have one). Tell this person how you're feeling and ask for help to make it through the moment/hour/day.

- Go directly to a hospital emergency room and seek help from a doctor, nurse, or other health-care provider.

- Call a help line, listed in your white pages.

  (If you live with someone you believe may be suicidal, lock away knives, guns, or other weapons, and empty the medicine cabinets of all medicines. You may also need to restrict access to car keys. Then call 911 and report your concerns; an emergency-services team can help get your loved one to the right professional.)

well-balanced meals. Weight gain may also come from a loss of interest in physical activities: exercising, sports, or a dozen other things that keep us active when we're feeling "ourselves."

A loss of interest in sex aggravates matters if we are in a sexual relationship. Again, the decreased desire for sex stems from general anhedonia.

Anhedonia was described by Dimitri F. Papolos and Janice Papolos in *Overcoming Depression:*

Joy, affection, desire, pride, humor are all drained away. What makes life worth living disappears slowly, relentlessly until nothing seems to be left. . . . Anhedonia creeps in and claims the person who once laughed with you, who once hugged you. . . .

Women suffering from depression also report feelings of self-blame or self-hatred, as well as physical symptoms such as headaches and gastrointestinal problems.

Who Gets Depressed?

More then nineteen million adult Americans older than eighteen suffer from some type of depression each year. And according to a recent joint study by the World Health Organization, the World Bank, and Harvard University, depression is the leading cause of disability in the United States and worldwide. Nearly twice as many women (12 percent) as men (7 percent) are affected by a depressive illness. There are reasons for this:

1. The social conditions for women are often more difficult than they are for men (discussed further in chapter 5), and women tend to seek help more often than men do.
2. Women in their twenties and thirties are at greater risk for postpartum depression, discussed in detail in chapter 4.
3. In later years, women are often grieving over the loss of their spouses.
4. There is genetic theory (criticized by many) purporting that depression may be inherited through the X chromosome; since women have two X chromosomes and men have only one, this theory suggests that it's only natural that women would suffer twice the incidence of depression. Most feminists find this to be simplistic, if not sexist, theory and reject it on the grounds that "biology is not destiny"—a famous feminist adage.

Statistics show that Americans born after 1940 more often suffer from depression and other mood disorders than those born before 1940. But such data say much more about the *social* structure that has emerged since 1940 than they do about people—more specifically, women and depression. There is no proof, however, that more women are depressed *today* than they were during, say, the Great Depression (no pun intended). That's because no one studied or "counted" how many women were depressed during that time; if someone did, it is likely she would have found high numbers of depressed women, given the lot of women at that time, as well as the economic misery of that period.

Causes of Depression

Since most episodes of depression are triggered by life events or circumstances, the causes of depression are different for everyone. In a *general* way, the direct answer to "what causes depression" is difficult circumstances. Understanding what's "difficult" is akin to understanding pain thresholds. What one woman finds difficult, another may not.

We also know that depression is on the rise—or, at least, the *diagnosis* of depression is on the rise. Not unlike other illnesses or diseases, when there is awareness and active screening for a particular condition, there is a rise in its incidence. (In other words, when you're looking for something, you'll find it.) Today, active screening is done primarily through diagnostic criteria listed in the American Psychiatric Association's *Diagnostic and Statistical Manual of Mental Disorders,* 4th edition *(DSM IV),* an often-criticized "recipe book" of psychiatric symptoms. But, of course, *not looking* for something doesn't mean it isn't there. The question remains: Is it better to seek depression and treat it, and end unnecessary suffering? Many health-care practitioners would answer "yes."

Although there is some agreement among health-care providers that depression is a biological state (in that, yes, brain chemistry is *altered* in depressed people), it is unusual for this to occur in the *absence* of an environmental trigger, which is defined as a life event or chronic situation. This can be an actual emotional trauma, such as a divorce or death; unresolved traumas from the past that were "buried"; anger that is being repressed (a significant contributing factor for women); stress from the workplace; physical illness; and a million other things. As mentioned in the Introduction, when a life event triggers depression, mental health-care experts refer to this as situational depression (also known as reactive, or precipitated depression).

Some depressing circumstances

It's useful to look at the life events that are common triggers of situational depression in women. Many of the symptoms of depression are understandable and *logical,* given some of the following situations. (In other words, you'd be crazy *not* to be depressed.) Keep in mind that this "top ten" list is not exhaustive but is designed to give you a comprehensive scope of women's experiences. (I've left birthdays *off* the list, but they are frequent triggers of depression because they represent aging, and feelings of loss of beauty, vitality, and power. Difficult birthdays are typically ones that end in five or zero.) Stress and fatigue, by-products of many of the following situations, are discussed in chapter 3.

Violence. One of the most identifiable difficult circumstances is violence. While statistics vary (as a result of the underreporting of violence), according to the majority staff of the Senate Judiciary Committee, University of Maryland Women's Studies Database, three out of four women will be victims of at least one violent crime during their lifetimes. In 1998, the number of women abused by their husbands was greater than the number of women who married. Domestic violence experts report that these assaults can range from physical and sexual to verbal, and that a single woman can have many assailants (most often men with whom she has relationships of trust—fathers, husbands, uncles, cousins, brothers, boyfriends). For example, 25 percent of women surveyed had been assaulted by a current or past sexual partner.

Domestic violence is said to follow a cycle, because it is not a continuous daily assault. It is a cycle with its own "hot" and "cold" phases. Tensions build, erupt, and then calm until the next cycle begins. The period of calm is what experts call the "honeymoon phase," where the "Mr. Good" appears until "Mr. Bad" resurfaces and takes over the abuser's personality.

Violence, in all its forms, can lead to feelings of self-blame, self-hatred, anxiety, guilt, loss of interest in formerly pleasurable activities (including sexual activities), as well as a host of physical symptoms, ranging from headaches to gastrointestinal problems, not to mention injuries due to physical assault.

Violence and pregnancy. Depending upon the population studied, it's estimated that 4 to 20 percent of women will be physically assaulted by a male partner or ex-partner during their pregnancies. And a 1994 report in the *Journal of the American Medical Association* suggests that 37 percent of all obstetrics patients may be abused during pregnancy.

In a survey of 6,002 households, psychiatrists Donna E. Steward and Gail Erlick Robinson discovered that a pregnant woman's risk of being abused was 60.6 percent greater than that of a nonpregnant woman. Assault by a partner during pregnancy is a high-risk situation. If you are battered during pregnancy, your baby is four times more likely to be born underweight; and you are twice as likely to miscarry. Some experts cite domestic violence during pregnancy as the leading cause of birth defects and infant death.

Studies have also shown that the younger and less financially stable you are when you become pregnant, the more likely you are to experience the *initial* assault from your partner. This first violent episode is triggered by the threat that the often unplanned child poses to the abuser. Women who are first abused in pregnancy suffer psychological trauma from the attack, which can include feelings of shock, numbness, withdrawal, and even denying that the episode occurred. At the same time, fear for the safety of the unborn child is often the predominant emotion. The abuse can also lead to stress, feelings of isolation (and possibly missed medical appointments out of shame), and depression—which can also trigger severe postpartum depression. Being in an abusive environment during pregnancy can also aggravate other chronic conditions, such as hypertension, diabetes, or asthma. Depression can also interfere with placental nourishment, as well as trigger premature labor.

If you are in a relationship with a batterer, the pregnancy may prompt a honeymoon phase with your partner, but it's likely that the battering will continue. Nearly 50 percent of abusive husbands batter their wives when they are pregnant. And the assaults usually escalate after the birth of the baby, when sleep deprivation pushes the abuser's buttons even more, causing him to lash out at a woman's preoccupation with the newborn, unavailability for sex, and normal adjustment to parenthood.

Poverty. Single women and women of color are far more likely to live in poverty than white men. After a divorce, a man's income increases by roughly 20 percent, yet a woman's income decreases by at least 50 percent. In 1995, the average wage per hour for an American male was $10.05, compared with $8.16 for an American female (or $538 compared with $406 median weekly). Difficulty paying bills and making ends meet lead to feelings of anxiety, sleeplessness, stress, guilt, irritability, and persistent physical symptoms. Poverty is tiring: Many women must work at two or three jobs in order to survive and cannot afford some of the conveniences that make life easier. This can lead to such symptoms as fatigue, loss of energy, and loss of appetite.

Women in debt is a new spin on poverty, and this poverty is often hidden by women who are living in seemingly comfortable surroundings, even though they have hit the limit on their credit cards to pay the rent in between jobs or contracts; are being harassed by creditors; and are one day away from having the car repossessed. That said, spending beyond one's means is often a sign of mania, which is discussed in the next chapter.

It's also important to note that many women who live in poverty or debt are also the "hidden homeless," even though they are not visible on the streets. Untold numbers of women camp out on the couches of friends and relatives, as they seek employment or a place to live.

Workplace stress and/or harassment. Even though it's the twenty-first century, women still must cope with sexual harassment, ageism, and sexism in the workplace, which often lead to loss of employment. Those women who are forced to work two jobs to make ends meet can be exposed to twice the abuse on the job in the form of harassment or stress, as well as the plain old stress caused by the long hours and commuting endured by *all* people in the workplace. (See chapter 3 for more details.)

Beauty standards. Impossible standards of beauty are another factor that makes life difficult for women. Aside from body-image anxiety (discussed in chapter 4), the physical symptoms caused by any resulting eating disorder can cause restlessness, irritability, difficulty concentrating or making decisions, loss of interest in formerly pleasurable activities, and feelings of self-doubt and self-hatred.

Hormonal factors. Hormonal changes related to the menstrual cycle, pregnancy, postpartum changes, and menopause could certainly be looked upon as organic causes of depression because hormones can alter behavior and moods. But many women argue that there are social stigmas attached to menstruation and menopause, which cannot be ignored. Heavy, painful periods (often signs of endometriosis) or an unexpected period (due to the unpredictability of menopausal changes) in the middle of a busy workday are not insignificant stresses. Menopause is a social symbol of aging in Western culture which, in itself, has a number of powerful feelings associated with it. (See chapter 4 for more details.)

Illness. A related factor in many cases of depression is chronic illness. Women living with arthritis, osteoporosis, colitis, HIV, AIDS, cancer, and other such chronic diseases can experience many of the symptoms associated with depression, such as loss of appetite, sleeplessness, and loss of interest in formerly pleasurable activities. To aggravate matters, medications used in a variety of situations, ranging from chemotherapy to AZT, can cause depression as well. (See chapter 8 for more details.)

Infertility. Roughly 20 percent of American couples are infertile. A study done by Harvard professor Dr. Alice Domar found that women who were undergoing fertility treatment experienced levels of depression that equaled those of women facing cancer or AIDS. First, the circumstance of infertility by itself can trigger all the feelings and symptoms associated with biological depression. Meanwhile, the hormonal changes created by fertility drugs can also trigger biological depression. Estrogen functions as a weak antidepressant, and when fertility drugs are introduced, your mood can head south. Then, the cost of treatment can place such a strain on your finances, it's, well, depressing. There is also grief involved with being labeled infertile, since women tend to mourn for their unborn children and must accept a change in identity from "mother-to-be" to "childless woman."

Pregnancy loss. This is a common trigger for depression in women of childbearing age. Overall, one in six pregnancies ends in miscarriage; but as women age, the miscarriage rate increases. Women who have struggled with infertility also miscarry at higher rates.

Divorce. Whether you were living in a common-law relationship or were married, the dissolution of a long-term relationship with an intimate partner leads to feelings of grief, sadness, loneliness, isolation, and often financial hardship—all fodder for depression.

When Depression Is a Symptom of a Physical Ailment

Sometimes the signs of depression are actually symptoms of an underlying chronic illness or condition, such as chronic fatigue syndrome, thyroid disorders, environmental or stress-related illnesses, or even simply a lack of sunlight. (This kind of depression is known as SAD, seasonal affective disorder, discussed in greater detail in chapter 3.) In these cases, depression is not triggered by a life event or life situations but by something purely organic, or physical.

For instance, about a year ago an old high school buddy called me, truly distraught over what she called "total body breakdown." She worked in what is referred to as a "sick building," which typically is a building built sometime in the mid- to-late 1960s/early 1970s, with sealed windows for "energy efficiency," recirculated air, harsh fluorescent lighting that triggers headaches and migraines, and an unending supply of dust irritants that wreak havoc on allergy and asthma sufferers. At first, she felt general malaise and fatigue, which she attributed to a flu. As her symptoms grew worse, she began to take more and more days off until she felt she couldn't work at all. Her energy was constantly depleted, and she found it next to impossible to do the laundry, wash dishes, or cook. She called me in the hope I would have some information for her (her call launched me into researching much of what you'll find in chapter 3). Unfortunately, her doctor decided the cause of her problems was internal rather than external, and she was diagnosed with depression. Antidepressants didn't seem to help her condition, and because of the side effects, they actually made her feel worse. After two years spent on the misdiagnosis merry-go-round, she eventually sought the help of a naturopathic doctor, left her job and "sick building" and, as of this writing, reports that she has much more energy, although she still doesn't feel like her old self.

Another variation you will recognize is my neighbor, a good example of the "double-duty" Everywoman. An advertising executive, she endures a one-hour commute to work each way in heavy traffic; she often works until the wee hours of the morning without compensation, all while struggling to raise two teenagers. In her case, real stress and fatigue were diagnosed as depression, but my neighbor (one tough cookie, I might add) refused to accept the diagnosis. While it is hard to distinguish depression from stress, my neighbor made some valid remarks: "How come my symptoms of so-called 'depression' vanish when I'm on holidays, but magically reappear when I return to work? To me, that's a sign that I'm working too hard, not a sign that I need medication. Prozac won't make my deadlines or kids disappear, and it certainly won't make my commutes to work any shorter. Sometimes a bad mood is a healthy re-action to bad traffic, demanding, unappreciative clients, and no child support from my ex-husband."

But when my neighbor realized that her bad moods were *inter-fering* with her ability to deal with demanding clients and affecting her interpersonal relationships, she decided it was time she found ways to *manage* her stress. She finds that yoga, massage therapy, and chocolate icing at certain times of the month have helped her to cope with her stressful life. In short, the skill of "tuning out the world" has helped her to tune it in at a softer frequency.

The Genetic Link

With so many likely triggers of depression, it's logical to ask: "Why isn't *everyone* depressed? *Why me?*" Some researchers believe that certain people have a genetic predisposition to depression. For example, let's say you had a genetic predisposition to lung cancer. If you never smoked, chances are you wouldn't develop lung cancer. But if you smoked, you could potentially "trip" the lung cancer "switch." Meanwhile, if you didn't have a genetic predisposition to lung cancer, you could smoke a pack of cigarettes each day until you were ninety and still might never develop lung cancer. It works the same way with depression. The "cigarettes" in this case are difficult life circumstances, unforeseen stresses and tragedies, and other random acts of misfortune. Some of these circumstances we can control; others are *beyond* our control, requiring us to tap into inner strengths, belief systems, and coping skills.

While no specific gene has yet been found for depression, the hunt is definitely on, yet critics contend that it is a potentially dangerous hunt. Although it's clear to researchers that depression has many causes, and no one gene will likely be found to cause various kinds of depression, the worry is that once certain genes are even linked to depression, then it may be easy to lose sight of the environmental triggers. In other words, instead of trying to enact legislation that may protect women from, say, domestic violence—a major "trigger" for depression—more emphasis will be placed on altering with drugs the battered woman's brain chemistry than helping her to leave her abusive environment.

Furthermore, who will control social harms associated with depression genes? What if we find that some minority or ethnic groups have more depression genes than other groups? This could potentially "blacklist" them from certain kinds of jobs. What if women are offered a prenatal test for depression genes and are given the opportunity to terminate pregnancies for fetuses that test positive for these genes? Would that be a good thing? These are unanswerable questions, and have yet to be posed at this stage. But the simple fact remains that life is difficult, and some people have less support and poorer coping skills than others to get through tough circumstances.

Why We Become Depressed

When we are faced with challenging an old way of being or thinking, depression may be the state that many of us enter in order to deal with the crisis and hopefully "emerge" more true to ourselves. Whether depression entails a slowing down or a complete halt, these symptoms may be necessary in order for us to change directions emotionally, coming closer to self-actualization. However, self-actualization may or may not lead to greater happiness or fulfillment, because ignorance is *still* bliss. Greater self-knowledge tends to "burst bubbles" and tears down walls you've spent *years* erecting to protect yourself. Unfortunately, human beings are driven to the path that leads to greater truth. Whether the truth is forced upon us through circumstances beyond our control or we (un)consciously set ourselves up to discover it, truthlike birth is born out of pain and suffering. Sometimes, when the pain and suffering are too great, we give ourselves an emotional anesthetic that numbs things for awhile. This can manifest as depression.

Even when a depression seems to come out of nowhere, it is your body and soul's way of getting you to *stop* and *think* about your life.

A depression may also be a state we enter to save ourselves from decisions or actions that can lead to bad consequences. For example, Antti Mattila, M.D., a Finnish researcher who has explored why we get depressed from a philosophical perspective, suggests that the inability to act or communicate has a larger purpose for people at the crossroads in life. When you find that your values and goals are shifting or stirring, and you're in a state of confusion, often the worst thing you can do is act or make a decision. That period of indecision is valuable, because it enables you to stop to reflect.

There may also be a larger purpose to the anxiety and melancholy that accompany the confusion or inaction we experience with depression. For example, the philosopher Kierkegaard believed that periods of depression (which he described as melancholy and angst) are simply part of authentic human existence; in short, a person who never knows melancholy will never know metamorphosis, either. And he described *angst* as a sign that one is realizing the field of possibilities that comes from free will. It is a time when we are contemplating our past choices or circumstances and thinking about ways to make new choices or *change* circumstances.

The philosopher Heidegger also believed that anxiety is part of the human experience, and suggested that it is an indication that the world (situations, relationships, contacts, etc.) isn't "working" for us anymore, forcing us to reconstruct.

In other words, when you're in a rut, or feel trapped by life's circumstances, sadness and suffering or depression can be your mind's and body's way of saying: "Wake up and change." In this case, the only way to *stop* the suffering would be to change the conditions of your life (as in "leave the jerk") or at least change the way you *view* the conditions of your life (as in "my infertility isn't a curse after all—it has actually allowed me to go back to school and change professions"). In other words, if you can't change your life, you can still change your *perspective* on it, which can be a huge life-altering event, even though the conditions of your life remain the same.

By now you should be able to gauge whether you're just sad or are actually depressed. And you should have a good idea of possible causes for sadness or depression. The next chapter will help you to sort through the types of depression and walk you through the medical jargon that surrounds a diagnosis of depression. Just as there are many different types of headaches (sinus, migraine, etc.), there are many different types of depression.

2

All Types of Depression

In order to communicate with your mental health-care provider and thus participate in your own diagnosis and treatment, you must be aware of each type of depression. You must also be aware of something else before you begin to sort through all the labels I'm about to hurl at you. Some therapists consulted criticized this chapter because they were concerned that I was endorsing the labels used by the *DSM IV (Diagnostic and Statistical Manual of Mental Disorders,* 4th edition), which, many therapists argue, is harmful to women. An excellent case in point is the labeling of premenstrual symptoms as a "disorder," which I'll discuss further in chapter 4. In general, critics of the *DSM IV* object to the characterization of behaviors *unique* to women as "not normal" (thus pathologizing them). For example, subtle forms of labeling are seen when traits traditionally viewed as unbecoming to men (such as passivity), or traits traditionally considered unbecoming to women (such as aggressiveness), are considered to be symptoms of a disease. Many critics question *who* decides what symptoms indicate a mental disorder. For example, if white males are in charge of setting the criteria, what kind of biases or prejudices do they bring to their task? These are good, valid questions all women should consider when they are being diagnosed and treated for depression.

Other experts consulted for this book pointed out that prompt and appropriate treatment for depression depends on an accurate diagnosis. In other words, you have to *name the beast* before you can treat it. Otherwise, people are likely to be misdiagnosed, poorly treated, suffer needlessly, and will ultimately be harmed.

So what's the answer? Well, if you read the *DSM IV* cover-to-cover, you'd probably be able to label everyone you know—male and female—with some kind of mental disorder. Similarly, if you read volumes of literature on cancer, you'd probably think everyone you know has the disease because of all the possible symptoms associated with it. Like it or not, most American women see doctors who practice within a Western medicine model infamous for technical jargon that alienates anyone who isn't a clinician or doctor. Much as I'd like to, I can't rewrite psychiatric medicine and soften or change the labels your doctors use when diagnosing and treating depression. But I *can explain* the labels so that you don't feel overwhelmed by your diagnosis. Let's walk through the valley of "psychobabble" together so you can at least *understand* what your doctor or therapist is telling you when she says you have one of the following mood disorders.

UNIPOLAR DISORDERS: THE MOODY BLUES

Mood disorders are divided into two groups: unipolar (one pole, or one mood) and bipolar (two poles, or two moods). Someone with a unipolar disorder has one low, or blue mood. The following are all considered unipolar disorders:

- *Major depression.* The symptoms I listed for depression in chapter 1 (page 7) refer to major depression, the "cold and flu" for mental health-care providers, because it is so common. The more severe the depression, the more numb you may be, making it difficult to "feel" anything—good *or* bad—for anyone in your life, or anything you do. This kind of depression most often leads to suicide or suicidal thoughts. And major depression by itself can manifest as a mild, moderate, or severe episode. To confuse matters, the next condition I discuss, called dysthymia, is often referred to as mild depression.

- *Dysthymia* (pronounced dis-thy-mee-ah). This is a chronic low mood that manifests as a "bad attitude" about life. The symptoms are vague but include an intolerance to stress, or stress "overwhelm"; feeling dependent on others; not being a warm or loving person; feelings of wanting to run away or quit; sensitivity to criticism; inability to have fun; or being grumpy all the time; feeling life isn't worth living; being overcritical; and constantly complaining. While this sounds like *a lot* of people you and I know, it is considered to be a mild form of depression. Mental health-care providers insist this is *not* just someone with a "bad" or "off-putting" personality but someone who can be helped. The symptoms here are awfully "slippery-slope" in that it's difficult to tell whether this label refers to normal reactions to stressful circumstances or to *over*reactions to stressful circumstances. This is a pretty recent label; before 1980, women with the symptoms of dysthymia were simply considered to have a personality/attitude problem, not an illness.

  Dysthymia may be proof that a person has been exposed to the despair and stresses of life to the extent that she can no longer (fully) enjoy hers. Studies show (there are no surprises here) that people with dysthymia are more likely to develop full-blown, or major, depression; and people with dysthymic relatives are also more likely to develop dysthymia. In other words, if your mother had a "difficult" personality, odds are you won't be able to cope with life as well—or as elegantly—

as someone with a mother who had a sunny disposition. Children who display symptoms of dysthymia (especially if they grow up in poverty and terrible circumstances) may be labeled with *early onset dysthymia.* According to the *DSM IV,* you may suffer from "dysthymic disorder" if you've had a depressed mood most days for at least two years, but your symptoms are less severe than those who suffer from major depression, and you experience two of the following:

1. poor appetite or overeating
2. too much or too little sleep
3. fatigue and low energy
4. low self-image or self-esteem
5. trouble concentrating and making decisions
6. hopelessness about the future

- *Melancholic depression.* This is similar to major depression but more serious than a "severe episode" of major depression. If you look at the list of symptoms of depression on page 7, and add the words *profound, extreme,* or *excessive* to each symptom, as in "profound loss of energy" and so on, this is known as melancholic depression.
- *Depression with catatonic features.* This is a rare and severe form of depression where individuals are immobile or in a trance of sorts. Think about the films that show women on psychiatric wards who stare into space and occasionally make odd grimaces, and this is what this label means. If you have the condition, you won't remember *anyone* discussing it with you. Tranquilizers and shock therapy (a.k.a. electroconvulsive therapy) are effective ways of treating this form of depression.
- *Double depression.* This is a confusing term that means you've probably been mildly depressed for some time, and now you're suddenly in the throes of a severe episode of major depression.

- *Agitated depression.* This is when you're anxious *and* depressed—all at once. You have many of the symptoms of major depression, but you have the added symptoms of anxiety disorders, such as not being able to sit still or feeling restless.
- *Psychotic depression.* This is depression with psychotic features: You're depressed—*and* you've lost touch with reality. This is a bad combination, characterized by visual hallucinations, hearing voices, having delusions ("false beliefs"), and hearing voices telling you that you're worthless. This is frequently misdiagnosed as schizophrenia, and the suicide risk is high in this kind of illness.
- *Recurrent depression.* You're depressed, or have been depressed, and your episodes of depression recur. What may also happen in this case is that antidepressant medications can precipitate or unmask manic episodes, which may be why your depression keeps recurring.
- *Masked depression.* This is an odd duck. Many psychiatrists do not even use the terminology *masked depression* and may even see some of these symptoms as hypomania (see bipolar disorder). In this case, you don't seem depressed at all but instead have one or more of the following symptoms: chronic aches and pains; oversocializing to *avoid* dealing with your own life (you're always going out—somewhere); thrill seeking; and impulse behaviors (flying into rages, sexual flings, shoplifting, or gambling). Moreover, you're always having accidents; you seek surgery for vague illnesses (known as malingering or faking). All of these behaviors involve avoidance of life problems.

These types of depression have one thing in common: They are characterized by one low mood instead of one high mood and one low mood, as is the case with bipolar disorders (which are discussed next).

BIPOLAR DISORDERS: FEELING GROOVY

Bipolar disorder is the new label for an older, probably more accurate one: *manic-depression,* which means that moods fluctuate between mania (incredible "highs") and depression (incredible "lows"). How "incredible" the high or low is can vary dramatically, which has given rise to the concept of different kinds of bipolar disorders—bipolar I and bipolar II.

When you have bipolar disorder, you may indeed go through life for awhile "feeling groovy." More than two million people in North America suffer from bipolar disorder, which psychiatrists believe is an inherited disease, because it is seen in families. In other words, it's not unusual to see this condition across the generations, as in a grandmother, mother, and daughter. Researchers believe that like multiple personality disorder, which is almost exclusively a disorder that is a "response" to child abuse, bipolar disorder may also be a response to other unusual conditions. Bipolar disorder occurs with greater frequency among high-achieving individuals and may be seen across the generations because of the special talents and gifts that are inherited across the generations. (There may also be pressure to achieve in such families. If your father was a brilliant scientist and your mother was a gifted classical pianist, you might feel some pressure to succeed in life, or at least measure up to your parents' successes.)

Episodes of mania are characterized by a speeding up, while the depression is the biological "payback" for the bursts of energy, creativity, and euphoria seen during the manic period. The genetic versus circumstantial aspect of bipolar disorder remains in question; to date, no genetic defect associated with bipolar disorder has been discovered despite intensive research efforts to find genes associated with this disease.

Women with bipolar disorder suffer from dramatic mood swings ranging from euphoria (known as mania), accompanied by irritability, to the depths of depression, hence the older, and perhaps more accurate term, *manic-depression*. For most, there are also periods in between when the mood is completely normal—neither depressed nor euphoric. (Clinicians are still arguing over what to call this disease; some feel "bipolar" disorder is inaccurate, giving the false impression that only two distinct moods are displayed in manic-depression, which is not so. Others feel that bipolar disorder is much less stigmatizing than the term *manic-depression*.)

Bipolar disorder usually appears during the teenage years or late adolescence—just as women begin to become sexually active and make their way in the world. As a result, it can lead to disastrous consequences in terms of sexual or intimate relationships and career-related decisions. Relationship breakups, job loss, alcohol and drug abuse, and even suicide are common among women suffering from untreated bipolar disorder.

The Myth of Mania

It's important to dispel one of the greatest myths about the highs felt in bipolar disorder: the myth of productivity. It is generally believed that the highs of manic episodes help the sufferer to achieve more, thereby being useful in some way. This just isn't so. The individual who is high is busy in unproductive ways, although she may *feel* while she's high that she is achieving more and being productive. The truth is, people in the throes of mania are scattered, unfocused, and can be destructive.

Socially, however, the highs may be of some use. A manic woman can be charismatic, energetic, bubbly, and magnetic, making friends easily. For some, manic episodes come complete with all the tools you need to be a great hostess, party-giver, entertainer, or life of the party. Mania also comes in handy if you're a connoisseur of good wine, gourmet food, and freshly cut flowers because the senses are heightened in euphoric states. For instance, it's not unusual to find manic women to be dinner-party divas—hosting lavish evenings for their friends (in reality, it's a good way for these women to use up their energy by cooking, planning, spending, and, ultimately, entertaining). *But pretty soon, the party ends.* The energy is still there—but without a productive outlet.

Signs of Bipolar Disorder

Some women recognize themselves in the signs below, but often it is family members or friends who notice the following:

- drug abuse (some common culprits: cocaine, alcohol, and sleeping pills—this is known as "comorbidity," and according to 1990 statistics, 61 percent of people with bipolar I have a history of drug abuse)
- erratic behavior characterized by wild spending sprees, sexual flings, and impulsive acts
- incredible bursts of energy and activity
- restlessness (constantly looking for something to do; being unable to focus for a long time on one activity)
- fast talking to keep up with a "racing mind" (ever seen Robin Williams, well known for his battle with bipolar disorder, in action?)
- acting and feeling high or euphoric
- extreme irritability and distractibility
- not requiring sleep (you feel there is too much to do in life and that sleep is a waste of time, even though lack of it may lead to irritability and agitation)
- the belief in unusual or unrealistic abilities and "powers" (e.g., it's not unusual for women with bipolar disorder to believe they are agents of God, or even God Herself)
- making decisions and judgments that seem out of character or "not like you"

* increased need or desire for sex
* behavior that pushes other people's buttons (aggressive or intrusive acts)
* total denial that "something's wrong" when confronted
* increasing sensitivity to sound, and easily irritated by various sounds
* feeling you are extraordinary or brilliant (even though this *may* be true)
* feeling at one with nature, and having heightened senses (everything smells, tastes, sounds, feels, and looks beautiful and exquisite)
* being told you are a workaholic because you are taking on too many projects at once
* calling people all the time for no good reason, and keeping them tied up with useless conversations

It's important to note that some of the therapists I consulted for this book questioned whether some of these established symptoms of bipolar disorder are simply "male" behaviors exhibited in women (arrogance, brashness, wit) that are pathologized. (In other words, should we label women "sick" for having characteristics typically associated with domineering personalities?)

Dr. Kay Redfield Jamison, author of *An Unquiet Mind,* an autobiography of a woman coping with manic-depression, describes her various manic episodes this way:

At first, everything seemed so easy. I raced about like a crazed weasel, bubbling with plans and enthusiasms, immersed in sports, and staying up all night, night after night, out with friends, reading everything that wasn't nailed down, filling manuscript books with poems and fragments of plays and making expansive, completely unrealistic, plans for my future. The world was filled with pleasure and promise; I felt great. Not just great, I felt really great. I felt I could do anything, that no task was too difficult.

And this:

> My normal Brooks Brothers conservatism would go by the board; my hemlines would go up, my neckline down, and I would enjoy the sensuality of my youth. Almost everything was done to excess: Instead of buying one Beethoven symphony, I would buy nine; instead of enrolling for five classes, I would enroll in seven; instead of buying two tickets for a concert I would buy eight or ten . . . When I am high I couldn't worry about money if I tried. So I don't. The money will come from somewhere; I am entitled; God will provide. Credit cards are disastrous, personal checks worse. Unfortunately, for manics anyway, mania is a natural extension of the economy. What with credit cards and bank accounts there is little beyond reach.

And this:

> When you're high it's tremendous. The ideas and feelings are fast and frequent, like shooting stars, and you follow them until you find better or brighter ones. Shyness goes, the right words and gestures are suddenly there, the power to captivate others a felt certainty. There are interests found in uninteresting people. Sensuality is pervasive and the desire to seduce and be seduced irresistible. Feelings of ease, intensity, power, well-being, financial omnipotence, and euphoria pervade one's marrow. But, somewhere, this changes. The fast ideas are far too fast, and there are far too many. Overwhelming confusion replaces clarity. Memory goes. Humor and absorption on friends' faces are replaced by fear and concern. Everything previously moving with the grain is now against—you are irritable, angry, frightened, uncontrollable, and enmeshed totally in the blackest caves of the mind.

The symptoms above will shift as the mood "crashes," and that person will then suffer from true depression, showing some or all of the symptoms of major depression (see chapter 1).

Shades of moods

The difficulty in understanding bipolar disorder is that a layperson tends to assume that the person suffering from this condition is either "pink" or "blue" (i.e., euphoric or depressed); but there are many shades of moods that women with this condition exhibit. For example, the episodes of depression can be mild, moderate, or severe, followed by normal moods, followed by a mild mania, known as hypomania, which can also turn into extreme mania.

There is no single pattern in bipolar disorder, either. Some women may suffer far more from depressive episodes than mania; others may only suffer from occasional depression. And frequently, the depression is combined with mania in a "mixed" bipolar state.

It's also important to note that many women who appear to have other problems, such as alcoholism or other addictions, are actually suffering from bipolar disorder; while many women who are diagnosed with bipolar disorder are actually alcoholics (i.e., if they stopped drinking, they'd be cured).

The Crash

If you go on wild spending sprees during your episode of mania, the bills generally don't arrive until you've crashed—giving you all the more reason to be depressed. Here's Kay Redfield Jamison on the subject of her crashes:

> From the time I woke up in the morning until the time I went to bed at night, I was unbearably miserable and seemingly incapable of any kind of joy or enthusiasm. Everything—every thought, word, movement—was an effort. Everything that once seemed so sparkling was now flat. I seemed to myself to be dull, boring, inadequate, thick-brained, unlit, unresponsive, chill-skinned, bloodless, and sparrow-drab. I doubted, completely, my ability to do anything well. It seemed as though my mind had slowed down and burned out to the point of being virtually useless. What is the point in going on like this? I would ask myself. Others would say to me, "It is only temporary, it will pass, and you will get over it," but of course they had no idea how I felt, although they were certain that they did. Over and over and over I would say to myself, if I can't feel, if I can't move, if I can't think, and I can't care, then what conceivable point is there in living? . . . Washing my hair took hours to do, and it drained me for hours afterward; filling the ice-cube tray was beyond my capacity, and I occasionally slept in the

same clothes I had worn during the day because I was too exhausted
to undress. . . . When I was manic, the tempo seemed slow; when I
was normal, frenetic seemed fine; when I was depressed, the pace was
impossible.

Types of Bipolar Disorders

Just as there are different types of unipolar disorders, there are different types of bipolar disorders: one more severe, in which people
suffer from extreme forms of mania (called bipolar I) and one less
severe, in which people suffer from a less obvious form of mania
known as hypomania (called bipolar II). In fact, many people with
bipolar II go through life undiagnosed because their mania may not
be extreme enough to be fully noticed by outsiders.

Bipolar I disorder

This is what is also known as full-blown manic-depressive illness
and is at least ten times more likely to occur if other family members have this disease. Roughly 60 percent of those diagnosed with
bipolar I also have problems with drug and alcohol abuse, which
makes it a much more difficult disease to control when substance/
alcohol abuse is involved. Evidence indicates that a stressful event
may trigger the first episode of mania (compared to later episodes),
followed by depression, or vice versa.

The manic episode typically comes on suddenly and quickly over
the course of a few hours or days. And each time a manic episode re-
curs, it will come on faster and faster. Since these episodes can last
from four to twelve months, if untreated, the behavioral patterns exhibited during mania can do a lot of damage to your life. In that
amount of time, you can destroy personal relationships, your job
and/or career, and your credit rating.

The depressive episodes are known as "crashes" because they generally come on fast, especially when they follow a manic episode. (In
unipolar disorders, depression typically develops slowly and gradually over the course of several weeks.) The depressive episodes in

bipolar I can last much longer (i.e., eight to twenty-four months) than the manic episodes, which can also do a lot of damage to your life.

Types of manias and mood states in bipolar I
Bipolar I euphoric mania. Less than 40 percent of all people with bipolar I have euphoric mania. Here, you have an inflated self-esteem, making grandiose statements about yourself, and are hugely overconfident. You believe you can do anything and have special or extraordinary powers. You may also have a magnetic personality, being charismatic, witty, and "infectious" with your mood, which causes people to be drawn to you. Then stage two hits, and you're driven by myriad projects and interests. At the same time, you're irritated by people around you, believing them to be "dense," "too slow," or even "too boring" to be around. You're talking fast, your thoughts are disorganized, people are getting in your way, and you don't like it. Stage three is when your thinking is so fast, *you* can't keep up, and you're suddenly panic-stricken and overtaken by fear and anxiety. Hallucinations and delusions at this stage are not uncommon.

Mixed states. You have symptoms of mania and depression all at once. You're in neither "pole" but in a sort of "pole purgatory," neither crossing completely to the North nor the South pole. This isn't fun. You are irritable, quick-tempered, hostile, agitated, anxious, discontented, sullen, and all the other bad feelings you can think of. A significant percentage of those with bipolar I have mixed states; women are more likely to be mixed than euphoric. Substance abuse and suicide are so common in mixed states because it is a state of discontent, unhappiness, misery, and agitation, and sufferers try to medicate themselves in order to cope.

Bipolar II disorder

This is a confusing diagnosis, and one that's difficult to pinpoint given the symptoms. Many women with bipolar II initially may be diagnosed with major depression. Usually the pattern is for symptoms of major depression to develop. After the bout of major depression appears to be resolving itself (with or without anti-depressants), symptoms of milder mania, known as hypomania, develop. Hypomania is not the same as euphoric mania. There are also women who are hypomanic all the time, which is their "norm"—but who do *not* have bipolar II, for the simple reason that there is no change in their mood.

Bipolar II represents about 60 percent of all people suffering from bipolar disorders. We also know that 14 percent of people currently diagnosed with major depression actually have bipolar II disorder. The irony is that the treatment for major depression—antidepressants—can trigger hypomania. So when you have bipolar II disorder, and you are told you are depressed and treated with antidepressants, it's not uncommon to find that you are growing more agitated, "speedy" in unproductive ways, or irritable because of the hypomania.

Women who are hypomanic have increased energy, a decreased need for sleep, and greater than normal self-esteem, although it is not as grandiose as seen in euphoric mania. Irritability and hostility are also common, as they are in later stages of euphoric mania, and mixed states are seen far more in bipolar II. This is one reason why so many women with bipolar II also turn to drugs or alcohol.

Because the illness is so frequently misdiagnosed and/or misman-aged (via psychotherapy alone or drug-addiction programs alone), at least 15 percent of people with bipolar II disorder will attempt or commit suicide as life becomes more miserable with each passing day. This is also true with bipolar I and unipolar disorders.

Your Mood Cycle

If you think of bipolar disorder as an "emotional menstrual cycle," it's easier to understand what is meant by *rapid cycling*—a term used to describe people who bounce from episodes of depression and mania throughout the year. The length of time between either mood is called your "cycle length," just as it is when reporting your menstrual-cycle length. After your initial manic episode or mixed-state episode, the time you spend feeling "normal" (i.e., neither depressed nor manic) is shorter and shorter, as the episodes occur more frequently. If you're having four or more episodes of mania or mixed states per year, you're known as a *rapid cycler*. Roughly 20 percent of people with bipolar disorders are rapid cyclers, but it is seen three times more frequently in women. Nobody knows how the menstrual cycle affects episodes of mania or mixed states, either, but curiously, people who are rapid cyclers may also have an underactive thyroid gland (called hypothyroidism), easily detected through a blood test and easily corrected with thyroid replacement hormone. Researchers at the National Institute of Mental Health (NIMH) have identified rare cases of people who are "ultrarapid cyclers" and have episodes of mania and depression (i.e., mixed states) every two days, which is often triggered by light and dark. But most psychiatrists have never seen this, and question this concept.

Almost Manic: Cyclothymia

Cyclothymia (pronounced cyclo-thy-mee-ah) is to mania what dysthymia (see page 25) is to depression. It is a subtle manifestation of manic features without being full-blown mania. Cyclothymia is evidence that mania is looming, but it is not yet full blown. Fifteen to 50 percent of people with cyclothymia "progress" to full-blown bipolar I or II. The symptoms of cyclothymia may again be applied to many people you and I know and include the following:

- *Thrill-seeking behavior.* This is when your behavior is avoidance-of-life related, demonstrated by promiscuity, substance abuse, gambling, or compulsive buying/shopping.
- *Uneven performances in school or work.* In this case, boredom and restlessness have led to a history of numerous career

changes and academic interests. You are continually moving
to different cities, have had countless fresh starts, and often
take on a "this time things will be different" attitude.

- *Many stormy romantic relationships/marriages.* Your
relationships are always in a crisis; you're always struggling
with your romantic partner in life, which causes a string of
failed relationships. You are often the "high-maintenance
friend in crisis."

- *You have great energy and charm.* Everyone *loves* to be around
you—until you become irritable, critical, hostile, easily
frustrated, and angry over small, trivial matters. People may
describe you as "moody," and you're often brooding or
depressed.

- *Interfering.* You butt in to your friends' and acquaintances'
personal lives. You seem to always know best, even though
your own life is a mess. People think you're arrogant or
brash.

- *You talk a lot—and go off on tangents.* You have great wit and
charm and are probably a great manipulator when it comes
to arguing and defending your point of view. People find it
hard to get a word in edgewise, and they leave the
conversations feeling uneasy, guilty, and manipulated.

TREATING DIFFERENT TYPES OF DEPRESSION: AN OVERVIEW

Consider the following scene: You've just been pulled by firefighters
from a burning building. You're struggling to breathe and are coughing and wheezing. You're rushed to the hospital. A doctor looks at
you and says: "Your wheezing and coughing are signs of a respiratory disorder—possibly asthma. I'm therefore going to prescribe
asthma medication."

What's wrong with this story? *How about the fact that you were just pulled from a fire?* Wouldn't it make much more sense for a doctor to say: "You're wheezing and coughing because you just inhaled smoke and were pulled from a fire. I'm going to treat your physical symptoms, but I think it's important that you have someone to talk to about your experience."

Indeed, how could a diagnosis of a respiratory disorder be made in isolation, without attributing the symptoms to the fire itself? It's absurd. Yet, that is exactly how depression is diagnosed for millions of North American women every year.

The physical symptoms of depression are often diagnosed in isolation of the "fire"—the life event that may have triggered those symptoms. This leaves women feeling *labeled* rather than *enabled*. Whether you wake up every morning to a wheelchair; to an abusive partner; as a woman of color facing racism; as a single mother struggling to make ends meet; as a woman coping with experiences of sexual abuse; as a fat woman living in a society that values thinness and impossible standards of beauty; as a woman turning fifty in a society that values only young women; as a woman facing infertility or cancer; as a lesbian teenager in a homophobic society; or as someone who's suffered the loss of a loved one through a breakup or death—these factors often make no difference to the doctor writing your prescription for an antidepressant. Shouldn't they?

That's not to say that it's so easy to *change* your circumstances. A woman of color cannot zip on her "white skin" to have a less stressful day for a change, nor can a survivor of sexual abuse change her past. But if you were suffering from a situational depression (see chapter 1) and were told: "You're suffering from a 'unipolar disorder,' which is caused by an imbalance in your brain chemistry," wouldn't you feel, deep down, as though a huge "chunk" was missing from the diagnosis? After all, *you* know yourself best. You know what's right for you because only you live in your body and in your situation. Trusting your instincts and accepting that it's okay to be the "expert on yourself" can often help you to fill in the gaps to which your doctor may be oblivious.

Wouldn't it make more sense to be told something like: "Given your circumstances, your symptoms are understandable. And, fortunately, we can treat your physical symptoms, but we also have to discuss some coping strategies for your life situation in order to prevent the recurrence of your physical symptoms." Ah, that's better. Let's face the fact that the fire is there.

In other words, no competent mental health-care provider should label you *without* sitting down and asking you some detailed questions about your life (family history, personal life, occupation, and stress). Yet, many women in the mental health-care system are indeed sent home without such a discussion and often feel they are labeled "out of context." By this, I mean the circumstances or situations that may have led to their symptoms often go unacknowledged by the health-care provider.

Short-Term Treatment Strategies

There is no one way to stop the suffering in depression. Different things work for different women. Less invasive solutions involve finding someone to talk to. This translates into finding counseling or psychotherapy, which I discuss in detail in chapters 5 and 6. Talk therapy may also work best in combination with antidepressants (see chapter 7) or self-healing strategies (see chapter 8).

If you're wheezing and coughing from smoke inhalation, there's nothing wrong with being prescribed medication that will help you to breathe in the short term. But you may also need to talk to somebody about the fire, or talk to other people who have also been in a fire. Depression is no different. Medication can help you to breathe or stop the suffering in the short term, but it can't give you insights for the long term or provide the emotional support you need to see what you need to see, learn what you need to learn, and go through what you need to *grow* through. If that is the path you want to take, chapters 5 and 6 will help you to find that special someone to talk to. Chapter 7 discusses medication in detail.

Long-term Solutions

Preventing a recurrence of a depressive episode involves prolonged therapy: long-term counseling and/or psychotherapy (see chapters 5 and 6) instead of short-term; long-term talk therapy in combination with medications (chapter 7) or herbs (chapter 8); lifestyle changes (ranging from stress-reduction techniques to dramatic changes involving residence, jobs, and interpersonal relationships). Since long-term solutions often involve making dramatic changes in your lifestyle, which can take a *long time* to come to terms with or to implement, counseling is often a key component in managing depression.

The "sharing" approach has been shown to be highly beneficial—particularly in cases where women share difficult circumstances or have difficulties in common (see chapter 6).

Family Support

Depression changes spousal/partner relationships, as well as other family relationships. When you're going through a depression, knowing that things won't fall apart can be the source of greatest comfort. Unfortunately, too many women are treated to "family harassment," in that they are not given the space to go through their depression. Being continuously told to "snap out of it," "get out of the house," "go for a walk," or "what you need is a nice big cup of . . . tea, soup, hot chocolate" isn't what family support is about. There are things family members can do that *are* supportive, which will give you the space to feel you are allowed to go through what you *are* going through.

. . . .

Family or friends may need some guidance on how to help. Here are some examples of what they can do for you.

1. *Become the homemaker without asking.* When family or friends look after as many of the meals or chores as they can, it takes pressure off you. You may have trouble asking for help and may worry about how to get everything done, which only adds to your burden.

2. *Join you in therapy.* If you want a family member or friend to go to support groups or counseling with you, they should go. This says "I want to understand what's going on with you."

3. *Check in instead of checking up.* Asking how you're feeling, or how your kids are faring, is fine and supportive. But badgering you with unwanted opinions or advice, or asking "what did you *do* today" in a tone that is judgmental, is *not* fine or supportive.

4. *Allow you to set the pace of your day.* When family members try to force you to go on an outing, eat, or do anything you don't feel like doing, it just puts more pressure on you and emphasizes your inability to function or cope.

5. *Be open.* Family and friends should be open to talking with you about your depression. People have different ways of coping, and some really choose to be more open about mood disorders. Sometimes the most supportive thing others can do is to listen without judgment; it takes a great deal of energy to keep depression a secret.

. . . .

A good health-care provider should first rule out whether your depression is a sign of an underlying physical problem, such as a thyroid disorder, allergies, or chronic fatigue. Questions about your occupation and overall physical health would help to eliminate a lot of misdiagnosed situational depression. If your depression is a symptom of another physical condition, the next chapter will get you on the right path to the right doctor.

Chapter

3

When Depression Is a Symptom of a Physical Ailment

If you look at the list of symptoms that comprise depression (see chapters 1 and 2), many of them are identical to symptoms of physical ailments, such as chronic fatigue syndrome, allergies and environmental sensitivities, thyroid disease, or just plain old exhaustion from overwork and stress. Just because you have a physical illness doesn't mean you can't also be suffering from a situational depression. Indeed, being ill is often the situation that triggers your depression. But when you're referred to a psychiatrist when all you need is thyroid hormone or a well-earned vacation, it can be enough to . . . well, drive you crazy.

This chapter is for the woman who falls into the cracks, and whose illness may be misdiagnosed as situational depression. This is the woman who can't find relief from her symptoms because nobody bothered to check her thyroid or to discern if she is allergic to the carpet fibers or industrial toxins in her workplace. Nor did anyone ask her how many hours a week she works, how much sunlight she gets, or when was the last time she ate a nutritious meal. In these cases, treating the organic disease or organic roots of her depression

symptoms *is* the cure. For example, one of the most common referrals psychiatrists get from family doctors are women who *appear* to
be depressed, when, in fact, they have an underactive thyroid gland.
A simple blood test and a little thyroid hormone magically restore
them to their vibrant, energetic selves, while the depression disappears. These are the scenarios this chapter will address.

A second group of women also falls into the cracks. These women
suffer from physical symptoms that appear to have no organic cause.
They may have irritable bowels or are plagued by the urge to
urinate—as often as sixty times a day—without "results." In these
cases, they are told that there is nothing wrong with them, that their
symptoms are a mystery. This is a situation that can be so frustrating and debilitating that a situational depression can arise. But
imagine the relief a woman in this situation would feel if her symptoms were validated and she were told: "You have a physical condition that has been triggered by stress. You're not alone; many women
like you experience these symptoms. And we have the data and studies to prove it." That's *exactly* what I will tell you in the latter half of
this chapter.

If you've been bouncing around from doctor to doctor with
bowel or urinary complaints, take heart: Two common conditions
that mercilessly plague women have been shown to improve when
stress is reduced—irritable bowel syndrome (IBS) and interstitial
cystitis (IC), an inflammation of the interstitium, the space between
the bladder lining and the bladder muscle. In this case, talk therapy
and some stress-reduction techniques may help you feel less physically sick, which will improve your emotional health.

NORMAL STRESS AND FATIGUE

Before I discuss chronic fatigue, it's important to understand how
sick you can feel when you're suffering from plain old fatigue and
stress, due to lack of sleep, overwork, and garden-variety annoy-

ances. The cure is obvious: Get more sleep, and don't work so hard. Trite advice for such demanding times, because most of us can't afford the cure if we want to keep paying the mortgage or rent.

Fatigue is one of the most common complaints doctors hear from their patients. It's no secret that these days women are tired and stressed. Most women have multiple roles, juggling career and family pressures. And if you're older than forty, chances are you have an ailing parent whom you care for as well.

There is a difference between feeling normal fatigue and chronic fatigue, which is characterized by low energy, lethargy, and flulike symptoms. This section outlines some of the factors responsible for normal fatigue, which can be remedied by making some lifestyle changes.

Sleep Deprivation

Women who have demanding jobs that require long hours are often sleep-deprived, which can have serious health repercussions. Recent research into sleep deprivation has found that it not only depletes the immune system (it depletes you of certain cells needed to destroy viruses and cancerous cells), but it can also promote the growth of fat instead of muscle and may speed up the aging process.

This happens because a lack of sleep increases levels of the hormone cortisol, the stress hormone. As cortisol levels rise, muscle-building human growth hormone and prolactin—a breastfeeding hormone released by the pituitary gland and responsible for milk production, and which also helps to protect the immune system—both decrease. Normally, cortisol levels should decline, while human growth hormone and prolactin should increase during sleep. Cortisol declines prior to sleep because it is the body's way of preparing for rest. Cortisol, which normally increases in the morning to make you more alert, is released by the adrenal gland in response to stress and is essentially an "alert" hormone that makes you take action. This is what causes you to be alert in important meetings, "close the sale or deal," or suddenly become incredibly articulate with someone on the phone after spending five days with two toddlers without any relief. The hormone subsides in the body as the stressful event passes.

A common reason women, in particular, cut down on their sleep is to get in their "workout time" before their days begin. It's not unusual for many working women to rise at five in the morning, for example, to exercise. This, according to sleep experts, only *compromises* health and increases stress. The benefits of the exercise may be canceled by the harm done by lack of sleep. A National Sleep Foundation survey revealed that two out of three people get less than the recommended eight hours of sleep per night; of that group, one out of three gets less than six hours of sleep.

There are two phases of sleep: rapid eye movement (REM) and nonrapid eye movement. Researchers believe we dream during REM sleep, which is an important component in mental health. Non-REM sleep is our deepest slumber, which is when, researchers believe, hormones are reset and energy stores are replenished.

Roughly 50 percent of people diagnosed with depression (see chapters 1 and 2) get too much REM sleep and not enough deep sleep, which is the "replenishing" sleep.

Raising a Family

Few women can escape the stresses involved with simply raising a family—especially when there's a shortage of affordable child care in this country. Stresses are increased when children get sick or suffer from chronic health problems, such as asthma or allergies. This often means women miss work, miss sleep, or run their child back and forth to doctors. Due to a decline in our air quality, the incidence of childhood asthma and allergies has skyrocketed; that places a working mother in difficult circumstances, because she is usually the parent who cares for a sick child.

We are also seeing more chronic ear infections in children, as well as an increase in childhood cancers. Again, this places tremendous stress on women who are raising families.

Lifestyle Factors

Caffeine

I'll make this short and sweet: Lots of studies show that caffeine causes anxiety and sleeplessness and is mildly addictive. It also exacerbates premenstrual symptoms (see chapter 4). Experts now recommend that you consume no more than 400 to 500 milligrams of caffeine per day, which is equal to two eight-ounce mugs of coffee or four cups of instant coffee. Of course, caffeine is also found in soft drinks, chocolate, and tea, so all sources of caffeine should be taken into account along with experts' recommendations.

Smoking

Many women turn to cigarettes to deal with the demands of stress, but people who smoke every day are twice as likely to suffer from depression as people who don't smoke. This may have nothing to do with smoking and *everything* to do with stressful circumstances. As discussed in chapter 1, people under a lot of stress are more likely to suffer from depression, while many of those people are likely to smoke to try to calm themselves. Other studies have found that people with major depression are three times as likely to be daily smokers. So, nicotine may also be a drug we crave in order to medicate our depressed moods.

Alcohol

If you have wine or other alcoholic beverages to unwind after a stressful day, be aware that alcohol can interfere with sleep patterns; it is a depressant. Initially, alcohol may make you tired, and you may think it's a sleeping aid; but it can wake you up later on, leaving you wide awake at two in the morning, and prevent you from falling back to sleep. Naturally, all of this can aggravate stress and fatigue.

Women also metabolize alcohol differently than men, so even when a man and woman are the same weight, because of fat distribution women will become intoxicated more easily than men. Alcohol is also tolerated by the same woman differently at different times in her menstrual cycle. She may become more easily intoxicated just before ovulation, which can aggravate premenstrual signs. Women also tend to be invisible drinkers and often drink alone. Moderate drinking is defined by fewer than twelve drinks per week and is not a daily activity. Moderate drinkers do not use alcohol to cope with stress, nor do they plan their recreational activities around it. If you think you're drinking more heavily, it is useful to keep a diary of your drinking. Often, just being aware of your alcohol-consumption patterns can be enough to make you change your habits.

Diet

When you're stressed and fatigued, you often don't eat well. By eating properly and choosing from a variety of foods—particularly all colors of vegetables—you'll be in better shape to cope. (See chapter 8.)

CHEMICAL REACTIONS

It's not your imagination that more people—particularly women—are suffering from a range of nondescript aches, pains, and allergies. For women who are *lucky* enough to be working, exposure to workplace chemicals and toxins is putting them at risk for occupational asthma and allergies. This can lead to chronic fatigue, which can mimic symptoms of depression.

According to the *Journal of the American Medical Association (JAMA)*, at least ten million North Americans suffer from chronic asthma; as much as 15 percent of asthma is directly caused by occupational exposure. Occupational asthma has a number of causes, many attributable to an occupational environment, *not* to external stimuli.

One of the most notorious chemicals is toluene diisocyanate (TDI), which is used in the plastics and oil industries. It is also found in plants that manufacture boats, recreational vehicles, and electronics.

High-rise office buildings are another source of asthma-causing substances and allergies due to poor air quality and air circulation; this is known as "sick building syndrome." Ventilation systems can be fodder for mold growth inside ducts; car exhaust when air-intake ducts are placed in parking garages; bacteria from bird feces if birds nest in or around the vents; or asbestos fibers and fiberglass, which are commonly used building materials.

Women who work with animals (the proteins in animal skin and urine can trigger asthma); health-care workers who have reactions to natural proteins in rubber latex gloves; and women who work in food plants and inhale dust from cereal protein and flour are also at risk for asthma and allergies.

Many women notice a significant drop in their energy and endurance levels as a result of chronic asthma and allergies from exposure to various man-made materials. Chronic fatigue can lead to anxiety and stress over lost time at work and lost productivity. A ten-year study by the National Institute of Occupational Safety and Health (NIOSH) reveals that asthma is among the leading job-related diseases in the United States.

The following materials, common in homes and workplaces, have been cited as hazardous to your health and/or well-being. This doesn't necessarily mean that all of the following are carcinogenic, but many of the items on this list cause headaches, rashes, and asthmatic symptoms.

- building materials that contain asbestos
- cleaning products and disinfectants

- urea-formaldehyde foam insulation
- adhesives (may contain naphthalene, phenol, ethanol, vinyl chloride, formaldehyde, acrylonitrile, and epoxy, which are toxic substances that release vapors)
- artificial lighting (can cause headaches)
- toners used in copy machines and printers
- particleboard furniture and space dividers
- permanent-ink pens and markers (contain acetone, cresol, ethanol, phenol, toluene, and xylene, which are toxic)
- polystyrene cups
- secondhand smoke
- synthetic office carpet (may contain acrylic, polyester and nylon plastic fibers, formaldehyde-based finishes, and pesticides due to moth-proofing for wool only)
- typing correction fluid (may contain cresol, ethanol, trichloroethlyene, and naphthalene, which are all toxic chemicals)

Unfortunately, occupational asthma is just one of the host of symptoms your body may exhibit in response to a toxic environment. The term *multiple chemical sensitivity* (MCS) was introduced in the early 1990s to explain a wide array of health problems and symptoms that appeared to be reactions to chemicals. Among the different symptoms associated with MCS are depression and chronic fatigue, sleep disturbances, mood swings, and poor concentration. People considered at risk for MCS include those who:

- work or live in energy-sealed buildings
- are exposed to fumes from carpets, pesticides, cleaners, and airborne allergens
- are exposed to industrial chemicals, such as those found in plants that process wood, metal, plastics, paints, and textiles
- are in constant contact with pesticides, fungicides, and fertilizers
- live in high-pollution areas

- work in dry cleaning, hair salons, pest control, printing, and photocopying

Reproductive Concerns

Women, of course, want to protect their reproductive organs. We know, for example, that if you're a dental hygienist and work in an unventilated area, you may be overexposed to nitrous oxide, which is linked to high rates of miscarriage. If you are exposed to certain solvents, ranging from those found in dry-cleaning businesses to the semiconductor industry, you may also be at risk.

The existence of chemicals that are classified as hazardous by the appropriate governmental bodies must be publicized to all employees in the workplace, with details of the relevant components, hazards, and handling instructions specific to that chemical. This in particular enables working mothers to decide whether they want to stop working while pregnant or find work in a hazard-free environment. And, of course, these hazardous chemicals may interfere with

••••••••••

In Canada, the Toxicological Index database (Infotox) provides peer-reviewed information concerning chemicals identified in the workplace that may affect pregnancy and breast milk; fifty-five hundred substances are included, of which 2.7 percent have been recognized as being transferred by milk.

There are also various drug and poison hot lines (listed locally) that provide considerable information on toxins that affect pregnancy and breast milk. Specific concerns can also be explored through the NIOSH-TIC database, maintained by the National Institute of Occupational Safety and Health (NIOSH), available on disk at various university and public libraries. NIOSH Information Dissemination can also be accessed directly by calling (513) 533-8287. Finally, consult the Centers for Disease Control and Prevention (CDC) in Atlanta, Georgia at (404) 639-3311.

••••••••••

breast-feeding. All foreign compounds that appear in your blood also appear in your breast milk. However, toxin exposure is less critical during breast-feeding than it is during pregnancy, especially during the early stages.

The easiest toxin to eliminate from the workplace is secondhand smoke. Smoke-free workplaces are definitely better places to work than smoke-*filled* offices. If your employer cannot guarantee a smoke-free environment, you should investigate whether your legal rights are being compromised.

ABNORMAL FATIGUE: CHRONIC FATIGUE SYNDROME

Seventy percent of all people who suffer from chronic fatigue are women younger than forty-five. Chronic fatigue syndrome (CFS) has been around longer than you might think. In 1843, for example, a curious condition called "fibrositis" was described by doctors. It was characterized by similar symptoms now seen in fibromyalgia (chronic muscle and joint aches and pains) and chronic fatigue syndrome (symptoms of fibromyalgia, accompanied by flulike symptoms and extreme fatigue). The term *rheumatism,* an outdated label, was also frequently used to describe various aches and pains with no specific or identifiable origin.

In the late 1970s and early 1980s, a mysterious virus known as Epstein-Barr was being diagnosed in thousands of young, upwardly mobile professionals—who at the time were known as Yuppies, primarily members of the baby-boom generation. People were calling this condition the "Yuppie flu," the "Yuppie virus," "Yuppie syndrome," and "burn out" syndrome. Many medical professionals were stumped by it, and many regarded it as a phantom or a psychosomatic illness. Because so many women were dismissed by their doctors as being hypochondriacs, or were not believed to be ill or fatigued, the physical symptoms triggered self-doubts, feelings of low self-esteem, and self-loathing, which often caused depression. But even with the most sensitive medical attention, depression seems to go hand in hand with CFS simply because the disorder leaves so many sufferers at home in bed, isolated from the active lifestyle so many of these individuals once had. In other words, some believe that in the case of CFS, depression is a normal response to feeling lousy every day of your life. It's an example of the "if you weren't depressed, you'd be crazy" adage I began to use as I researched this book.

Many people with CFS were also misdiagnosed with other diseases that shared some of the symptoms we now define as CFS. These diseases included mononucleosis, multiple sclerosis, and HIV-related illnesses (once called AIDS-related complex, or ARC), Lyme disease, postpolio syndrome, and lupus. (If you were diagnosed with *any* of these diseases, please look at the established symptom criteria for CFS below. You may have been misdiagnosed, which is a common scenario.)

In the early 1980s, two Nevada physicians, who treated a number of patients sharing this curious condition (after a nasty winter flu had hit the region), identified this condition as "chronic fatigue syndrome." This label is perhaps most accurate, and the one that has stuck.

But there are some other names for CFS, such as the U.K. label, M.E., which stands for myalgic encephalomyelitis, as well as post viral fatigue syndrome. CFS is also known as chronic fatigue immune deficiency syndrome (CFIDS), because it's now believed that CFS sufferers are immune-suppressed, although this is still being debated. But, for the purposes of this chapter, I'll refer to the simpler label that seems to tell it like it is: chronic fatigue syndrome.

The Symptoms of CFS

The term *chronic fatigue syndrome* refers to a *collection* of ill-health symptoms, the most identifiable of which are fatigue and flulike aches and pains.

It wasn't until 1994 that an official definition of chronic fatigue syndrome was actually published in the *Annals of Internal Medicine*. The Centers for Disease Control and Prevention (CDC) have since published official symptoms of CFS. Although many physicians feel the following list of symptoms is limiting and requires some expansion for accuracy, as of this writing, the official defining symptoms of CFS include:

1. *An unexplained fatigue that is "new."* In other words, you've previously felt fine and have only noticed in the last six months or so that you're always fatigued no matter *how* much rest you get. The fatigue is also debilitating; you're not as productive at work, and it interferes with normal social, personal, or academic activities. You've also noticed poor memory or concentration, which affects your activities and performance.
2. In addition to this fatigue, you have four or more of the following, which have persisted for at least six months:
   * sore throat
   * mild or low-grade fever
   * tenderness in the neck and underarm area (where you have lymph nodes, which may be swollen, causing tenderness)
   * muscle pain (called myalgia)
   * pain along the nerve of a joint, without redness or swelling
   * a strange and new kind of headache
   * a sleep that leaves you unrefreshed (a sign of insufficient amounts of non-REM sleep (as discussed on page 46)
   * fatigue, weakness, and generally unwell for twenty-four hours after you've had even moderate exercise

A word about exercise tolerance

Some CFS experts feel that "poor exercise tolerance" (this means that even modest exercise is followed by exhaustion and malaise) is perhaps the *hallmark* symptom of CFS. Research into CFS has uncovered that there is indeed a biological reason for this that has to do with a deficient flow of oxygen and energy to your cells during exercise. Normally, oxygen increases in our bodies with exercise; in CFS sufferers, the opposite has been found: Oxygen seems to decrease with exercise. Without oxygen during exercise, various "poisons" (accumulated substances we produce naturally, such as lactic acid and magnesium) can build up and reduce the efficiency of our tissues and organs. Why this happens remains to be discovered, while the issue of *whether* this is happening at all still needs to be confirmed and further documented, according to many other scientists.

What Your Doctor Should Rule Out

Since there are so many *other* causes of fatigue and malaise, before you're diagnosed with CFS, your doctor should rule out the following:

- multiple sclerosis
- an underactive thyroid gland (known as hypothyroidism)
- sleep disorders (such as sleep apnea or narcolepsy)
- side effects from any medications you're taking
- hepatitis
- major depression or manic-depression, which predates your symptoms (see chapters 1 and 2)
- eating disorders
- substance abuse or alcohol abuse within two years of your current symptoms
- obesity-related fatigue and malaise (if you're very heavy, a number of the symptoms of CFS could be related to your size—see chapter 4 for more information on obesity)
- Lyme disease
- sexually transmitted diseases, including HIV or syphilis

- fatigue related to your menstrual cycle (fatigue is often a symptom of PMS and estrogen loss as women approach menopause); anemia, due to heavy menstrual flow, is a common cause of fatigue
- pregnancy or postpartum-related fatigue (this is discussed in chapter 4)
- allergies—delayed symptoms of an allergic reaction can be joint aches, pains, eczema, and fatigue; foods and environmental toxins can be classic triggers

If none of the above is responsible for your condition, you may be suffering from CFS. It is also possible you may be diagnosed with a frustrating label: *idiopathic fatigue,* which means that your fatigue is of "unknown origin." This is not very helpful, and if your symptoms persist, you should find out why you don't meet CFS criteria.

Fibromyalgia Versus CFS

Fibromyalgia is a soft-tissue disorder that causes you to hurt all over—all the time. It appears to be triggered and/or aggravated by stress. If you notice fatigue and more general aches and pains, this suggests CFS. If you notice *primarily* joint and muscle pains *accompanied* by fatigue, this suggests fibromyalgia.

It is sometimes considered to be an offshoot of arthritis, and it's not unusual to be misdiagnosed with rheumatoid arthritis. Headaches, morning stiffness, and an intolerance to cold, damp weather are common complaints with fibromyalgia. It's also common to suffer from irritable bowel syndrome or bladder problems.

Causes of CFS

There is no official, known cause of CFS. But there are several theories, including everything from viral agents infecting the population to airborne environmental toxins and poisons that can impact the immune system.

Some CFS sufferers have an impaired immune system similar to what happens with HIV infection. This suggests that there *may* be some viral agent(s) at work. But other CFS sufferers have an overactive immune system, suggesting that CFS may be an autoimmune condition. That means your immune system manufactures antibodies that attack your body's own tissues. Autoimmune diseases are triggered by stress.

The pain and inflammation many CFS sufferers report are more likely due to the overactive immune system, while the flulike malaise and fatigue are more likely due to an underactive immune system, which is why CFS continues to remain a mystery to researchers.

When a body is poisoned by environmental toxins, however, it's possible that different toxins can trigger different reactions in different immune systems, which may explain the paradox. Gulf war syndrome, for example, is characterized by a wide array of symptoms. Different bodies may also react differently to the same toxin.

Stress appears to be a major trigger of CFS. When we are under stress, our bodies produce the hormone adrenaline, which increases our heart rate, blood flow, and blood pressure. Adrenaline may aggravate the inflammation and pain in many CFS and fibromyalgia sufferers.

Some experts who treat CFS and fibromyalgia believe that a lack of non-REM sleep may also be a factor in this disorder. In fact, many have gone on record to say that chronic fatigue syndrome is really a sleep-related disorder. One Canadian study deliberately deprived a group of medical students of non-REM sleep for several nights. Within the next few days, each of the study participants developed symptoms of CFS and/or fibromyalgia.

Treatments

Since experts agree that CFS is an environmental illness triggered by stress, it follows that diet and lifestyle modification would be an effective treatment. Some CFS experts believe that since so many CFS sufferers have candida, adjusting the diet is a logical first step. *Candida* is a parasite that normally inhabits the digestive tract. This parasite can overgrow, spread to other places in the body, and damage the immune system. (Certain "trigger foods"—foods that typically trigger allergies, or fungal infections caused by an overgrowth of the fungus *Candida albicans*—include processed foods and foods high in sugar or yeast.) When these foods are eliminated and replaced with more nutritious, vitamin-packed, organic foods, CFS symptoms frequently improve. To date, diet modification is the most effective treatment CFS experts recommend. They also suggest cognitive therapy, which is a type of counseling that helps you to "shift" your thinking or focus. (See chapter 6 for details.)

Often, a move to a cleaner environment is also useful (changing jobs or telecommuting if you believe you're being exposed to workplace toxins; moving from an urban center to a suburb or rural area).

Downshifting, a term coined to describe people who simplify their lifestyles by shedding the urban "noise and toys," often works wonders to eliminate some stress and improve CFS. This may involve moving to a smaller home or apartment, with a lower monthly payment; leaving a job; buying that farm you've always wanted; or just cashing in your investments to take a long trip. (This was known in the 1960s as "dropping out.")

CFS experts and fellow sufferers caution you about taking antidepressants (discussed in chapter 8)—often the first thing a medical doctor prescribes. Since antidepressants have many side effects that can aggravate CFS symptoms, they are reportedly not the best solution as a first-line treatment for CFS. The general advice is to clean up the diet and lifestyle first to see if your symptoms improve. Symptoms of depression in CFS often resolve when you start to feel a little better physically, which enables you to get out of the house.

Numerous alternative therapies have been reported to work with CFS. Check out chapter 8 for starters. Then, review my list of CFS resources at the back of this book. Many of these organizations have Web sites and monthly newsletters with the "latest" treatment trends. I hesitate, as of this writing, to recommend much of what I came across in my research because it is simply not yet substantiated. But like so many herbs and alternative therapies, from glucosamine sulphate (for arthritis) to St. John's wort (for depression) (see chapter 8), just because they're unproven in traditional scientific studies doesn't mean they don't work. Time will tell.

THYROID DISORDERS

The thyroid gland is responsible for making thyroid hormone, which drives the function of every cell in your body. If your gland is either overproducing or underproducing thyroid hormone, your energy levels and emotional responses will be affected. When your thyroid gland makes too much thyroid hormone, you suffer from *hyper*thyroidism. When your thyroid gland does not make enough thyroid hormone, you suffer from *hypo*thyroidism. In most cases, autoimmune diseases cause the thyroid gland to malfunction, which means that your body produces antibodies that attack the thyroid gland.

Hyperthyroid symptoms often imitate those of major depression and bipolar disorder (see chapter 2). Until the mid-1970s, women with hyperthyroidism were diagnosed as hysterical, depressed, or emotionally unbalanced. They were often referred to psychiatrists. But as stress-related ailments became more prevalent in the 1980s and 1990s, women with hyperthyroid are now often told they're under too much stress, which again does not treat the underlying physical disorder.

Hypothyroidism is linked to depression more frequently than hyperthyroidism. Sometimes, psychiatrists find that hypothyroid patients can exhibit certain behaviors linked to psychosis, such as paranoia or auditory and visual hallucinations (hearing voices, seeing things that aren't there).

The most common autoimmune thyroid diseases are Graves' disease and Hashimoto's thyroiditis. Graves' disease causes your thyroid gland to be overactive, while Hashimoto's thyroiditis causes your thyroid gland to be underactive. Women suffer from thyroid disorders about ten times as frequently as men, and therefore it is women who suffer from continuous and classic thyroid misdiagnosis.

Before you accept a diagnosis of depression or another mood disorder, request that your mental health practitioner perform a thyroid function test so that mood problems related to thyroid disease can be ruled out. If thyroid disease is the cause of your mood disorder symptoms, as soon as your thyroid problem is treated, you'll find your mood disorder will vanish. That said, it is possible for people to have both a thyroid condition and a mood disorder (or other mental illnesses, too). In these cases, the psychiatric symptoms may result after a thyroid condition has been treated, or persist despite thyroid treatment. In short, someone with a thyroid condition is not necessarily exempt from depression or other psychiatric illnesses.

Symptoms

Symptoms of thyroid disease come in two groups; which one *you* suffer depends on whether you're hyperthyroid or hypothyroid.

If you're hyperthyroid . . .

Your body functions speed up, your heart rate increases, and you may lose weight but eat more. You may also notice excessive perspiration, an intolerance to heat, irregular periods, and diarrhea. Many of the same symptoms are seen in depression, such as exhaustion (from an overworked physique), insomnia, irritability, restlessness and nervousness, anxiety, and general fatigue (caused by the insomnia). It is because of the emotional symptoms exhibited in hyperthyroidism that so many women are diagnosed with mood disorders. This is particularly true after a pregnancy. Obviously, when these emotional symptoms are caused by a *physical* problem, no amount of psychotherapy will make you feel better—which may just exacerbate the symptoms. This becomes a nightmarish merry-go-round for the misdiagnosed.

If you're hypothyroid . . .

Your body slows down, creating some classic physical symptoms which include constipation, bloating and fluid retention, a decreased appetite, lack of sex drive, dry hair, dry skin, intolerance to cold temperatures, and irregular periods. The emotional symptoms of hypothyroidism are different—extreme fatigue and lethargy regardless of how much sleep you get, as well as symptoms of depression.

Treatment

A simple blood test will confirm whether you are hyper- or hypothyroid. Treatment for hyperthyroidism depends on what is causing the gland to become overactive, but ultimately your thyroid gland will probably be chemically "deadened." You'll be put on synthetic thyroid hormone (levothyroxine sodium), which replaces the natural hormone your thyroid makes. In the second scenario, synthetic thyroid hormone replenishes or "tops up" your diminished supply.

In addition to thyroid disease, many kinds of autoimmune diseases plague women. These include multiple sclerosis (more common in colder climates), lupus, and rheumatoid arthritis. However, it is thyroid disease that is the most common culprit in a misdiagnosis of depression, and thyroid disease which is the most easily treated.

SEASONAL AFFECTIVE DISORDER (SAD): LIGHT-DEPRIVED

I'm sure by now you've read a lot about seasonal affective disorder (SAD). This is a fairly recent label that wasn't used until 1987, even though mood disorders have long been known to be triggered by changes in seasons. The person with SAD will notice atypical symptoms of depression during the winter: She sleeps too much and eats too much (thereby gaining weight). Then she begins to "wake up" in the spring and can even be slightly manic (known as hypomanic). (Occasionally, the reverse occurs, and the depression comes on during the summer months instead, where the symptoms of major depression present themselves. Some of this may be related to extreme discomfort in humid, hot weather; inability to sleep as a result; increased pollutants in the air; and all the other miseries of humid, hot urban summers.) In short, SAD has many of the features of "hibernation"—oversleeping and storing up high fat or carbohydrates for the cold winter. It's this "bear and squirrel" behavior in humans that can be debilitating.

SAD strikes women in their twenties and thirties and is more typically seen in regions at higher latitudes. Light at the end of the tunnel—literally, is in sight for women with SAD.

Living or working in areas that are light-deprived can also lead to SAD. For example, people who spend weeks or months at a time on submarines exhibit symptoms of SAD. And here's a true urban tale: A friend developed a bad case of SAD when she moved into a basement apartment without windows. Since she was looking for a cheap "crash pad" for a couple of months while she was in a transition period, she wanted something serviceable but didn't consider the "no window" factor as being problematic. It was. Within a couple of weeks, she began craving sweets and junk food and became quite blue, irritable, and apathetic: She was depressed. Several friends commented that she should move to a place with windows. She did. Her symptoms vanished within about a week. She was amazed at how dramatically her basement flat had affected her mood.

Treating SAD

Light can be like a drug. If you've been diagnosed with SAD, you may have been prescribed light rather than pills (medications may also be effective). Often, the "cure" for SAD is to re-create the kind of light you'd naturally be exposed to on a nice summer's day. Sitting under your chandelier won't do. However, it isn't necessary to have sunlight or sunlike light. You can get the light you need with a "light box," which utilizes bright, full-spectrum fluorescent or incandescent lights, covered with a sheer material to protect your eyes. Maximum effectiveness occurs when you sit approximately a foot and a half away from the lights for 30 to 120 minutes each day.

For this therapy to work, you need to keep your eyes open, so napping isn't a good thing. However, there is an experimental device known as a dawn simulator, which can work while you sleep. Most people start to feel better in a few days of 30-minute light treatments.

However, there are some side effects: Mild headaches or eyestrain are not unusual, and sometimes mild mania (from the production of serotonin) may occur. If you're taking a drug that makes you sensitive to bright light, you are not a good candidate for this therapy. See your doctor for information on purchasing a light box.

Bright-light therapy has also been shown to help depression that isn't necessarily a result of SAD but is related to a disorder known as circadian rhythm sleep (disorders having to do with how the brain perceives time and light, which are often termed the *biological clock*). In this case, light therapy during the day has been shown to help with sleep problems.

BATHROOM BLUES

The signs of stress aren't always visible in your mood or disposition. Your body may be reacting to stress much more than you realize. Irritable bowel syndrome (IBS) and interstitial cystitis (IC) are disorders that affect mostly women and are believed to be triggered by stress. Thus, by reducing your stress, you may be able to find significant relief from these disorders.

Hazards of Not Being Able to Go to the Bathroom

Sometimes bathroom-related stress is caused by not being able to get to a bathroom. Hats off to the ABC news program "20/20" for exposing one of the most ignored occupational hazards women put up with daily: not enough, or poorly designed, bathrooms in the workplace. Well, here's a news flash for business and industry: Women have a uterus that presses down on the bladder, which biologically necessitates more frequent urination. Frequency increases, of course, with pregnancy, fibroids, and other below-the-belt nuisances women endure. Heavy periods also often necessitate frequent trips to the bathroom. Being forced to "hold it" is unhealthy physically and psychologically. Physically, women are at high risk for developing urinary incontinence, urinary tract infections, and interstitial cystitis. The latter is associated with chronic pelvic pain, frequent urge without "results," and sometimes incontinence.

The most shocking example of how pervasive this bathroom problem is comes from the program's report on the practices of a Fortune 500 company. One of its central plants in the United States had only one toilet for more than a hundred female employees. There was not enough time on their breaks for these women to wait in line to go to the bathroom. The penalty for coming back from the break "late" was docked pay. The result was that many of these women were forced to wear incontinence briefs (a.k.a. "adult diapers") just so they could continue working without being tormented by the urge to urinate.

Restraining yourself from the urge to defecate also presents some nasty health hazards for women. For example, many more women than men are diagnosed with irritable bowel syndrome, which is often characterized by diarrhea and actually thought to be caused by stress. Many women also suffer from inflammatory bowel disease (a much more serious condition that occurs when one or more parts of the small or large intestine becomes inflamed), which also leads to frequent bouts of bloody, mucous-filled diarrhea. Both conditions may be aggravated by stress and menstruation.

These practices cause enormous psychological damage to women, of course. When grown women are forced to wear diapers, they suffer from low self-esteem, unexpressed anger, and myriad negative feelings and thoughts that can trigger the symptoms of depression discussed in chapter 1.

In many workplaces, women have to actually ask permission from their superiors to go to the bathroom. Again, this infantilizes women and should not be tolerated. Because more women than men work in visible yet vulnerable areas, such as reception or secretarial/assistant positions, sometimes getting up and leaving their desk is not possible. In these cases, adequate coverage from a second or third person should be provided. Many women also report that their superiors note the number of times they go to the bathroom. Sometimes these logs come back to haunt women in performance reviews in the form of "frequent absences from the desk." If you can relate to this section, it's worth noting how much aggravation and stress are added to your day simply because you do not feel at liberty to go the bathroom when you want to.

Irritable Bowels?

A most confusing label has come into vogue and now defines the bowel habits of twenty-five to fifty-five million North Americans, two-thirds of whom are women. The label is irritable bowel syndrome (IBS), which refers to unusual bowel "patterns" that alternate between diarrhea and constipation, and everything in between. IBS is also referred to as irritable or spastic colon; spastic, mucous, nervous, laxative, cathartic, or functional colitis; spastic bowel; nervous indigestion; functional dyspepsia; pylorospasm; and functional bowel disease. The problem with using the term *irritable* is that irritation is *not* what's going on. It also sounds too much like *inflammatory*, which is not what's going on, either. In fact, inflammatory bowel disease (IBD) is a different condition, one that is serious, chronic, and *does* involve an inflammation of parts of the small or large intestine.

Worse, many family doctors say "IBS" instead of "we don't know what's going on—but have you tried fiber?"

The term *irritable bowel syndrome* came into use to describe a bowel that is overly sensitive to normal activity. In other words, when the nerve endings that line the bowel are too sensitive, the nerves controlling the gastrointestinal tract can become overactive, which makes the bowel overly responsive or "irritable" to normal things, such as passing gas or fluid. In other words, the bowel may want to pass a stool before it should. The bowel, in a sense, becomes too "touchy" for comfort. However, since we tend to think of irritable when used clinically—as something that is red, irritated, or inflamed—this label is more confusing than defining. IBS has nothing to do with irritation, inflammation, or any organic disease process. It is about nerves.

The term *IBS* also implies that a diagnosis of your symptoms has been made and that there is a definite cause—and cure—for your condition. This is not so. IBS is a diagnosis made in the absence of any other diagnosis. There is no test to confirm IBS, only tests to rule out other causes for your symptoms. The term *functional bowel disorder* is beginning to catch on instead of IBS, because "functional" means that there is no disease. No matter what you call it, roughly half of all digestive disorders are attributed to IBS. After the common cold, IBS is the chief cause of absenteeism from work. Many doctors compare IBS to "asthma," because there are a number of causes with the same outcome. Asthma may be related to allergies or a hundred other things. Similarly, IBS has many different causes that are difficult to pin down. However, most experts agree that stress and dietary factors are most likely the chief culprits.

IBS symptoms

IBS symptoms are characterized by frequent, violent episodes of diarrhea, which will almost always strike after a stressful situation. (People often experience IBS symptoms before job interviews or plane trips.) More than 60 percent of IBS sufferers report that their symptoms first coincided with stressful life events, while 40 to 60 percent of people with IBS also suffer from anxiety disorders or depression, compared to 20 percent of people with other gastrointestinal disorders. Stressful life events that can bring on IBS include the death of a loved one, separation/divorce, unresolved conflict or grief, moving to a new city or job, as well as having a childhood history of physical or sexual abuse.

Many people find that their symptoms persist well beyond the stressful life event and that the episodes invade their normal routine. It isn't a matter of one, single stressful event that precipitates IBS; it could first present itself after you've been in a stressful job for a long period of time or have been subjected to the normal stresses of "life in North America" for a long period of time. The episodes of diarrhea are often accompanied by crampy, abdominal pains, or gas, which are relieved by a bowel movement. The pain may shift to the abdomen as well. After the episodes of diarrhea, you may then be plagued by long bouts of constipation, or the feeling that you're not emptying your bowels completely. Again, IBS refers to an irregular bowel *pattern* rather than one particular episode. The pattern is that there is no *normal* pattern of bowel movements; it is often one extreme or another.

Your stools may also contain mucus, which can make the stool long and ropelike or wormlike. The mucus is normally secreted by the colon to help the stool along in a normal movement. In IBS, your colon secretes too much mucus.

Blood mixed with your stools means "this is *not* IBS but something else." Some people can also suffer solely from diarrhea, or solely gas and constipation. Other symptoms include bloating, nausea, and loss of appetite. Fever, weight loss, or severe pain is not a sign of IBS.

Many people find it confusing that IBS can cause both constipation and diarrhea, which seem to be opposite ends of the spectrum. But what is happening is that instead of the slow muscular contractions that normally move the bowels, spasms occur, which can either result in an "explosion" or a "blockage." It's akin to a sudden gust of wind: It can blow the door wide open (diarrhea) or blow it shut (constipation). It all depends on the direction of the wind.

It's important to note the timing of your diarrhea; in IBS, your sleep should not be disturbed by it. The episodes will always occur either after a meal or in the early evening.

The following distinguishes IBS from infectious diarrhea or inflammatory bowel diseases:

- finding relief through defecation
- noticing looser stools when the bowel movement is precipitated by pain
- noticing more frequent bowel movements when you experience pain
- noticing abdominal bloating or distention
- noticing mucus in the stools
- feeling that you have not completely emptied your bowels

What to rule out

The symptoms of IBS are obviously vague in that they can be signs of many other problems. Therefore, before you accept a diagnosis of IBS, make sure your doctor has taken a careful history to investigate:

- dietary culprits: food allergies, lactose intolerance, or just plain poor diet (i.e., high fats/starch; low fiber)
- intestinal bacterial, viral, or parasitic infections (where have you been traveling? what are your sexual habits?)
- overgrowth of *C. difficile,* a common cause of infectious diarrhea

- yeast in the gastrointestinal tract (called candidiasis), which is notorious for causing IBS symptoms (eating yogurt every day should clear this up)
- medications
- gastrointestinal disorders, such as dysmotility, where the stomach muscles are not moving properly, which causes bloating, nausea, and other problems
- enzyme deficiencies (the pancreas may not be secreting enough enzymes to break down your food)
- serious disease, such as inflammatory bowel disease or signs of cancer

Stress and IBS

It's possible to have a well-balanced diet, rule out all forms of organic disease, yet still suffer from IBS while under stress. In the same way that you can sweat, blush, or cry under emotional stress, your gastrointestinal tract may also react to stress by "weeping"—producing excessive water and mucus, and overreacting to normal stimuli, such as eating. What often happens, however, is that there is a delayed gut reaction to stress, and you may not experience your IBS symptoms until your stress has passed. Apparently, under stress your brain becomes more active as a defense. (For example, when we're running away from a predator, we have to think and act quickly, so our heart rates increase, and we sweat more.) During this defensive mode, the entire nervous system can become exaggerated (that's what causes butterflies in the stomach). The nerves controlling the gastrointestinal tract therefore become highly sensitive, which can cause IBS symptoms. Studies show, for example, that IBS symptoms are more common on weekday mornings than afternoons or weekends, and IBS symptoms do not appear while you're sleeping.

Women and IBS

Why is IBS more common in women? For one thing, women menstruate and experience normal mood fluctuations related to their natural menstrual cycles. Mood changes are common premenstrual symptoms that may create more emotional stress and, hence, IBS symptoms. Another factor is uterine contractions during menstruation. When the uterus contracts, it often stimulates a bowel movement. The first day of a woman's period is often a day where she has several loose bowel movements. (A common symptom of labor is diarrhea and vomiting. This occurs because of the intensity of the uterine contractions, which create ripples throughout the gastrointestinal tract.)

Women who experience painful periods or endometriosis may also experience IBS symptoms more intensely. In endometriosis, parts of the uterine lining grow outside of the uterus into the abdominal cavity, which often triggers painful bowel movements, diarrhea, or constipation during or just prior to menstruation.

Finally, women are more prone to eating disorders and laxative abuse, as well as domestic abuse (resulting in continuous emotional upset and stress), all of which wreak havoc on the gastrointestinal tract.

Bladder Problems

Another stress-related condition women suffer from is interstitial cystitis (IC), which is the inflammation of the interstitium, the space between the bladder lining and bladder muscle. This can cause chronic pelvic pain, urinary frequency, and a shrunken, ulcerated bladder. The bladder itself is lined with a protective layer that is secreted, like mucus, by the cells that line it. This layer protects the inside of the bladder from acids and toxins in the urine and prevents bacteria from sticking to the bladder wall. If this layer is damaged, as is the case with IC, infection can result.

IC symptoms include frequent urination (as many as sixty times a day). In addition, you may feel a bruising kind of pain around your clitoral area, and may find that acidic foods, chocolate, red wine, aged cheese, nuts, yogurt, avocados, and bananas—and sometimes antibiotics—seem to exacerbate the pain. IC starts as a normal urinary tract infection (known as bacterial cystitis), but after a few bouts of cystitis, the urine cultures will all be negative.

There are several theories as to the causes of IC, including increased progesterone levels. In fact, postmenopausal women on progesterone may notice cystitis symptoms more often than premenopausal women. If you have IC, you'll need to see a urologist. There are numerous treatments that include anti-inflammatory drugs and bladder relaxants.

STRESS REDUCTION

Since so many of the health problems discussed in this chapter are manifestations of stress, what can you realistically do to lower your stress? Being told to simply "take things easy" and "relax" is not a solution, because indeed, if we weren't so stressed, we *would* relax.

Stress reduction entirely depends on the source of your stress. The only way to control stress that is beyond your control is to shift your response to it. And, for many women, this takes time and may require some work with a qualified counselor, which is discussed in chapters 5 and 6.

If you are the source of your own stress because you're too hard on yourself, or are a perfectionist, work on lowering your self-expectations and forgive yourself for not being perfect. Again, seek the help of a therapist or counselor. In the meantime, here are some suggestions for reducing some sources of daily stress:

1. Isolate the exact source of stress to see if there's a solution. (Taking the time to think about what, in fact, the real problem is can work wonders.)
2. See the humor in difficult situations, and try to look at lessons learned instead of beating yourself up.
3. When times get tough, surround yourself with supportive people, such as close friends and family members.

4. Don't take things personally. When people don't respond to you the way you'd like, consider other factors. For instance, maybe the other person has problems unrelated to you that are affecting her behavior. (See the "Cognitive-Behavioral Therapy" section in chapter 6.)

5. Focus on something pleasant in the future, such as a vacation, and allow yourself time to daydream and plan.

6. Just say no. If you can't take on that small favor or extra task, just politely say "I'd love to, but it's impossible. . . ."

7. Make time for yourself. Spend time alone and block out everyone once a week or so. Go for a long walk, and get in a little exercise.

8. Make lists. Some people find list making really helps; others find it is just another "chore." But if you haven't been a list maker, try it. It might help you to become a little more focused on and organized with the tasks at hand.

9. Look at some alternative-healing systems, such as massage and Chinese exercises such as qi gong (pronounced "chi kong") or tai chi.

10. Eat properly, and get enough sleep.

A Little Hedonism Goes a Long Way

I know this sounds glib and trite and looks like it's been torn from the pages of the latest fluff magazine, but many women report that small pleasures can help them unwind. If you have children, try to schedule in the following pleasures at least once every couple of weeks:

1. Aromatherapy. Who *cares* if it doesn't have the medicinal benefits it claims to (although, for many women, it does). It smells nice and makes you feel pampered and special. Splurge on a diffuser, buy some "tea lights," take a bath, turn the lights off, and soak up the atmosphere for twenty minutes.

2. Take a bath *anyway.* Bubble baths are important. (If you have sensitive skin, ask a dermatologist or family doctor to recommend something that soothes it, such as Epsom salts or baking soda.) Many women make this a nightly ritual. If you really want to be decadent, take a glass of wine or a favorite food into the tub with you.

3. Schedule some sex. There's nothing like a good orgasm to help you release steam. If you don't have a sexual partner, get a vibrator (which can be ordered discreetly through various magazines).

4. Modern meditation. Okay, so not everyone can get into meditating properly, complete with chants and incense. So here's a compromise: Put on your favorite music, turn out the lights, and light a candle. It's amazing what this can do for your mental health.

5. Go for a walk around the block without thinking about it as exercise. We're talking "stroll," not a brisk walk that gets your heart rate up. This is a great way to just let your mind wander and reset your batteries.

6. Do a chick-flick night. Whether it's seeing *Gone With The Wind* for the fiftieth time or salivating over your favorite male or female lead, be decadent. Make popcorn, fondue, or whatever turns you on. The rule is not to feel guilty about having your own time with the VCR.

Many of the disorders in this chapter are soothed by validation and behavior modification. The next chapter continues with the same theme. When mood swings and depression are related to body image and female biology, validating the negative feelings generated by society's expectations of women and then changing our response to those expectations can calm us.

Chapter 4

Body Image, Hormones, and Cycle-Logical Issues

Women have a hard time with "out-of-body" experiences because we seldom stop *thinking* about our bodies. Whether it's an unhealthy fixation on our weight and physical appearance, the need to plan our lives around our menstrual cycles, making choices about our fertility, or experiencing the normal changes of our reproductive life cycles, our moods are intricately wound around how *we* feel about our bodies and how our bodies make *us* feel. This chapter explores the role body image plays in depression and then discusses hormonal factors that contribute to premenstrual, postpartum, and menopausal depression.

BODY IMAGE

Most women are depressed by what they see in the mirror. A third of American women believe they are overweight. Fifteen percent of young women have substantially disordered eating attitudes and behavior, and more than five million Americans suffer from an eating disorder. A *New York Times* poll found that 36 percent of girls ages thirteen to seventeen wanted to change their looks. A 1995 survey of girls in grades nine through twelve conducted by the Centers for Disease Control found that 60 percent of them were trying to lose weight and that 5 to 10 percent of girls fourteen and older suffer from eating disorders.

During a recent lecture, a man asked me to describe what it feels like to be a woman in our culture. I told him that it begins the moment we get up in the morning: continuous bombardment of beauty and fitness images from all forms of media. The result is that we are never beautiful enough, thin enough, or young enough to feel good about ourselves. Wherever we go, our appearance is watched and judged. Although women may be able to make peace with their appearance and accept their bodies, it is almost impossible for most women to feel truly beautiful.

The man was stunned and said: "This can't be true; it sounds so painful to be a woman." I then turned to the audience, where about a hundred women were sitting, and asked them if there was anyone who disagreed or who felt that what I had just said was inaccurate. No woman raised her hand. Instead, they quietly nodded to me, and some mouthed "it's so true."

Women's bodies are objects in our current culture, used to uphold and impose impossible standards of beauty. No woman is immune to this powerful psychological attack. We have created a culture in which women see their bodies as objects, too. Experts on women, health, and body image see a literal separation between mind, body, and spirit, sometimes known as mind/body dualism.

Women's relationships with their bodies are complex. Their bodies are their source of power. When the body ages or is otherwise deemed to be less attractive, this translates as a loss of power. When women rely on their bodies to empower them, it interferes with their real autonomy—the power to run their own lives.

By focusing on our bodies, we have lost many of our strengths as women. Some authors suggest this is a deliberate ploy by the male-dominated world to distract us from the business of real liberation, which, as Gloria Steinem has said, is a revolution, not public relations.

Because our body sizes can be manipulated and changed through eating, food, dieting, starving, and exercising, the body has become a live sculpture for millions of women, who essentially "sculpt" their bodies, using food as the "clay" in order to try to get the ideal size and shape. But since food is more than just clay—it is either a source of comfort or torture—many women have developed complex and often contradictory behaviors to have their comfort and clay too. (Of course, face-lifts, liposuction, breast augmentation, and other cosmetic surgeries—including injecting poison into the face, known as Botox treatments to eliminate wrinkles—are serving this "live sculpture" theme. For the purposes of this chapter, I limit the discussion to the issue of weight.)

If a woman wants to sculpt herself into a thin body, then she has to control how much clay she uses. That could mean she either severely limits the food she ingests or she purges after eating. If she wants to surround herself with flesh and comfort and make her body large, then she may binge on food without purging. If she wants to sculpt herself into a skeleton, which she perceives as a symbol of her self-restraint and control, then she will deny herself comfort at all costs and simply refuse food altogether. She would rather die than show that she wants comfort.

Since almost all of her worth is invested in her outer appearance (whether she admits it or not), feelings of self-loathing and low self-esteem are driven by her perception of her body image. When a woman is depressed, her feelings of low self-esteem cannot be separated from her body image. Matters grow even more complicated when we address social issues, such as the aftermath of sexual abuse. When her body has been invaded, a woman often manipulates her body size to make it less appealing to future attackers.

This section looks at the *behaviors* involved in sculpting various body sizes, and the meaning of different body sizes. There are just as many women, for example, who have an interest in being large as there are women who desire to be thin. This section will not tell you how to get down—or up—to your desired weight but will help to outline some of the reasons *why* you may desire the weight you strive for. By understanding why you want the body you want, you may be better able to understand how your perception of your body

Signs of a Body-Image or Eating Problem
- preoccupation and obsession with food and weight
- narrowing your food choices as the days pass (i.e., this week it's no fat; next week it's no carbohydrates, etc.)
- insisting you're fat when you're not
- feeling guilty or ashamed to eat in public
- exercising to lose weight rather than to be fit
- overly concerned about your appearance
- noticeable mood changes in association with your appearance (i.e., feeling depressed or sad after you've eaten a big meal)
- seeing only two types of bodies: fat or thin versus healthy, normal, or average
- self-loathing after eating
- avoiding public or family gatherings because you don't look good enough
- not participating in activities that require you to wear shorts or bathing suits
- avoiding sexual relations because you hate your body

image and the resulting behavior are driving you to despair. The chart on page 78 can help you to identify whether or not body image could be contributing to your depression.

What It Means to Be Thin

At one point in our culture, to be thin meant to be poor and hungry; a plump woman was a wealthy, successful woman. But two significant trends emerged to change the perception of "thin." First, food-distribution patterns changed in North America, and nutritious foods became more expensive than low-nutrient, fattening foods. Fat started to be associated with the lower class. Second, as women began to flood the workplace, their bodies became masculinized. The successful woman was a tall, thin, mannish woman who did not show evidence, on her body, of being female or of harboring reproductive organs. The beauty standard that we see on runways and in magazines reflects the masculinization of the female form. Since women instinctively realize that their bodies must be controlled in order to look masculine, they have associated feminine curves with a loss of control. The successful woman can look like a man because she *controls* her food intake. The unsuccessful woman cannot control her food intake and therefore takes on the rounder shape, which is rejected by society. Controlling food is synonymous with self-control, self-discipline, and, ultimately, success—another facet of the power struggle.

For many women, controlling the shape of their bodies gives them a sense of accomplishment. The irony is that sometimes a thin body leaves the impression of ineffectiveness, delicateness, and frailty.

Achieving thinness

Two percent of the female population in North America view starving and purging as a normal way to control weight. Experts estimate that this number is actually much higher, because many women successfully hide their disorder for years. The two most common eating disorders involving starvation are anorexia nervosa ("loss of appetite due to mental disorder") and bingeing followed by purging, known as bulimia nervosa ("hunger like an ox due to mental disorder"). Women will purge after a bingeing episode by inducing vomiting or abusing laxatives, diuretics, and thyroid hormone. The most horrifying examples occur in women with Type 1 diabetes, who sometimes deliberately withhold their insulin to control their weight.

Another type of purging behavior is overexercising. Today, rigorous, strenuous exercise has become socially acceptable feminine behavior. A skeleton with biceps is the current ideal, an image that is reinforced by several female celebrities.

Eating disorders are diseases of control and primarily affect women, although in recent years more men have become vulnerable. Bulimics and anorectics are usually overachievers in other aspects of their lives and view excess weight as an announcement to the world that they are "out of control." This view becomes more distorted as time passes, until the act of eating food in public (in bulimia) or at all (in anorexia) is perceived to be equivalent to a loss of control.

In anorexia, the person's emotional and sensual desires are channeled through food. These desires are so great that the anorectic fears that once she eats she'll never stop, because her appetite/desires will know no natural boundaries; her fear of food drives her disease. Many experts also see eating disorders as an addiction to perfection; the sense of control the eating-disordered woman gains through this behavior is the drug.

Most of us find it easier to relate to the bulimic than the anorectic; bulimics express their loss of control through bingeing in the same way that someone else may yell at her children. Bulimics then purge to regain their control. There is a feeling of comfort for bulimics in both the binge and the purge. Bulimics are sometimes referred to as "failed anorectics" because if they could, they'd starve. Anorectics, however, are masters of control. They never break. I once asked a recovering anorectic the dumb question, "But didn't you get *hungry*?" Her response was that the hunger pangs made her feel powerful. The more intense the hunger, the more powerful she felt; the power actually gave her a high, which reinforced the addiction theory.

The onset of anorexia has traditionally been seen during adolescence, when the female body is changing dramatically. Controlling her food intake is viewed by the teenage anorectic as controlling her puberty—trying to stop her body from changing into that of a woman's. However, this disease is also seen in a number of older women, in their thirties and forties. Here, the woman may be expressing her desire to stop her body from changing as well—but, in this case, the change she is trying to stop is age itself. Many older women who are anorexic are overlooked because they are not "young," even though the shame and struggle of their eating disorder may be more pronounced because of their age.

What It Means to Be Fat

Many people see fat and the act of getting fat (i.e., overeating behavior) as a public refusal to play by the rules when it comes to society's expectations of women today. If you recognize yourself here, you might wish to explore what being fat means to you—and what might be driving your addiction to food.

As women, we might still find ourselves purchasing and preparing most of the food for our families. We are nurturers and providers. But we are also, according to the media by virtue of the images they present, expected to reach impossible standards of beauty, fitness, and weight. Most of us can't meet these standards, and the result is often a feeling of powerlessness. Some women choose to manipulate their own body shape and size in order not to succumb to this feeling. By eating more food and thus gaining more weight, these women are actively resisting an impossible goal. In this case, the act of getting fat expresses an unconscious desire to gain control over one's life.

Psychotherapists urge women who want to lose weight to try to understand what conscious or unconscious needs are being met by the fat. Some believe that fat both isolates a woman and publicly proclaims her a failure. This sad truth is confirmed by therapists who work with women on weight-loss issues. Unfortunately, however, being overweight is often used to psychological advantage. In other words, the fat can "excuse" a woman from being successful in both the sexual (i.e., love) and the financial (i.e., career) arenas. Not only is the fat woman not accountable for her lack of success, but success is also something that is not expected of her.

Fat, in this case, lets a woman stay put. If she equates thinness with success, then fatness becomes the reason for all her own failed attempts at success. Fat is protective; it even serves to protect women from the horror of looking at her own demons and fears and, in so doing, keeps her from identifying just what it is she really wants.

When fat means "mother"

Some women—especially those who have gained weight later in life—associate fat with the act of mothering and being mothered. It's natural to seek situations or relationships that "mimic" the ones we experienced in childhood; this also gives us a chance to resolve certain relationships. When fat actually does mean "mother," it's worth exploring what the fat is replacing. After all, our mothers' breasts initially nurture us, and it is through our mothers that we learn about food and food behaviors. Our mothers are also the source of love, comfort, emotional support, and sense of what is acceptable. Even when we do not get this from our own mothers, we still associate "mothering" with these behaviors. Therapists have observed that this association is a dangerous one, because it gets tangled up in mother-daughter relationships and can have varied meanings and consequences for the overweight woman. Some daughters use fat as a way to rebel against their mothers' standards or as a means of expressing anger at their mothers for inadequate nurturing. Fat can also be used as a cry for help or as a ready replacement for the help a mother might normally provide. In the latter, fat expresses an unconscious desire to carry the soothing and nurturing aspects of "mother" with us wherever we go.

When fat means "screw you"

Fat can also be combative. Many women regard their fat as an expression of anger at impossible standards of beauty, restrictive sexual roles, and expectations. Fat doesn't protect, it offends. Deliberately. Fat can be very much an expletive—a big "screw you" and a challenge to anyone who dares to penetrate the layers.

The Act of Getting Fat: Compulsive Eating

When we hear eating disorder, we usually think about anorexia or bulimia. There are many people, however, who binge without purging. This is also known as binge eating disorder (a.k.a. compulsive overeating). In this case, the bingeing is still an announcement to the world that "I'm out of control." Someone who purges her bingeing behavior is hiding her lack of control. Someone who binges and never purges is *advertising* her lack of control. The purger is passively asking for help; the binger who doesn't purge is aggressively asking for help. It's the same disease with a different result.

There is one more layer when it comes to compulsive overeating, which is considered to be controversial and is often rejected by the overeater: The desire to get fat is often behind the compulsion. Many people who overeat insist that fat is a consequence of eating food, not a *goal*. Many therapists who deal with overeating disagree and believe that if a woman admits that she has an emotional interest in actually being large, she may be much closer to stopping her compulsion to eat.

Many women who eat compulsively do not recognize that they are doing so. The following is a typical profile of a compulsive eater:

- eating when you're not hungry
- feeling out of control when you're around food, either trying to resist it or gorging on it
- spending a lot of time thinking or worrying about food and your weight
- always desperate to try another diet that promises results
- feelings of self-loathing and shame
- hating your own body
- obsessing over what you can or will eat, or *have* eaten
- eating in secret or with "eating friends"
- appearing in public to be a professional dieter who's in control
- buying cakes or pies as "gifts" and having them wrapped to hide the fact that they're for you
- having a "pristine" kitchen with only the "right" foods
- feeling either out of control with food (compulsive eating) or imprisoned by it (dieting)
- feeling temporary relief by "not eating"
- looking forward with pleasure and anticipation to the time when you can eat alone
- feeling unhappy because of your eating behavior

Drug Treatment for Obesity

Drug treatment for obesity has a pretty shady past. Throughout the 1950s, 1960s, and even 1970s, women were prescribed thyroxine— thyroid hormone—to speed up their metabolism. Thyroxine is a dangerous medication for people with normal functioning thyroid glands and can cause heart failure. Request a thyroid-function test before you accept this medication.

It used to be common practice for doctors to prescribe ampheta-mines or "speed" to increase the body's metabolism. They, too, are dangerous and can put your health at risk.

Antiobesity pills

An antiobesity pill that works by a system of reward and punish-ment was recently approved by the U.S. government. Orlistat (Xenical) blocks the absorption of almost one-third of the fat that people eat. But there's a heavy price to pay for eating fat: You'll no-tice rather embarrassing diarrhea each time you eat fatty foods. Talk about a deterrent! To avoid the drug's side effects, simply avoid fat. But the pill can also decrease absorption of vitamin D and other im-portant nutrients.

Orlistat is the first drug to fight obesity by working through the intestine instead of the brain. Taken with each meal, it binds to cer-tain pancreatic enzymes to block the digestion of 30 percent of the fat you ingest. Its long-term effects on the pancreas are unknown. Combined with a sensible diet, people on Orlistat lost more weight than those who did not take the drug. Orlistat is not intended for people who need to lose a few pounds; it is designed for medically obese people. (Orlistat was also found to lower cholesterol, blood pressure, and blood-sugar levels.)

One of the most controversial antiobesity therapies was the use of Fenfluramine and Phentermine (Fen/Phen). Both drugs were ap-proved for use individually more than twenty years ago, but since 1992, doctors have tended to prescribe them together for long-term management of obesity. In 1996, U.S. doctors wrote eighteen mil-lion monthly prescriptions for Fen/Phen. And many were issued to people who were not obese. This is known as "off-label" prescribing. In July 1997, the U.S. Food and Drug Administration and re-searchers at the Mayo Clinic, and the Mayo Foundation made a joint announcement warning doctors that Fen/Phen can cause heart disease. On September 15, 1997, "Fen" was taken off the market. The Fen/Phen lesson: Diet and lifestyle modification are still the best ways to weight control and good health. (More bad news has surfaced, revealing that Fen/Phen wreaks havoc on serotonin levels, which only reinforces this message.)

A Fen/Phen "replacement" drug, sibutramine (Meridia) was approved in November 1997 by the U.S. Food and Drug Administration and was still pending approval in Canada at this writing. Sibutramine was first developed in the late 1980s as an antidepressant, but, like Fen/Phen, it controls appetite through the brain's interpretation of "feeling full." Sibutramine is a monoamine reuptake inhibitor. (See chapter 8.) Sibutramine differs from Fen/Phen in that it does not interfere with the heart.

Depression, Stress, and Weight

Negative body image and the resulting depression create a vicious cycle. Although depression is often associated with a decreased appetite or interest in food, many women turn to food for comfort when they are sad, while symptoms of depression often accompany a diagnosis of an eating disorder. Remaining sedentary, which is often the case in depression, can also lead to weight gain. So as the body weight increases, women who are depressed have that much more to be depressed about.

Stress is also a factor in weight gain. A Yale University study suggests that the desire to reach for potato chips when you're under stress is activated more by feeling anxious than feelings of hunger, which may explain why women eat more and gain weight when they're under stress. The stress hormone cortisol is the culprit. This study showed that women who secreted the most cortisol were more attracted to high-fat foods than women who secreted lower levels. (However, this study has been criticized by other researchers for being somewhat simplistic.)

Research published in the *British Journal of Nutrition* supports the theory that low-fat eating can lead to anger, hostility, and sadness.

That simply demonstrates what we already know: That you may reach for higher fat foods in order to feel better. In fact, American research using monkeys has actually shown that low-fat diets resulted in more aggressive and angry behavior.

Do You Have a Body-Image Problem?

Few women today can admit to liking their bodies. Many distort their body size. When does your body image become a problem that requires intervention with therapy or counseling? When your obsession over your body interferes with other aspects of your life, you should seek help. For example, impulsive weighing, spending a lot of time worrying about your weight, and practicing one of the eating behaviors discussed in this chapter (starving, bingeing and/or purging, or overexercising) are signs that you need help, even if you don't exhibit signs of depression.

Most women have a desired weight goal set at roughly ten pounds *less than* their ideal weight; many women who think they are overweight are either at an ideal weight or ten pounds underweight. Normal body fat for a healthy woman is 22 to 25 percent; most models and actresses have roughly 10 percent body fat. To help establish a reasonable weight for *you*, experts suggest you ask yourself five questions:

1. What is the lowest weight you have maintained as an adult for at least one year?
2. What is the largest size of clothing you feel you "look good" in, and how much do you need to weigh to wear that size?
3. Think of someone in your life who is your age and height (versus a model or actress) and who appears to be a "normal" weight. What does she *actually* weigh?
4. What weight can you live with?
5. What does your cultural background value in terms of body size and shape?

HAVING THE TIME OF YOUR MONTH

If you use the term *PMS* (which stands for premenstrual syndrome, *not* premenstrual symptoms) in front of a psychiatrist, you'll be told that it is outdated. In 1994, a new term was introduced to replace PMS: *premenstrual dysphoric disorder (PDD)*. This simply means "unhappy before your period."

The symptoms of PDD include profound mood swings; sudden, inexplicable sadness; irritability; sudden or inexplicable anger; feelings of anxiety or being "on edge"; depression; hopelessness; and self-deprecating thoughts. In addition, women also present some or all of the physical symptoms described on pages 90 to 91, such as tender breasts and bloating. To be diagnosed with PDD, these symptoms would then need to disappear once women began bleeding. While only 3 to 4 percent of women meet these criteria, more than 90 percent of all women when asked about "PMS" will say they suffer from it. In the psychiatric literature, even women with hysterectomies and oophorectomies (removal of their ovaries) were found to experience these symptoms.

But *nobody* uses the term *PDD* unless they're well versed in medical jargon. Furthermore, many feminist critics are outraged by the fact that a normal biological process is even called a "disorder" by psychiatrists, because it suggests that normal physical changes around menstruation are somehow a mental disorder. As of this writing, discussions about *what* to call premenstrual changes are still being debated in psychiatric circles. So for the purposes of this chapter, I'll simply use the phrase *premenstrual signs* to discuss the physical and emotional changes women experience prior to their periods.

Almost all women in their childbearing years have premenstrual signs. It's often difficult to define all of them; ten doctors will have ten different opinions about what these signs really are, while ten menstruating women will describe ten different *collections* of signs. There is also the question of "medicalizing" what is really a normal

and natural condition, considering the hormonal symphony that women "conduct" each month. Therefore, treating premenstrual signs is somewhat controversial. *Should* they be treated? And is it right to think of these signs as a "disease" or disorder, medicating them with tranquilizers, water pills, or synthetically produced hormones? (Even if you want your doctor to prescribe medication for your premenstrual changes, you should still consider this question.) Traditionally, women's complaints about premenstrual signs have been viewed as either psychological or have been written off as part of the woman's biological lot. Many women have difficulty admitting they suffer from them, fearing that this might compromise their position in the workplace. But almost all women experience some premenstrual signs. It's how *you* experience these signs and how severely they affect *you* that determine whether these premenstrual signs are healthy and normal or whether they warrant medical intervention or other therapies because they are interfering with your ability to function.

Who Cares About Premenstrual Signs?

Ninety percent of women who menstruate experience premenstrual signs of some sort. Of this group, half will experience the more traditional premenstrual signs, such as breast tenderness, bloating, food cravings, irritability, and mood swings. For many women, these signs are often perceived as a signal that their bodies are "in tune" or "on schedule" and that all is well. In other words, these signs are natural markers of a healthy menstrual cycle.

Of the remaining 45 percent of women who experience premenstrual signs, 35 to 40 percent experience the same signs of the first group but in a more severe form. In other words, they have *tender* breasts so sensitive that they hurt if someone lightly touches them; severe bloating to the extent that they gain about five pounds before their periods; instead of just food cravings, they may suddenly find that they have voracious appetites; instead of just being irritable, they may find that they become impossible to be around. Believe it or not, even these more severe signs are considered to be normal experiences.

However, the remaining 3 to 4 percent of women who experience premenstrual signs suffer from incapacitating symptoms that affect their ability to function. It is this group that suffers from what used to be known as premenstrual *syndrome* (and still is, by those who don't use the current PDD label). In other words, roughly one in ten women suffers from premenstrual signs that occur one to fourteen days before her period, which significantly interfere with interpersonal relationships and daily activities, and which disappear at or during her menstruation.

The physical changes
This list isn't exhaustive, but women report the following physical premenstrual signs:

- breast swelling and tenderness
- increased appetite and weight gain
- abdominal bloating (which may also cause weight gain)
- constipation or diarrhea
- headaches
- acne or other skin eruptions
- eye problems
- joint and muscle pain (also review chapter 2)
- backache
- sugar and salt cravings
- fatigue (also review chapter 2)
- hoarseness
- racing heart (review the section below on hyperthyroidism)
- clumsiness and poor coordination
- nausea, menopausal-like hot flashes
- chills, shakiness, and dizziness
- changes in sex drive (either more or less)

- sensitivity to noise
- insomnia
- asthma
- seizures

Emotional changes

Of course, it is the emotional premenstrual signs that cause the most problems. They include:

- irritability, anger, and rage
- sudden mood swings
- restlessness
- melancholy
- anxiety
- emotional overresponsiveness
- loss of control
- depression (see chapter 1 for a review of all the symptoms that constitute the various forms of depression)
- suicidal thoughts (rare)
- nightmares
- forgetfulness
- confusion (rare)
- decreased concentration
- withdrawal
- inexplicable crying
- inward anger
- physical or verbal aggression toward others

On the positive side . . .

There *is* a positive side to all these signs: Some women report increased energy levels and sexual drive, as well as bursts of creativity during this time. Even increased levels of anger and aggression can be viewed as constructive, particularly in business. Rents and bad debts are often collected at these times.

Do You Have a Premenstrual "Disorder"?

Chances are, if you menstruate, you experience some of the physical and emotional premenstrual signs described above. These emotional changes, however, often negatively impact your personal life and are also more difficult to link to your periods. If you think this inexplicable behavior and these feelings may indeed be caused by premenstrual signs, the best thing you can do is chart them. Through charting, you'll become more aware of your body and emotions at various stages in your menstrual cycle. In fact, charting your changes is the *only* way your doctor can diagnose a premenstrual disorder—if you are seeking some kind of diagnosis. Although, while many women recoil at the thought that menstruation is being turned into a disease, large numbers of women do seek explanations for certain behaviors, and for them, a diagnosis of PDD is often the validation that allows them to lead happier lives.

Currently, psychiatrists divide premenstrual changes into those that are emotional, behavioral, and physical. Emotional changes include irritability, mood swings, anxiety, depression, decreased interest in usual activities, decreased libido, and the desire to be alone. Behavioral changes include increased appetite or food cravings, fatigue, insomnia, hypersomnia (oversleeping), agitation, poor concentration, and poor motor coordination. Finally, physical changes include bloating, cramps, breast swelling, muscle aches, fluid retention, acne, constipation, and a host of other signs already discussed.

Generally, psychiatrists have found that women who *do* complain about these premenstrual signs and believe they're suffering from some kind of premenstrual disorder tend to have another psychiatric illness—such as situational depression, anxiety, or a psychotic disorder—that's being *exacerbated* by premenstrual signs. So psychiatrists rely on charting the menstrual cycles to see if there is truly an association with their patient's reported symptoms and their menstrual periods; they also chart to make sure the symptoms disappear

attitude and feelings—a fabulous indicator of how quickly her PMS signs came over her and took hold of her life. Clearly, the woman of January 17 would be difficult to live and work with. Let's see how she feels after her period (see the chart below).

The woman of February 4 is far happier, less stressed, and more optimistic. She even has the wherewithal to observe how differently she was acting just eighteen days ago, about thirteen days before her period. (Indeed, not all women experience premenstrual changes *exactly* fourteen days before their period. It can vary. Fourteen days is just a rough number used when discussing an average twenty-eight-day cycle, which most women *don't* have.)

· · · · · · · · · ·

Cycle Day: 5 (bleed—day 1 of the cycle—occurred on January 30)

Calendar Date: February 4

Physical state
    appetite = 3
    cravings = 0
    breasts = 0
    bloat = 0
    weight = normal
    backache = 0

Emotional state
    mood = 1 (feeling really great)
    irritability = 0
    energy = 10 (I actually did the laundry)
    sex drive = 8
    stress = 1

Special circumstances
    "Was reading my earlier charts. Don't know what came over me a couple of weeks ago."

· · · · · · · · · ·

Tender Breasts Affect Your Mood

If you take any male and fluctuate his hormone levels the way ours do before our periods, he would experience the same mood swings and variations in body temperature, appetite, and weight. Indeed, if you study male moods for thirty days, you're also likely to find a wide variety of ups and downs. Certain women are affected more than others. The important thing to remember about premenstrual changes is that most of them imitate the changes of pregnancy. Each cycle ends with your body deciding whether to shed the lining or not to shed the lining. From the time your period starts in puberty, your body is waiting to get pregnant. All the hormones triggered during pregnancy are triggered before your period. This is normal. So, if you are among the 90 percent of women who experience premenstrual signs, it's important to put them in perspective and realize that it's just "you," not a syndrome or a disease. As one family practitioner put it to me, "tender boobs affect your mood." In other words, when you're physically bloated and tender, you won't be in as good a mood as you normally would be. Similarly, when you have a headache, your mood is also affected: You're in a lousy one. Does this mean you have headache syndrome? No. You're just reacting normally to physical discomfort.

In most cases, premenstrual changes are simply what it feels like to be a woman in her reproductive years. Our rush of hormones and premenstrual changes are like our own personal clocks, telling us what our reproductive organs are up to. In fact, women I've interviewed who are taking synthetic hormones (as a result of surgical or natural menopause) report how odd it feels to be even-tempered all the time.

Psychiatrists agree that there have been lots of confusion and negative myths associated with premenstrual signs. Although many women will be sent for psychiatric evaluation for their premenstrual signs, psychiatrists report that it's actually *rare* to see a woman who has severe enough symptoms to be incapacitated by them. How rare? Only about 3 to 4 percent of the general female population will be diagnosed with a truly premenstrual disorder.

Treating Premenstrual Changes

What do psychiatrists suggest as a treatment for premenstrual signs or even a premenstrual disorder? *Validation.* Women who feel they have severe premenstrual symptoms respond well when they have a physician who validates their symptoms and feelings. In addition, these women have responded well to the diet changes discussed below, as well as lifestyle adjustments to accommodate their changes. (In other words, don't schedule a board meeting before your period or plan a dinner party for forty.)

Natural remedies

Before you resort to medication, you can take a variety of natural steps to reduce your symptoms. The most important step is to pay attention to nutrition.

Many doctors feel that a change in diet about fourteen days before your period (again, this date may move forward or back) can help alleviate your symptoms. They recommend that you experiment with reducing or eliminating sugar, salt, caffeine, and alcohol about two weeks before your period is due. Sugar and caffeine are stimulants, which may aggravate your premenstrual changes, and alcohol is a depressant, which may contribute to an already depressed mood before your period. Salt causes you to retain water, so reducing your salt intake will help to reduce bloating. They also recommend eating small, frequent meals. This means eating three meals and three nutritious snacks without going longer than three hours without eating. (Insulin requirements often change around menstruation, which can lead to hypoglycemia. This can exacerbate symptoms.) Around this time, stock up on grains and beans, fish, chicken, fresh fruits, and vegetables. Highly processed food and junk food should be avoided, as should dairy products, fats, and red meat.

Doctors also recommend adding vitamin B_6 to your diet. This can be purchased over-the-counter. Taking 50 to 200 milligrams is the usual recommendation. It's also a good idea to take vitamin B_6 in a complex containing the other B vitamins in equal amounts.

Another natural ingredient some doctors suggest is evening prim-rose oil, taken orally in capsule form. It's been reported that women find evening primrose oil particularly helpful for changes such as breast tenderness, depression, irritability, and bloating, although studies show no difference between evening primrose oil and placebo (which means "dummy pills"). The dosage begins at one or two capsules twice a day during the first two weeks of the cycle and is increased to six capsules a day in the last two weeks of the cycle. Evening primrose oil is usually available in health-food stores (your doctor will know where it's available in your community).

Pampering yourself helps to relieve stress, and learning various re-laxation techniques can also help. (See chapter 9.) Many women find talking to a counselor or social worker helpful when they are feeling moody and hopeless. Regular exercise is also key. Exercise re-leases endorphins in the brain which have a calming effect. Yoga is also recommended in helping to reduce the severity of premenstrual changes.

Alleviating premenstrual signs with drugs
There are certainly drugs to help with premenstrual changes severe enough to interfere with your ability to function.

Antidepressants have been shown to have an almost immediate effect on premenstrual changes. Intermittent serotonin reuptake in-hibitors are usually prescribed in these cases. (See chapter 8.)

A more drastic drug that you should watch out for is danazol (Cyclomen), a synthetic male hormone derivative that shuts down ovarian functions completely and causes pseudomenopause. A small amount of estrogen is often added to danazol therapy to prevent estrogen depletion. Danazol is potent, expensive, and has many side effects. The problem with premenstrual treatments is what one woman may find severe, another may interpret as moderate. (Or, what one doctor feels warrants danazol, another may not.) The only time danazol should be used is if premenstrual symptoms are so severe they are causing true disaster in a woman's personal or professional life. So, unless your symptoms drive you to murder, steal, or commit suicide, danazol is not a good idea. If you suffer from what you think are severe, incapacitating premenstrual changes and this is the therapy your doctor suggests, *get a second opinion.* (See chapter 5 on where to get help.)

HAVING A HARD TIME AFTER HAVING A BABY

Having a baby changes your life. It also changes you, and it may lead to dramatic shifts in mood. You have probably heard of the postpartum blues, which is sometimes confused with postpartum depression, a phrase that has been used incorrectly by the media. This confuses three *separate* psychiatric conditions that occur in the postpartum phase: maternal blues, depression, and psychosis. I'll also discuss a postpartum thyroid condition that is often misdiagnosed as postpartum depression.

A connection between depression and pregnancy was recognized as early as 1840. First, normal fatigue and feelings of letdown, in that you've been excited and preparing for the birth, are common and normal. True postpartum psychological and emotional disturbances range from what are known as "maternal blues" and true postpartum depression, where one experiences symptoms of major depression or clinical depression (discussed below), to something known as postpartum psychosis, the kind of diagnosis made in a situation where a woman loses touch with reality and becomes psychotic. She believes, for example, that her newborn is evil or abnormal in some way. Postpartum psychosis occurs in one to two of every one thousand deliveries, which is not as uncommon as we have been led to believe.

Maternal Blues

As many as 70 percent of all women after delivery suffer from maternal blues. This condition is common and nothing to worry about. It is mild and short term and usually occurs within the first ten days (averaging three or four) after delivery.

Symptoms of the maternal blues are frequent crying episodes, mood swings, feelings of sadness, low energy, anxiety, insomnia, restlessness, and irritability. Women who experience these feelings should feel comforted that they are normal and will pass. They only last for a couple of weeks.

What causes maternal blues?

Maternal blues are most likely caused by enormous hormonal shifts in your body. However, there isn't any *real* proof that what you're feeling is hormonal. Since we *do* know that hormonal shifts definitely cause premenstrual, as well as menopausal mood swings, and we *do* know that estrogen levels are depleted after childbirth, it's likely that hormones *are* the culprit.

Nevertheless, other causes result from the enormous lifestyle shift, including an increase in stress and responsibility, worry about your newborn, physical discomfort associated with the postpartum "physique," and possible exhaustion following labor and delivery.

As noted, some women experience a kind of letdown. During pregnancy, there is excitement and anticipation about the big day. Then the "big day" arrives, you experience an enormous physical strain, and all the energy and excitement you've invested in the experience needs an emotional outlet. So you cry. Similar feelings tend to follow weddings and big trips. In this case, though, while one kind of adventure is over, another is beginning.

New family conflicts often surface after delivery, too. If this is a first grandchild, the emotional tug-of-war between the two (or more) sets of grandparents may contribute to your stress. And don't forget—baby naming, baby-naming ceremonies, christenings, choosing godparents, circumcision decisions, and bris planning all take their toll on your stress levels and can create dismal conflicts that are *never* settled. This one's hurt; that one's offended; *he* disapproves; *she* can't believe you did this or that. . . . You get the idea. Often, these family wars interfere with you and your partner's relationship and enjoyment of the newborn.

If you're on maternity leave, your sudden change in daily activities may be a shock to your system, and you may have difficulty adjusting to your new schedule (or the horrors of daytime television).

And, too often, babies are planned as a way to patch up relationship problems between partners. This is disastrous and usually yields more holes than patches.

Interestingly, in some studies, a significant number of new fathers suffer from an adjustment disorder after the arrival of the newborn, sometimes called the paternal blues. This definitely suggests that the causes are not rooted in hormonal changes but in lifestyle changes.

What should you do?

Unless you're feeling so bad you cannot function, give it a couple of weeks to see if you feel any better. If these feelings persist, you should seek counseling and explore whether your feelings are truly related to your postpartum condition or are perhaps related to other problems that are only now surfacing. Pregnancy can mask relationship problems (that you may not have been aware of) or expose relationship problems. The pregnancy also masks lifestyle ruts that will eventually resurface after the baby arrives. In other words, don't expect old problems to disappear just because you've had a baby.

Postpartum Depression (PPD)

Postpartum depression is more serious and persistent and affects between 10 to 15 percent of the postpartum population. This depression can begin at any time after delivery, from the first few hours afterward, to a few weeks after. These symptoms include sadness, mood changes, lack of energy, loss of interest, change in appetite, fatigue, guilt, self-loathing, suicidal thoughts, poor concentration, and foggy memory. When these feelings last for more than a couple of weeks, the consequences can be negative, which lead to problems with bonding and relationships. However, women don't go from the maternal blues to depression. In fact, you can feel well after delivery and then suddenly develop postpartum depression.

Causes of PPD

The causes of postpartum depression are possibly similar to those cited as causes for the milder maternal blues. But women at risk for this more serious depression are those with a family history of depression and women who have a poor support system at home (being spouseless; having a bad relationship with a partner; and being a teenage mother).

Many studies have looked into psychosocial issues revolving around PPD. In one study of educated, white, middle-class, married women in their early thirties who returned to work within the first year after delivery, marital adjustment and child-care stress significantly influenced the severity of their PPD symptoms. Those with lower self-esteem and greater stress reported more severe PPD symptoms. In fact, mothers with low self-esteem were thirty-nine times more likely to suffer from PPD than those with high self-esteem. Studies on teenage mothers also confirm these figures. Teen mothers typically have more frequent bouts with PPD than adult mothers because they have poor social support systems and lower self-esteem. These studies also revealed that inner-city, low-income women developed PPD at double the rate of middle-class women. Not surprising, single mothers with no partners were at particular risk for postpartum depression.

Unfortunately, PPD can also affect a baby's temperament during the first year, as the baby intuitively responds to the mother's "vibes." The reverse is true, of course, when women are coping with a colicky or difficult baby. Women with PPD who are caring for older children as well as the new baby report feelings of being overwhelmed by their child-care duties. They also report feelings of guilt, loss, and anger. Irrational thinking, robotlike "going-through-the-motions" was a common experience in one study.

Treating PPD

If you do begin to notice these feelings, treatment is available from a qualified mental health practitioner. (See chapter 5.) You may just need some counseling, or you may need to be put on antidepressant medication. Counseling can vary from short-term "sorting out your life" chats (interpersonal therapy) to cognitive-behavioral therapy. (See chapter 6.) It depends on the severity of your symptoms. In addition, there are now a number of postpartum support groups, where you can talk to other women in the same boat. This may help you to put all your feelings into a healthier perspective. If you are taking medications for your condition, you must discern whether they are compatible with breast-feeding. (Most antidepressants prescribed today are fine, but it's wise to double-check.)

Research shows that women who experienced postpartum depression once have a 30 to 60 percent chance of reexperiencing it with a subsequent pregnancy. As a result, some hospitals offer antidepressant therapy to women with a history of PPD, with drugs such as nortriptyline hydrochloride. These antidepressants are administered twenty-four hours after delivery for a period of roughly twenty weeks.

When postpartum depression goes untreated, it can have consequences for the baby. Some psychiatrists report that it can interfere with bonding as well as cognitive and behavioral development. In some instances, a therapist may suggest that you have some extra help at home until you get on your feet again.

Postpartum Psychosis

Postpartum psychosis is serious and requires hospitalization. This affects a *small* portion of women and usually begins in the first month after delivery. Basically, this is when you're out of touch with the world around you. *HINT: If you're able to read this book, you probably don't have postpartum psychosis.*

This condition usually indicates other psychiatric disorders, but women *can* suddenly develop the following psychotic symptoms: delusions that the child is dead or defective, denial that the birth ever took place, or hearing voices (inside their head) that tell them to harm the infant. Accompanying symptoms include sleep disorders, intense confusion, loss of energy, and hence, difficulty caring for the child. At-risk women are those with a history of a psychotic episode, a past diagnosis of postpartum psychosis, or a history of bipolar disorder. (See chapter 2.) This is a serious psychiatric illness that needs to be treated with medications and therapies. In some cases, the infant may need to be cared for temporarily by another family member.

Postpartum Thyroiditis

Some women diagnosed with postpartum depression are not depressed at all but are really suffering from a thyroid condition common in the postpartum phase called postpartum thyroiditis (inflammation of the thyroid gland). This is often a short-lived condition that tends to clear up on its own a few weeks after delivery.

In recent years, this health problem has begun to change the way postpartum depression is perceived by the medical community. Postpartum thyroiditis occurs in roughly 10 to 18 percent of all women after delivery, many of whom will be relieved to know that their feelings of depression have a *physical* cause. For more information on thyroid disorders, see chapter 3 or refer to my book *The Thyroid Sourcebook for Women.*

DEPRESSION AND MENOPAUSE

As estrogen levels begin to dwindle, women experience physical symptoms such as erratic periods, hot flashes, and vaginal dryness. There isn't solid evidence suggesting that estrogen loss leads to the emotional symptoms of menopause, such as irritability, mood swings, and melancholy, but since estrogen functions as a weak antidepressant, it's not surprising that moods may swing as estrogen decreases. Some experts believe that emotional symptoms during menopause are actually caused by a rise in follicle-stimulating hormone (FSH), the hormone that signals the ovaries to "spit out" the follicle, which refers to the egg in the early stage of the cycle. As the menstrual cycle changes and the ovaries' egg supply dwindles, FSH is secreted in high amounts and reaches a lifetime peak in an effort to move the remaining eggs—as much as fifteen times higher than in women of childbearing ages. This is the body's way of trying to "jump-start" the ovarian engine. This is why the urine of menopausal women is used to produce the potent fertility drug human menopausal gonadotropin.

One reason the link between estrogen loss and mood swings is fuzzy is because of what happens during menstruation. Our premenstrual symptoms are caused by *peak* levels of estrogen and progesterone; the symptoms are relieved when the flow starts and the estrogen and progesterone levels *drop.* In other words, there is paradox at work: How can high levels *and* low levels of estrogen cause mood swings? The mood swings may have more to do with an imbalance of estrogen. In addition, decreased levels of estrogen can make you more vulnerable to stress, depression, and anxiety because estrogen loss affects REM sleep. When we're less rested, we're less able to cope with stresses that normally may not affect us. (See sleep deprivation in chapter 2.)

Ironically, the only other time in a woman's life when her FSH levels are as high as they are in menopause is during puberty. (This may be why the classic mother/daughter "hormone clash" tends to occur when a daughter is entering puberty and the mother is entering menopause. At this stage, both mother and daughter are more sex-hormone matched in terms of hormonal levels than at other times in their relationship.) In fact, the erratic up-and-down moods of puberty mirror the mood swings that can characterize menopause for the same reasons.

Every woman entering menopause experiences a change in her menstrual cycle. However, not all women experience hot flashes or even notice vaginal changes. This is particularly true if a woman is overweight. And, of course, many women go through menopause without experiencing changes in their moods. It is an absolute myth to assume that mood swings always accompany menopause or that women who suffer from premenstrual symptoms always experience more severe menopausal symptoms.

The Menopause Blues

Most mental health experts agree that the blues women experience during menopausal years are rooted in the psychological fear of aging, and the stress of the physical symptoms of menopause, such as hot flashes. If you're taking hormone replacement therapy (HRT) because you think it will cure your depression, you're mistaken. Hormone therapy will only relieve your night sweats and any resulting insomnia, as well as anxiety related to your menopausal symptoms. Since you'll be better rested and calmer, you'll be able to cope with daily stress more effectively and positively. But if you are depressed to the extent that you can't function normally, you need to seek counseling, treatment, or support groups of other women who have experienced menopause. (Review chapter 1 for the symptoms of depression and chapter 5 on where to find help.)

Some HRT "recipes" may mix antidepressant medication or tranquilizers, which may help to relieve depression. Doctors sometimes prescribe these HRT recipes if their patients seem depressed or anxious—without the patient's knowledge. It's important to *ask* what is being prescribed. If you do need these drugs, it's better to take them separately—independent of your estrogen—under a psychiatrist's supervision, not a gynecologist's. So make sure you know what you're getting in your estrogen pills before you take them. And if tranquilizers have been added to the HRT recipe, remember that they can cause dizziness, confusion, and drowsiness.

While the feminist adage *biology is not destiny* (meaning that, just because you own baby-making equipment doesn't mean that you have to spend your life "serving" it) is true, women are still destined to experience their biology. Feminist therapists consulted for this book were concerned that this chapter reinforces chauvinist myths about women and hormones, sending the message that women are either slaves to their hormones or are at the whims of their hormonal cycles. But when we understand how hormones and the life events surrounding our reproductive life cycles influence our moods, we gain insight into another feminist adage: *The personal is political.* This means that within one woman's story about her feelings and struggles with her body lies the story of all women's feelings and struggles with their bodies. And within *that* story lies the social history of women and, by extension, the history of women and depression, which has led to a revolution in women and psychotherapy.

The History of Women and Psychotherapy

When we look at various ways to manage and treat depression, it's important to know where we've been before we can understand where we're going. The social history of women has everything to do with the history of women and depression, psychiatry, and psychotherapy. Simply put, social history is the "way it was" for women: social conventions, sexuality, marriage, societal roles, and, most important, how women have been *perceived* by men. How women have been treated for mood disorders at various times in history is a reflection of how women's roles—and the *perception* of their roles—have shifted through the ages.

Up until the 1950s, depression in women was usually diagnosed as hysteria (literally meaning *womb disease,* but a term that meant different things in different centuries—often contradictory). The most profound example of how psychiatry and women's social history is intertwined is to look at the way *hysteria* (a term that remained in the vernacular of medicine from the fourth century B.C. until 1952, when the American Psychiatric Association finally stopped using it) was diagnosed and treated. Next to fevers, hysteria was listed as the most common women's disease and thought to be a disease caused by sexual dissatisfaction (or longing) commonly diagnosed in virgins, young widows, and nuns, all of whom were discouraged from the terrible sin of masturbation. Marriage was considered a cure. Yet, it clearly failed to cure many women. Hysteria was also thought to plague women who had more passionate natures.

In her book *The Technology of Orgasm: Hysteria, the Vibrator, and Women's Sexual Satisfaction,* author Rachel P. Maines meticulously documents physicians' standard treatment for hysteria: manually stimulating the clitoris during the office visit and bringing the "hysterical" patient to orgasm. This treatment was documented as early as the first century A.D., and continued well into the twentieth century. In fact, bringing women to orgasm was the "bread and butter" of many physicians from the time of Hippocrates until the 1920s. In the late nineteenth century, it was documented that 75 percent of the female population required these treatments. Vibrators were invented by physicians as a medical device to save time—since apparently, so *much* of it was spent with patients who "came once a week" for these treatments. In short, what we now consider to be a normal sexual fulfillment was a medical treatment for women.

Eventually, the vibrator evolved as a consumer sex product, putting into the hands of women what, Maines says, was the "job nobody wanted." Thus, many of the symptoms of sexual dissatisfaction, which characterized hysteria, simply disappeared as the function of the clitoris became more widely known as did the fact that most women cannot reach orgasm during intercourse without direct clitoral stimulation—a fact that surfaced through the research of Alfred Kinsey and Shere Hite.

Too much information? Well, if you think of talk therapy (see the next chapter) as a product you're purchasing or investing in to aid your mental health, it's useful to understand the origins of that product, and what came before it. What this chapter does is give you some information that's not only nice to know but also hard to find: the background and history of women and psychotherapy.

This chapter also discusses the ways in which the feminist movement influenced how women were treated in psychotherapy. The first book to criticize women's treatment in psychotherapy was *Women and Madness,* by Phyllis Chesler, which was published in 1972. Chesler's book completely turned the psychoanalytic and psychiatric profession upside down, as she exposed the deeply embedded sexism of a system that had been essentially mistreating and incarcerating women for centuries. She also exposed the so-called symptoms of depression or hysteria as simply *healthy* responses to a sick role that women were playing in society. Chesler dared to say, yes, oppression is *depressing.* She dared to state the obvious.

When the women's movement reemerged in the late 1960s and early 1970s (in academic circles this is known as "postmodernist" or "second wave" feminism to distinguish it from the first wave, which was at the beginning of the twentieth century—the movement that got women the vote)—it liberated women from many of their so-called mental illnesses.

Freedom from oppressive marriages, relationships, careers/workplaces, or parents, and freedom to act as adults and make their own choices did amazing things for women's self-esteem. As you read about the history of women and psychotherapy, think about how difficult it still is to liberate *yourself* from situations that undermine your freedom to make your own decisions or rob you of your self-esteem and self-worth. While we've come a long way, we still have a long way to go.

A BRIEF HISTORY OF WOMEN AND "MADNESS"

The first European "madhouses," as they were called, were nothing short of prisons for the wives and daughters of men. As early as the sixteenth century, wives were thrown into madhouses or royal towers by their husbands as punishment for not conforming or behaving. Soon, private madhouses became popular for-profit institutions designed as drop-off centers for rich husbands to dump their wives. The practice became so widespread that Daniel DeFoe criticized it in 1687, calling attention to the "vile practice now so much in vogue among the better sort, as they are called, but the worst sort, in fact, namely the sending of their wives to madhouses at every whim or dislike."

By the seventeenth century, prostitutes, poor women, unmarried pregnant women, and young girls joined wives in the first mental asylum in France, called the Salpetriere. Women continued to populate mental asylums throughout the nineteenth century. Until the 1970s, the majority of women in mental hospitals either were committed involuntarily or while they were in a coma following an unsuccessful suicide attempt.

One of the most famous cases of involuntary confinement involved Elizabeth Packard, whose husband committed her to an asylum in 1860 because she dared to question religion. Packard was kidnapped by her husband, who then withheld her children, income (from her inheritance), clothes, and books. She began keeping a diary of asylum events (or, rather, horrors) and never referred to it as a hospital but always a prison. It is Packard who first made the analogy of institutional psychiatry and the Inquisition.

Many feminist writers observe that the players in the drama of mental hospital "scenes" mimic the witchcraft trials. The male doctors star as the "Inquisitors"; a subservient female nurse stars as the "Handmaiden," while a female patient stars as a "Witch," possessed by unhappiness, powerlessness, and dependence. These images still pervade mental health. In a 1998 article on depression in a women's health magazine, the visual accompanying the article was that of a woman lying on a hospital bed, with wires attached to her head and a plastic device inside her mouth. Scientific-looking male doctors with beards and glasses hovered around her. The article was discussing brain research and the differences between male and female brain responses to cortisol, a hormone produced while under stress. (See chapter 3.)

By the twentieth century, male psychiatrists were acting as agents for husbands unhappy with their wives. This differed from the seventeenth century in that the husbands now appeared to be innocent bystanders while the psychiatrists recommended institutionalization. By 1964, the number of American women seeking psychiatric services climbed to unprecedented rates, and adult female patients exceeded the number of adult male patients.

As of 1992, women accounted for roughly two-thirds of psychiatric consumers; 84 percent of all psychotherapy patients were reportedly women, while out of all new patients in psychotherapy each year, 60 percent were reportedly women.

The Career Psych Patient

The phenomenon of the "career," or long-term psychiatric patient began to emerge in Western culture between 1950 and 1970. During this period, not only were more women suffering nervous breakdowns than men, but, curiously, more married women suffered from psychiatric diseases than single women. The symptoms that compose depression, for example (see chapter 1), are in fact feminine behaviors that were adopted to survive under sexist, oppressive conditions. Real oppression of women caused real distress and unhappiness. Feminist scholars also note the following:

- There was limited social tolerance for women who behaved differently from what was expected within their social roles (hence, they were judged to be neurotic and psychotic). That is, women were frequently perceived as "sick" when they rejected the female role (and frequently, when they accepted the role by adopting passive behavior, they were *also* told they were "sick").
- Women in urban North America (which favored the nuclear family over the extended family) who outlived their

husbands, and who reached menopause, were left "unemployed" at an early age. With the extended family shrinking after World War II, they were left without a family to rear; there was no role for women.

• Women tend to seek help more than men and tend to report their distress more willingly than men.

These three factors helped mobilize women into psychiatrists' offices to seek help for feeling unfulfilled with the roles of wife and mother.

Asylum Life

Of course, the outdated term *asylum* (meaning psychiatric institution) rarely offered asylum, as Phyllis Chesler noted. There are numerous studies and documented horrors of mental institutions, notorious for sexual crimes and sexual abuse against women. Chesler reported that between 1968 and 1970, there were numerous reports of prostitution, rape, and impregnation of female mental patients by the professional and nonprofessional staff—and by male inmates.

One of the most damaging features of the traditional mental asylum is that it forced adult women back into adolescence. Women were punished for expressing sexuality or sexual aggression much as a teenager is punished by her parents. The wards of mental asylums were traditionally sex-segregated, while homosexuality, lesbianism, and masturbation were discouraged or even interrupted by force. "Heterosexual dances" put on for the patients mimicked 1950s high school proms. Female patients were chaperoned and frustrated. The process of being institutionalized infantilized women.

Women in Male Therapy

Of course, not all women who saw psychiatrists were sent to mental asylums; many were treated as outpatients in private practice. And, as discussed above, many were treated for hysteria by being brought to orgasm in the doctor's office. There have been some changes since those days. More female physicians (and psychiatrists) have helped to shift the perspective on women's mental illnesses. In the 1960s, 90 percent of all psychiatrists were men. In 1992, 73 percent of all American medical doctors were men; 86 percent of all psychiatrists and 84 percent of all psychologists were men.

Chesler noted the following in 1972 about psychiatric clinical practice: The profession was dominated by men; it encouraged traditional myths about normalcy and "abnormality," sexual stereotypes, and female inferiority; the profession perpetuated negative views of women, couching them in scientific and medical jargon; and the institution of private therapy mirrored the female experience in a male-dominated culture. In other words, many women simply became passive children in the presence of the therapist-father or passive wives serving the therapist-husband.

It's also important to remember that psychoanalysis was conceived in the minds of men. The result was a warped understanding of female psychological development:

1. Girl discovers she doesn't have a penis.
2. Girl believes she once had a penis but lost it via castration, which she views as a form of punishment (although she doesn't know what she did to deserve this punishment).
3. Girl regards herself as inferior and develops "penis envy."
4. Girl never gets over her sense of inferiority and constantly desires to be a man.
5. Girl "acts out" her anger over not being a man by seeking revenge on the man who has the penis she lacks.

The psychological development of the male was also distorted by psychoanalysis. The "male plot" goes like this: boy starts out in life believing that girls are the same as boys; discovers, alas, that they are not; views the girl as a "castrated" boy; fears the girl because she has obviously done something wrong to be castrated; can't understand how the girl can live without a penis; and spends his life fearing or dreading *her* penis envy, which he knows will one day target *him.*

Consider how psychoanalysis might have developed if equally close-minded women had been in charge, reversing "penis envy" into "womb envy," depicting, say, a boy's development as one in which he continuously acts out the loss of the womb (i.e., the inability to give birth) by "creating destruction" in his external environment (weapons or bombs) and taking out his hostility on women (rape and violence).

We need to remember that the female penis-envy "plot" is not describing "typical" female psychological development; it is interpreting female psychological development in the traditional man's world—a world run by men who simply couldn't imagine a rich and fulfilling life as a woman. As a result, women got the message, early on, that they would never be as valued or worthy as men. The flip side, of course, was that any woman growing up in a male world who did not feel inferior and envious of a penis (the "tool" of success in this world) must, in fact, be crazy.

The penis-envy plot has caused a lot of harm for women in therapy. Male "fathers" of psychoanalysis typically saw women as repressing their desires to be male (and thereby more sexually aggressive) as being at the core of every female neurosis or psychosis, a fact that is documented by Maines's vibrator research. That's why sexual abuse (or sexual relations—depending on who you talk to) among male therapists and female patients, was, until the last few decades, rampant.

Chesler reported that in the 1970s many individual therapists throughout New York and California systematically had sex with their patients. Moreover, many bullied their patients into having sex with them when there was no attraction. It's also no secret that many psychoanalysts in Freud's time had love affairs or married their female patients. One American psychiatrist, James L. McCartney, actually endorsed sex between male therapists and their female patients. McCartney was later thrown out of the American Psychiatric Association for publicly favoring "overt transference." Seems he would seek permission first from parents or husbands of patients before he had sexual contact.

Chesler noted in 1972 that a typical situation would be for the male therapist to create a sort of "harem" of women patients (not to mention their support staff of secretaries, a legal wife, and a mistress on the side). Often, the therapist's accusation of a woman being repressed was used to manipulate her into bed with him.

When Chesler interviewed eleven women about their experiences as psychiatric patients, ten out of the eleven had had sex with their therapists; five of the incidents were initiated and continued in the therapists' office; seven of the women continued to pay for the sessions after sexual contact. The therapists were generally fifteen years older than their patients. These women described being hurt and humiliated by the sexual contact (the therapist was usually emotionally detached and cold throughout contact), which was usually terminated not by the patient but by the therapist.

Feminists noted that traditional psychotherapy only mirrored the inequality most women faced in their marriages. Help came from a male authority figure when the woman would express her distress, but the solutions were not real solutions to the problems causing the distress. The distress was caused by external forces in the woman's political and social role in the world. Yet, she was told, the solution to her distress lay within, which only served to make her more impotent.

A class thing

Some authors propose that the traditional psychotherapy to which women were (and still are) subjected served a specific socioeconomic function for the white, male-dominated society. As North America became urbanized and young couples became increasingly more isolated, psychotherapy served to keep marriages together for the purpose of socializing children into urban society, hence "keeping the system going." The opening paragraph to Betty Friedan's 1963 book, *The Feminine Mystique*, illustrates this theory:

> The problem lay buried, unspoken, for many years in the minds of American women. It was a strange stirring, a sense of dissatisfaction, a yearning that women suffered in the middle of the twentieth century in the United States. Each suburban wife struggled with it alone. As she made the beds, shopped for groceries, matched slipcover material, ate peanut butter sandwiches with her children, chauffeured Cub Scouts and Brownies, lay beside her husband at night—she was afraid to ask even of herself the silent question—"Is this all?"

Feminist critics of psychotherapy argue that it treats unhappiness as a disease and fails to recognize real ethical, political, and social causes of unhappiness and oppression for women. Women who dared to ask "is this all?" were treated as if they were sick because they did not find the role of wife and mother fulfilling. Working-class women who had no time to ask "is this all?"—because they were too busy working—did not generally seek psychotherapy; they were not the ones questioning the status quo.

FEMINISM AS A CURE?

If you were a twentysomething middle-class woman in 1960 and you did not plan to marry, your career choices were limited. You could be a teacher, nurse, or secretary. Women who deviated from these three choices were met with opposition from parents and peers. By 1970, much had changed, and many more middle-class women were choosing higher education and many different careers.

Think back to the era of "The Mary Tyler Moore Show" (the groundbreaking TV sitcom about the single thirtysomething Mary Richards who was the heroine of so many of our mothers). Its theme song, "You're going to make it after all," was the anthem of thousands of women who were liberating themselves in that time period, or who were just coming of age. When the women's movement (again, known as second wave feminism) took shape in the 1970s, many women made positive changes in their lives. They left oppressive marriages. They returned to school and obtained skills. Some left oppressive jobs and got better skills and higher-paying jobs, and many were also able to get credit and loans for the first time, which gave them economic power. Many women began to use contraception and took control of their reproductive choices. The landmark abortion case, *Roe v. Wade,* made abortion safe and legal in the United States by 1973, allowing women even greater reproductive choice and freedom. In essence, feminism enabled women to become more self-sufficient, and this, for women, was more therapeutic than the psychotherapy of yesteryear.

Feminism also made women freer. It made them happier, better able to express their anger, and gave them back their self-esteem. In essence, the women's movement helped to expose the sickness of the traditional woman's *role* in Western society, which, many feminists insist, was reinforced in psychiatric hospitals and by psychotherapy.

The Stigma of Sexual Abuse

As women's voices began to be heard in therapy, stories of sexual abuse and/or violence in childhood, adolescence, and adulthood (via a partner or spouse) began to surface. These stories were not coming so much from women whose memories had been repressed (see chapter 6) but whose *voices* had been repressed.

When one examines the history of oppressed peoples, sexual abuse, violence, and oppression go together. For example, African-American history is flooded with sexual abuse and violent crimes; African-American women were repeatedly raped and abused by white male slaveholders. Today, rape is recognized as a war crime—and is known to be a punishment of choice by conquering armies. Thus, from a historical perspective, it's no surprise that women, as an oppressed group, suffered from such crimes.

As more women came forward with their stories, it led to what is called the "recovery movement." People—men and women—were deriving strength from the voices of women recovering from abuse or incest. Even the *DSM IV* (*Diagnostic Statistical Manual,* discussed in chapter 1) felt the effects, and it applied the term *post-traumatic stress disorder* (known as shell shock in World War I and battle fatigue in World War II) to such victims. This term originated in the 1970s to describe psychological trauma experienced by Vietnam war veterans but was extended to anyone suffering the effects of trauma. Many feminists saw the use of this terminology in women's experiences as a victory, because finally, women were seen as suffering similar effects as prisoners of war, for example. Recurring night terrors, sleeplessness, and bursts of anger were listed as symptoms. But the problem was yet more labeling and diagnosing. Critics attacked the *DSM IV* label because it looked upon post-traumatic stress disorder as an anomaly outside the realm of normal women's experiences, when statistics showed the opposite was the case. (See chapter 1.)

For many therapists, the incest/abuse recovery movement replaced other focuses that continued to oppress women, such as general societal roles, and how women's lives, work, and families were intertwined within those roles. Many therapists were said to have been lost to the recovery movement as a result. Another problem that surfaced with the recovery movement was a cheapening of women's experiences. As the talk shows caught onto the recovery audience, more pseudotherapy was being done on the television "talk soup," and more psychobabble began to infiltrate living rooms, obscuring the real issues rather than offering real support or solutions.

Why Are Liberated Women Still Depressed?

If women are so liberated, why is depression still so prevalent? In the first place, liberation isn't a panacea; there are still the issues of human experience, angst, wants, and longing. (See chapter 1.) And, in the second place, women are not all that liberated. Not yet.

Women's liberation has enabled women in some ways but disabled them in others. For example, it has allowed women to enter the male world on *male* terms, which for many women involves deep sacrifices. The notion of the liberated career woman who has it all has led to a new, impossible fulfillment norm—the Superwoman (sometimes known as Supermom). The Superwoman is beautiful, thin, successful, and has the perfect husband and family. She has chosen just the right career, and chosen to have children at just the right time—biologically. She has no problem fulfilling her dual roles as lawyer, doctor, or accountant by day, perfect homemaker by night. The Superwoman of the late twentieth century is perhaps a more dangerous ideal to women today than the Perfect Homemaker of the mid-twentieth century. Superwoman sends the message that women can have it all in a world where we not only *cannot* have it all but often have not much, if anything.

And with Superwoman comes the Supermodel—a seventeen-year-old girl whose image is distorted by computers, lighting, and deceptive photography. She is supposed to be what a thirty-five-year-old woman strives to look like. The worst legacy of the Supermodel is that a woman still makes more money with her body than her mind, and little girls grow up preferring to be skeleton-thin models rather than striving for meaningful careers. This is a real problem with what has been called the "backlash" of feminism. Since the corporate world is still a masculine one, a masculine body type has become the feminine ideal, which was discussed in chapter 4.

How far have women come in the workplace, anyway? Here are the latest statistics, from the U.S. Census Bureau (U.S. Department of Commerce), Status of Women Canada, Statistics Canada, the Feminist Majority Foundation, and the Center for the Study of Women in Society: The average female worker in the United States earns seventy-six cents for every dollar a man earns. Just 2.6 percent of corporate officers in Fortune 500 companies are women; 4.3 percent of corporate officers are women in the Fortune Service 500 in spite of the fact that 61 percent of all service workers are women. It's estimated that at the current rate of increase, it will take until the year 2466 before women reach equality with men in the executive suite.

It's also worth noting that there is still inadequate day care for millions of North American families, which often forces women out of the workplace.

Women have seen a 360-degree turn when it comes to psychotherapy. Its earliest forms saw women who rejected their roles as sick, while today, woman-centered approaches to therapy see the role women are asked to play as sick. In other words, a new approach to women in psychotherapy has identified depression as perhaps being a clinical name for the effects of male domination of women. Women are seen not as being medically sick but as being sick and tired of a sick role. This is still a controversial perspective, and not all mental-health experts agree that this is an accurate, or even helpful, perspective. But armed with a little bit of history of women and psychotherapy, it may make it easier for you to find that special someone to talk to.

Chapter

6

$\mathcal{F}$inding Someone to Talk to

How do you *know* when you need help? If *you* feel you need help, you should seek it—even if family members or friends discourage you. Help can come in the form of counseling—talk therapy—and perhaps medication. It can become a daunting task to figure out *who* you should seek, which is why many women simply do not find the proper help. This chapter will help you to navigate your way through the sea of talk therapists and the styles of talk therapies. Medication issues are discussed in chapter 7, while alternative therapies are discussed in chapter 8.

IN SEARCH OF A GOOD THERAPIST

When you're looking for a therapist, you should focus on finding someone you can relate to, someone who is a good fit. You want to avoid winding up with a therapist who is not helpful. Unhelpful therapy does not mean that your therapist is incompetent or unethical; it means that the style of therapy is not well-suited to you, and/or your therapist is not someone with whom you feel entirely comfortable. There can be many reasons for this, and they are often difficult to nail down. In other words, what one woman finds to be helpful therapy another woman may not. Therapists and styles of therapies are highly individual, and so is their impact.

Locating Names

Where do you begin if you are seeking help on your own? There are two general routes: referral or "going shopping." If you have a good primary-care physician (general practitioner, family practitioner, internist, or, in some cases, a gynecologist whom you see more regularly than your primary-care doctor), that physician can refer you to a few different therapists who specialize in depression or mood disorders. You're more likely to be referred to a psychiatrist or psychologist in this case. Chances are, if you like your referring doctor, you'll probably like one of the therapists she refers you to.

Many women can't count on their primary-care physicians for such referrals. In some cases, they may feel uncomfortable disclosing their wish to seek counseling; in other cases, they may not have a primary-care doctor at all—or one they like. Thankfully, there are many options available:

- *The employee assistance program.* This is a program many workplaces now offer. The employer pre-pays a group of therapists for X number of hours of therapy. You call a toll-free number, which is kept completely confidential, whereupon you have the option of seeing various licensed therapists on a short-term basis. Some therapists may specialize in addiction or stress management, while others may specialize in depression. This is relatively risk-free: if you don't like who you see, you simply don't return. And it hasn't cost you anything.
- *Community family services or women's health clinics.* Several communities operate family and child services or women's

clinics, where you can call to book an appointment with a
staff social worker. In some cases, you may be able to drop in
unannounced, but calling ahead of time is always best. These
services are usually not free, but you will be charged
according to your ability to pay.

- *Hospitals.* If you're feeling overwhelmed and know you must
speak to someone immediately, you can go straight to a
hospital and request a consultation with a mental health
professional in that hospital. Mental health professionals who
work in hospitals include psychiatrists, clinical psychologists,
psychiatric nurses, and social workers. You can sign yourself
in as a voluntary patient if there is room. You can also be
treated as an outpatient, which is a popular alternative for
many women. Hospitals usually won't admit you unless
you're threatening suicide or have attempted suicide in the
past. (And sometimes even under these circumstances you
may be sent home, due to hospital cutbacks.) See the "When
You Feel Life Isn't Worth Living" section in chapter 1.

- *Crisis lines.* If you're feeling overwhelmed and need to speak
to somebody right away, calling a crisis telephone line,
usually listed in the front of your white pages, is an option. A
crisis counselor can also refer you to other people or places
for more long-term counseling.

- *Community services listings.* Most urban areas have a
community information services book or at least a list of
community services phone numbers. You can find these in
public libraries.

- *Friends.* You may or may not feel comfortable going to a
therapist recommended by a friend. Confidentiality would be
the main concern, but if you trust your friend and see that
she has been helped by a particular therapist, you may feel
good about going to this professional. As noted, successful
therapy is so personal that most experts in mental health will

tell you *not* to use "hairdresser rules" for therapists, but it often depends on the circumstances. You should be careful about "gurus" or people who seem to have tremendous influence on the friend who has been helped. There are a variety of cultlike therapists with no formal training who practice dangerous mind games and brainwashing on the vulnerable. Look for credentials. This is not to say that only people with credentials are valid therapists, but it guarantees that the therapist has had some formal training and is adhering to some code of ethics.

* *The phone book.* You can find plenty of private practice therapists who should advertise their credentials up front. If you don't see degrees after her name, this may be a sign that the therapist has no formal training in therapy.

Looking for Credentials

When you're shopping for a therapist, one of the most confusing words is *doctor,* because it can mean either a medical doctor or a PhD, which technically stands for doctor of philosophy. People obtain PhDs in a number of academic disciplines ranging from A (as in anthropology) to Z (as in zoology). Furthermore, just because someone is a trained medical doctor doesn't make him or her a psychiatrist or a trained therapist.

An interesting example of credential confusion is the education of certain so-called "doctors" who dish out advice over the airwaves. Most people assume that radio or TV doctors are either psychologists or psychiatrists. But if you look at some of their credentials, you'll find that the term *doctor* is often misleading. For example, obtaining a PhD in any field gives one the right to call oneself a doctor but does not guarantee training in the area of mental health. Someone who obtained his PhD in chemistry, for example, can call himself a doctor and counsel people about their problems over the radio, but that doesn't mean that this person has done his graduate work in the area of mental health. Some questionable PhDs may indeed take the same marriage and family counseling certification courses that many other therapists take but do not necessarily hold PhDs. But because we can slide doctor in front of some names, the power of the title suggests that some hold more substantial credentials in the field of therapy than they actually do.

Even the "right" letters don't mean that a therapist is properly trained in therapy. For example, a social worker who has a Master of Social Work (MSW) could obtain such a degree by taking some general courses in social work theory but may not have any training specifically related to counseling or therapy. Or, a social worker may have spent most of her professional life in policy jobs and has no exposure to counseling or therapy. Letters may also be meaningless if that therapist obtained them through a disreputable university, college, or society.

But looking at letters is certainly a start, which helps you to sort out what type of training your therapist has likely received. The following professionals should have the corresponding credentials:

- *Psychiatrist.* This medical doctor specializes in the medical treatment of mental illness and is able to prescribe drugs. Many psychiatrists also do psychotherapy, but this isn't always the case. The appropriate credentials should read: Jane Doe, M.D. (medical doctor), F.A.C.P. (Fellow, American College of Physicians) F.R.C.P. (Fellow, Royal College of Physicians). That means this doctor has gone through four years of medical school and has completed a residency program in psychiatry, which, depending on the state, lasted approximately four years, and is registered in the American College of Physicians and Surgeons (or, if trained in Canada or the United Kingdom, the Royal College of Physicians and Surgeons).
- *Psychologist and Psychological Associate.* This professional can be licensed to practice therapy with either a master's or

doctoral degree. Clinical psychologists have a Master of Science degree (MS) or Master of Arts (MA) and usually works in a hospital or clinic setting but often can be found in private practice. Clinical psychologists can also hold a PhD (Doctor of Philosophy) in psychology, an EdD (Doctor of Education) or, if they're American, a PsyD (Doctor of Psychology), a common degree in the United States. Psychologists often perform testing, assessments, and plan treatments. They can also do psychotherapy and may have hospital-admitting privileges; they should be registered with their state licensing board. Licensure is required in all fifty states. Licensure requirements are generally uniform across states and authorize the psychologist to diagnose independently and treat mental and nervous disorders upon completion of both a doctoral degree in psychology (PhD, PsyD, or EdD) and a minimum of two years of supervised experience in direct clinical service. In some states, psychologists can also prescribe drugs.

- *Social Worker.* This professional holds a BSW (Bachelor of Social Work), and/or an MSW (Master of Social Work), having completed a bachelor degree in another discipline (which is not uncommon). Some social workers have PhDs as well. A professional social worker has a degree in social work and meets state legal requirements. The designation CSW stands for Certified Social Worker and is a legal title granted by the state. A designation of ACSW refers to the National Association of Social Workers (NASW), a nongovernmental national credential, and stands for the Academy of Certified Social Workers. Unlike the CSW, which, in addition to the exam, requires graduation (in most states) from a master's-level program, the ACSW requires two years of supervised experience following graduation from such a program. Some social workers have a P and R: These letters stand for CSWs who have become qualified under state law to receive insurance reimbursement for outpatient services to clients who have group health insurance. Each initial refers to different types of insurance policies. The P requires three years of supervised experience, while the R requires six years.

- *Psychiatric Nurse.* This is most likely a registered nurse (RN) with a *bachelor* of science in nursing (BSc), which isn't absolutely required. She probably has, but doesn't necessarily need, a *master's* degree in nursing as well. The master's degree could be either an MA (Master of Arts) or an MS (Master of Science). This nurse has done most of her training in a psychiatric setting and *may* be trained to do psychotherapy.

- *Counselor.* This professional has *usually* completed certification courses in counseling and therefore has obtained a license to practice psychotherapy. She may have (it is not required) a university degree. Frequently, though, counselors will have a master's degree in a related field, such as social work. Or, they may have a master's degree in a field that has nothing to do with mental health. The term *professional counselor* is used to represent those individuals who have earned a minimum of a master's degree and possess professional knowledge and demonstrable skills in the application of mental health, and psychological and human-development principles in order to facilitate human development and adjustment throughout the life span. As of January 1999, the District of Columbia and forty-four states had enacted some type of counselor-credentialing law, which regulates the use of titles related to the counseling profession. The letters *CPC* stand for Certified Professional Counselor and refers to the title granted by the state legislative process. The letters *LPC* stand for Licensed Professional Counselor and refer to the most commonly granted state statutory counselor credential. No matter what letters you see, however, it's always a good idea to ask your counselor what training she has had in the field of mental health.

- *Marriage and Family Counselor.* This is somewhat different from the broader term *counselor.* This professional has completed rigorous training through certification courses in family therapy and relationship dynamics and has also obtained a license to practice psychotherapy. This professional should have the designations MFT or AAFMT. MFTs have graduate training (a master's or doctoral degree) in marriage and family therapy and at least two years of clinical experience. Forty-one states currently license, certify, or regulate MFTs.

A word about fees

It's important to discuss fees with your therapist up front, so you know what services are covered by your health plan. In general, mental health services in hospitals are covered by health plans, as are services provided by psychiatrists. But social workers or counselors in private practice are all fee-for-service. Call the National Association of Social Workers (NASW), at 1-800-638-8799 to determine what a social worker or counselor in private practice should charge and to obtain a copy of the NASW Code of Ethics. If you want to see someone in private practice but can't afford it, some community-provided counseling services charge you based on ability to pay. Experts consulted for this book agreed that it is considered bad practice for a counselor to agree to see someone who cannot (or will not) pay for her services. This person is offering a service, not a charity, and the professional relationship should be respected. As of this writing, psychiatrists typically charge roughly $100 to $175 per hour/session; clinical psychologists charge roughly $85 to $120 per hour/session; while social workers charge $65 to $110 per hour/session.

If you have health coverage through a managed-care plan, you may be in for a rude awakening when it comes to coverage of psychiatric services. Most plans cover only thirty days of inpatient psychiatric care per year, and twenty outpatient visits to a psychotherapist. This is fine if you require only short-term therapy, but for most people suffering from depression or mood disorders, this coverage is inadequate. Some plans offer "conversion of benefits," meaning that you can convert your thirty days of inpatient coverage to thirty *extra* days of outpatient visits, which gives you fifty covered outpatient visits.

An *important* consideration for anyone using psychiatric services covered by a health insurance plan is confidentiality. Managed-care facilities require frequent record reviews by psychiatric services providers, which means that confidentiality between you and your mental health-care provider may be compromised. Discuss this aspect of treatment when you discuss fees and costs; it's important.

Going for a Test Drive

Okay, you've found someone you think is qualified to be your therapist. That doesn't mean you've found the right therapist. Ask yourself the following questions when you first sit down with this professional. If you find you're answering "no" to many of the questions below, you should ask yourself whether you're really with the right therapist. There is no magic number of negative responses here, but these questions will help you to gauge how you truly feel about this therapist.

1. Is this someone you feel comfortable with?
2. Is this someone you can trust?
3. Is this someone you feel calm with?
4. Is this someone you feel safe with?
5. Does this person respect you (or treat you with respect)?

6. Does this person seem flexible?
7. Does this person seem reliable?
8. Does this person seem supportive?
9. Does this person have a supervisor or mentor with whom they consult on difficult or challenging cases?

Red flags

You should be cautious about engaging a therapist when . . .

- she does not do a formal assessment, known as a workup, which rules out organic causes for your symptoms, for example, thyroid disease. If your therapist is not a physician, she may not be trained to do as formal an exam as a physician would, but she may still be an excellent therapist. However, a therapist *should* ask you where you've been prior to this appointment, and at least inquire about whether you've had a physical exam.
- if you're seeing a medical doctor or psychiatrist, she prescribes antidepressants or other medications on your first visit. This may be warranted in some circumstances, and many psychiatrists will make a decision about medication on a first visit if you've already been seen by another physician or counselor. But, as a general rule, some sort of workup and discussion is necessary before you're handed a prescription and sent home.
- you are diagnosed or labeled with a disorder of some sort within a few minutes of your first visit. This is a situation that would only occur if your therapist is a medical doctor. Again, you may be clearly suffering from an identifiable mood disorder, but some discussion and workup should occur before you're immediately diagnosed.
- she is adamantly opposed to prescribing any sort of medication, period (this isn't good, either; some people require medication *and* talk therapy).

- she believes in only one kind of approach or theory and seems inflexible to any other approach, theory, or school of thought, such as a woman-centered approach. This is okay if the therapist is clear and open about the fact that she only believes in one approach, explains to you why she believes it's helpful, and points out the limitations of her work. In this case, you've been informed about the pros and cons and are free to decide if the one-school-of-thought approach is for you.
- she does not ask you about your relationships, school, and work histories, or other aspects of your personal history.
- she uses a lot of jargon or technical language that intimidates you. (How can you possibly expect to talk to someone when you can't understand what she's saying?)
- he (or she) suggests you have sex together in order for you to work through your sexual problems. (This is malpractice and should be reported. And yes, while it is rare, women can abuse women.)

Does your therapist's age or lifestyle matter?

The only time the age or lifestyle of your therapist matters is if it matters to *you*, because it will affect your degree of comfort with her. Although younger therapists certainly have fewer life experiences than older therapists, everyone knows there are just as many wise thirty-one-year-olds as there are fifty-six-year-olds with limited wisdom. Younger therapists may be more flexible, caring, less "burned-out," and more up-to-date in terms of codes of practice and ethics. Older therapists may have more experience but may also be more rigid in their approach. But older therapists may be more sensitive to fears of death or aging than a younger therapist. Meanwhile, a childless therapist may be less apt to understand the stresses of a woman with children. Gender preference may also be a factor. If you're a lesbian, you may be more comfortable with a therapist who is gay or lesbian. However, finding someone who is similar to you in some ways because you want the automatic feeling of acceptance isn't a guarantee that this is the right therapist. Other dynamics are also important: You may be uncomfortable with a father figure, for example, or a mother figure, but you may be equally uncomfortable with someone the same age as your son or daughter. Although most people strive to find a peer in a therapist, a therapist and client are not equal in this context. In other words, looking for a therapist who is like you may not be the best criteria when you're looking for a therapist. There is enormous value in finding a person with the right therapeutic distance.

STYLES OF THERAPY

You may wish to review chapter 5 on the history of women and psychotherapy to understand some of the trends that have emerged in woman-centered approaches to therapy and the shady history of women and psychotherapy. But *all* of the following styles of therapy, discussed in alphabetical order, can *include* a woman-centered approach, even if you don't choose a feminist therapist.

Biologically Informed Psychotherapy

First, only medical doctors can prescribe medication. This is bio-psychiatry, where your therapist believes depression is a medical problem, triggered by some life pressure or stressor. Medication combined with talk therapy is the preferred approach, and if you are believed to be suffering from seasonal depression, or SAD (seasonal affective disorder—see chapter 1), light therapy may be used instead of medication, which I discuss in chapter 7.

This doesn't mean your therapist is against "talk therapy," however. She may combine with medication one of the styles of therapy discussed below. But instead of seeing your depression as stemming solely from a social situation, a therapist who practices biopsychiatry sees your depressive thinking, for example, as a side effect of depression. This is viewed as a medical condition. If you are thinking about suicide rather than looking at your personal situation or life events as having triggered this thought or desire, a therapist from this school would say: "That's your depression talking (i.e., your disordered brain chemistry), not *you*." Thus, your depression is removed from your circumstances and treated like a medical condition, such as pneumonia. The belief is that once your brain chemistry is restored, you will begin to think rationally and reasonably again, and may even be able to (or open to) shift your perspective on life, which could be done through talk therapy.

This is not unlike an approach used to treat anorexia nervosa, for example. A woman suffering from anorexia may benefit enormously from talk therapy. But if she weighs less than sixty pounds and is physically starving, there is no way for her to "hear" what is being said, let alone participate in talk therapy. She will therefore need to be fed and to be physically restored before she can hear anything.

If you are incapacitated by your depression, for example, and cannot get out of bed, talk therapy is not useful; your therapist's main goal in this case would be to help you to *get out of bed*, and thus restore your functioning. This may be done through medications, such as antidepressants. (See chapter 7.)

Biopsychiatry does not mean that the therapist believes medication will fix everything; she believes that it can facilitate productive talk therapy.

Cognitive-Behavioral Therapy

This is more oriented toward upbeat thinking and correcting what is referred to as disordered thinking. Instead of dwelling on negative thoughts, this form of therapy is based on the premise that "how you think can affect how you feel." For example, if a friend cancels a lunch date with you, or somebody doesn't return your phone call or E-mail, you may be apt to take it personally and make assumptions that you are not liked by that person. That thought then leads you to feel badly about yourself, which reinforces feelings of low self-esteem or even self-loathing. A cognitive-behavioral therapist will ask you to consider other reasons for the cancellation or unreturned call. Perhaps there are problems overwhelming your friend that have absolutely nothing to do with you. Perhaps a last-minute deadline came up, or it may be that problems and stresses in your lunch date's personal life necessitated the cancellation. In other words, not everything you perceive to be negative is really negative, and not everything you take personally is personal.

Ultimately, the premise of cognitive-behavioral therapy is this: If you think negative thoughts about yourself and believe you're a failure or that your life is doomed, you are more apt to be sad. On the other hand, if you think positive thoughts and believe in yourself, you are more apt to be happy. Although this approach might sound "easy" and to be a "quick fix," changing your perspective on life can be powerful. But again, in the midst of a depression, this may have limited success. Essentially, what's past is past, and you can decide *today* to be a more positive person, which in turn can attract more positive experiences into your life.

Feminist Therapy

Feminist therapy means woman-centered therapy. Feminist therapy is not one specific style of therapy but an overall philosophy that takes into account women's social roles and social situations when looking at the symptoms that comprise women's depression. (You may wish to review chapter 5 to understand the origins of this approach more thoroughly.) I am not saying this is the *only* approach to therapy, and plenty of female therapists do *not* embrace feminist therapy. The following goals represent a feminist approach to therapy.

1. Developing a sense of self, independent of male authority or idealized visions of what a woman is supposed to be; the task is not for a woman to develop a "masculine persona" but to celebrate her own feminine persona and to see her traits as inner strength rather than an inability to compete in a male world.

2. Seeing that the *personal is political,* as the adage goes. Feminist therapists listen for the connections between the personal story and the outer world in women's lives. The therapist uses feminist values to help shift a woman from being a victim to being a person who sees how the world *around* her is creating her feelings of victimization—which is therefore validating.

3. Seeing that depression is really the internalization of oppression. *(This does not mean, however, that you should walk around depressed and not seek help.)*

4. Seeing that feelings of low self-esteem, worthlessness, inadequacy, powerlessness, poor body image, anxiety, depression, and/or sexual dysfunction are symptoms of female subservience in a man's world. In other words, they are normal, adaptive responses to the world around you rather than symptoms of a disease or sickness. *(Again, this does not mean that you should just shrug off your feelings of depression and low self-esteem and not seek help. In other words, cold symptoms may be normal reactions to a common cold virus, but you still must care for yourself by resting and drinking plenty of fluids to get better.)*

5. Seeing that self-sacrificing behaviors are normal feminine, nurturing behaviors rather than symptoms of a disease. Labels such as "codependent" are not helpful and should be dismissed as psychobabble.

6. Seeing that physical ailments are valid and should be trusted as another way of "knowing." In other words, women's bodies may be trying to tell them something about the

environment or the toxic lifestyle to which they have become numb. For example, many women who have chronic fatigue or environmental sensitivities (see chapter 3) should see their symptoms as visionary or intuitive rather than invalid and phantom. There is a link between femi- nine intuition, ecology, and environment, which feminists have called eco-feminism. Women such as Rachel Carson, author of *Silent Spring,* who warned of the dangers of pesticides as early as 1964 and was declared a heretic by the pharmaceutical industry, are examples of how women's physical ailments and body intuition were dismissed to the world's peril.

7. Seeing that human emotional pain is not a medical problem but a normal response to one's environment. In other words, pain in response to a bad situation is normal, not sick.

8. Understanding that grief is grief. Grieving the death of a loved one is not different from grieving one's poverty or life circumstances. Yet, in the medical world, some things are more worthy of grief than others, which can mean that you are labeled "normal" for some kinds of grieving but "sick" for other kinds.

9. Connecting to other women as a group. What you suffer, other women suffer. You are not alone but part of a community. The solution cannot be found on an individual level but must be arrived at collectively. In other words, one black person in 1950 could not overturn centuries of racism and segregation. It took a movement.

A therapist doesn't have to be a female therapist to offer a woman- centered approach, either. If you are interested in seeking help with a feminist therapist, contact women's centers or even women's stud- ies programs at local universities for names. Alternatively, use the guidelines for finding help on page 124, and simply tell your thera- pist that you are interested in a feminist approach.

Interpersonal Therapy

This specific approach to therapy is based on the idea that malfunctioning relationships surround your depression. In other words, where there's depression, there are "screwed up" relationships in your life that are interfering with your quality of life. You and your therapist will explore current relationships and recent events that may have affected those relationships, such as loss, conflict, or change. You may also explore the roles various people play in your life and what your expectations are of them, and vice versa. Your therapist works in a supporting role to help you to develop better strategies to cope or negotiate with key people in your life. This can help to resolve conflicts. Much of this has to do with setting reasonable expectations from relationships, as well as looking at how one might have misinterpreted the actions of others.

Psychoanalysis

It's important not to confuse psychoanalysis with psychoanalytic therapy, which is similar to psychodynamic therapy (see below). Psychoanalysis is an intensive therapy that usually involves three to four sessions per week and is not recommended for people in the midst of a depression, because you are not able to function well. This therapy, best suited to the time after the crisis has passed, is designed for people who are ready for self-discovery. It is a journey into your childhood based on the premise that your current problems stem from deep wounds from your childhood. For example, as an adult, you may be reenacting unmet needs you had as a child. Or you may discover that behavior such as pleasing your parents is being acted out in your workplace or in your personal relationships. In the previous chapter, I discussed how women in the past were frequently harmed through psychoanalysis because it tended to reinforce father figure/little girl relationships. But, properly done, it is not something women have to fear, and many excellent psychoanalysts are women.

Psychodynamic Therapy

Psychodynamic therapy deals with the ghosts or relationships and events from your past, the dynamics of your upbringing, as well as present events and relationships. Here, your thoughts, emotions, and behavior over a lifetime are examined. Patterns of behavior and aspects of your personality are discussed as possible sources of both internal and external conflict. Couples or groups are often involved in psychodynamic therapy. The adage *the past is history, the future a mystery, and the present a gift* works well in this context.

GETTING THE MOST OUT OF TALKING HEADS

How do you know when talk therapy is helping? Therapy is a two-way street; a good therapist recognizes this and should, without your prompting, begin your course of talk therapy by laying her cards on the table with respect to her goals and your expectations. Once therapy begins, some therapists also like to use the blank-slate approach, which means that the therapist says little, in the hopes that you will project onto that slate, providing important clues about your relationships and your relationship dynamics. There are some hallmarks of good therapists, which include:

- *Genuine caring.* Your therapist should demonstrate a basic concern for your welfare, the ability to empathize, and the ability to communicate that empathy.
- *Accepting your criticism.* If you become angry or critical, your therapist shouldn't take it personally and should be able to accept solid criticism in good measure. You need to feel assured that you can get angry or critical in a session without feeling that your therapist will hold it against you or retaliate somehow. (If your criticism is not valid, a therapist should feel free to interpret your anger.)

- *Giving you reliable service and undivided attention.* Your therapist should not frequently cancel sessions, change sessions, take phone calls during sessions, or use your time to discuss fees or payments. Nor should your therapist cut you off in the middle of an epiphany because time's up. (Epiphanies, one presumes, don't happen every day; they should be respected.) That said, you shouldn't take advantage of your therapist and manipulate her for more time. Obviously, if a therapist cannot give you an extra minute now and then, there's a problem. But there are clients who can overstep the boundary and constantly go overtime, which interferes with someone *else's* time. And that's not fair, either.

- *Refraining from discussing her own problems.* Your therapist isn't your hairdresser. It's not tit for tat. You shouldn't be expected to listen to your therapist's personal problems during your time with her.

- *Practicing within a code of ethics.* Your therapist should keep your sessions confidential, should not be tape-recording, videotaping, or staging your session in front of a one-way mirror, where her colleagues are watching without your knowledge. If your session is being recorded or observed by others (which may be the case if the therapist is in training, is training someone else, or would like to consult with someone else about your case), it must be done with your full consent. Otherwise, these are indications that you cannot trust your therapist, and you should find help elsewhere.

Repressed Memories Versus False Memories

Obviously, therapists have access to your mind, which can put them in a powerful position. One of the most controversial issues to have emerged in the last decade is the phenomenon of repressed memories, and a questionable condition known as false memory syndrome. If you are having nightmares or flashbacks about abuse you suffered as a child, this is a sign that you may have repressed painful memories, which are only now surfacing.

But there have been reports of people who have no memory or inkling of abuse who, with the aid of a therapist, begin to visualize horrible scenes and are told they are memories. This is known as false memory syndrome. Experts consulted for this book were sharply divided about this subject. Some believed it to be nothing more than media hype and felt that its incidence was so small in the therapeutic community that they wondered why I was devoting any space to it at all. Some felt it was important to raise the issue but to distinguish false memory syndrome from the real phenomenon of repressed memories.

British psychiatrists felt strongly enough about this issue to pub-lish a report attacking the practice known as recovered memory techniques, which can supposedly lead to false memories. According to the Royal College of Psychiatrists, memories recovered through hypnosis, dream interpretation, or regression therapy are almost al-ways false. False memories of abuse undermine the real experiences of children who have suffered abuse. False accusations also destroy families and interpersonal relationships, causing far more damage and creating enormous dependency on the therapist, who, in this scenario, frequently becomes the client's only friend or trusted rela-tionship. According to this report, people who have been abused re-member; that's the problem—they *can't* forget. Therapists consulted for this book maintained that repression of memories also exists and that not everyone remembers entirely but that flashbacks and night-mares are common features of repressed memories.

Talking Versus Drugs

A common scenario for many women is going through talk therapy for years without any real progress, which raises the issue of whether talk therapy alone is less effective than medications, or less effective than the combination of medications and talk therapy. (Of course, it can simply mean the woman is seeing the wrong therapist.) The opposite scenario is medication without any talk therapy, which is not good, either. The experts consulted for this book agreed that in cases of severe depression, a combination of medication and talk therapy is best. In cases where patients are dealing with a particular crisis, or in mild to moderate depression, talk therapy alone has been shown to be helpful. For example, cognitive therapy, in some studies, is shown to be just as valuable a treatment for mild to moderate depression (see chapter 1) as antidepressants.

Most mental health professionals agree that if you've never experienced depression before, are not severely depressed, or don't seem to be suffering from any major physical symptoms—such as sleep disturbances or appetite problems—then talking to someone without being put on medication is certainly worthwhile. If you don't seem to be improving after having been in therapy for four to six months, then it's time to ask yourself whether you're with the right therapist and whether you might benefit from another approach.

When Is Therapy Finished?

Most mental health experts agree that good therapy should have a beginning, middle, and an end. People shouldn't languish for years in therapy, stuck in some sort of limbo. However, sometimes there is a natural phase in therapy where you need to be "stuck" before you can go forward. As a general rule, if you're not learning anything new and your discussions seem to just repeat old issues and insights, it's time to revisit your initial goals in therapy and look at other approaches. It's also important to keep in mind that with some chronic mental illnesses or physical conditions, people may benefit from a "light talk" therapy. Here, the goal is to discuss day-to-day functioning rather than developing deep insights. In other words, for some people, talk therapy makes it possible to do even the simplest of tasks, such as banking, for example.

The Rent-a-Friend Problem

Many women form strong, deep ties to their therapists, developing deep, trusting friendships. Having romantic thoughts for a therapist is also not unusual, but it may be an issue that your therapist raises. Otherwise, it could be the big, pink elephant sitting in the room that no one is talking about. But the alliance or trust you've built with your therapist is not a good reason to stay in therapy. In some situations, it may be possible to decide *when* you're going to leave at the beginning of your therapy, but this may not be reasonable. In a general way, however, you establish goals with your therapist and decide together whether you will be coming for a short or a longer term.

The problem with having deep, intimate discussions with a really nice, reasonable, practical, insightful person at regular intervals is that you'll probably grow and want to *continue* to grow. The question you must ask yourself is whether your relationship with your therapist is interfering with the fostering of other friendships or intimate relationships. In other words, are you paying your therapist for "friendship" and/or "romance" rather than paying him or her for *therapy?* That can be a tough question.

There comes a point when you can be *alone* and grow. In other words, you don't have to be in therapy to have personal insights. With therapy, there is no such thing as "going all the way," because there is no end to our personal and spiritual growth. It's impossible for this book to define an appropriate course of therapy. Every woman is different. But good therapists work toward liberating you from the dependency on counseling and help you to feel more self-reliant. A good therapist, in short, should give you roots *and* wings.

SUPPORT GROUPS

Professionals who provide counseling for women report that the support and confidence gained from other women, including woman-centered counseling (see chapter 5), is helpful.

This isn't just true for depression. Several studies have shown the value of support groups and support systems in treating many physical diseases, including cancer. One study found that women with end-stage breast cancer who joined a support group actually lived longer than women who did not. And women who share common conditions, such as infertility, AIDS, and pregnancy loss, for instance, find support groups helpful.

Since depression has so many causes, support groups for depressed women are not as useful as support groups for, say, women who are living with violence or women who are battling obesity. In other words, finding or establishing a group of women that share your *circumstances* is the key to finding good support. Otherwise, you may wind up in a group where your *circumstances* are not understood. For example, if you were going through a divorce, someone coping with cancer may not find your circumstances "reason enough" for you to feel depressed. Or, someone with AIDS may find someone with a treatable cancer unreasonable in her feelings of depression.

Community and cultural norms are also an important factor in finding the right support group. For example, stigmas about depression may vary dramatically from culture to culture, while perspectives on what constitutes community and support may also differ. In some cultures, large, extended families may be the norm, which may substitute for a support group. For these reasons, white women may cope differently with depression than black or Hispanic women. East Indian women may cope differently than Asian women, while African-American women may cope differently than Caribbean or Somali women.

Where Do You Look for Support?

If you're struggling to make ends meet, for example, you won't likely find an ad in the paper inviting "all poor women" to a support group. But if you live in a poor community, responding to community-based programs ranging from crafts groups to yoga is the way to support. In fact, community-outreach workers use the arts, crafts, fitness, and computer classes as tools to attract women within the community who could benefit from support. What often takes place in community-based programs is a great deal of talking and sharing during, prior to, or after the activity. These are places where you make friends, find someone you can talk to, and, most important, find that you're not alone in your situation. Community programs are a way for women to say to their abusive husbands "Back in an hour; I'm going to my yoga class" instead of "I'm going to talk about you to a bunch of other women."

The old joke about women going to the bathroom in twos is accurate; women go together to the bathroom because it's a place where they can *talk*. Women *need* other women to talk to. This is how for centuries we've coped with the hardships of life. One study found that women tend to have four to six close friendships with other women; men have zero or one close friendship with another man.

When women talk informally to try to put their feelings into perspective, these are some of the things they talk about.

1. *Sexism.* In case you haven't noticed, we live in a sexist society where men still enjoy more privileges than do women. Ask other women how they feel about that. Your conversation won't change the world, but your feelings about the world might be validated. And that feels good.
2. *Powerlessness.* You know what? You feel powerless because you're "set up" to feel powerless—by those in power. Most women have little power in their workplace, home, or community. So it's no wonder you feel inadequate. Talking about this may help you to find a perspective that actually empowers you. By the way, this is not to say that there are no powerful women in the world; it's just that they are few and far between. And there are plenty of women in power who feel powerless, too.

3. *Ambivalence over assertiveness.* I know it's the twenty-first century, but women in many cultures are taught to be docile and passive in a world that is aggressive and harsh. Again, talking about it won't necessarily change you into a go-getter, but it will probably help you to realize that you're not the only one who has been taught to feel that aggressiveness and assertiveness are unfeminine. Therefore, your reluctance to assert yourself is perfectly understandable, given the message you're sent from birth: You do not have a voice, and when you speak, negative consequences follow.

4. *Absurd standards of beauty.* Spend an afternoon with a fashion photographer and makeup artist and they'll tell you a few things. What you see in the magazines is fiction and fantasy, with the aid of heavy makeup, carefully constructed lighting, and computer-aided touch-ups. Model's bodies, too, are to some degree unreal. In fact, it's common for fashion models to self-induce vomiting prior to a photo shoot (the makeup artists can smell the vomit on the model while she's in makeup). Is that beautiful? Talk about *that* with other women. One makeup artist put it best when he told me: "I can't even watch television or read a magazine anymore because I know how ugly this business is and how desperate the women are who participate in this sham. We [makeup artists and photographers] spend hours distorting these women and dare call it 'beauty.'"

When it is the Caucasian face that is objectified and held up as the global standard of beauty, what are you supposed to do if you're not Caucasian? Does this standard of beauty make sense to you? And when seventeen-year-old girls are objectified and held up as the standard for what a thirty-five-year-old woman is supposed to look like, isn't that *insane*? Tall women (models must be at least 5 feet 9 inches to get work) are taller than the average *Caucasian* woman. So if you're of average height for a Caucasian, you're not considered beautiful enough for the Western standard. But, of course, most women on the planet are not Caucasian. The average height for Asian women, for example, is shorter than the average Caucasian height. Again, our beauty standards are not sane.

The message of seeking comfort in validation is not to confirm your suspicions that life is horrible and hopeless but that you're not the only one who feels that life is a struggle. This should give you the courage to move forward and make some changes (or, at least, make some friends who have common concerns) instead of shrinking in a corner, feeling you're the "only one."

When you're in the midst of a depression, are experiencing disordered thinking, are unfocused, and are unable to function, talk therapy is often not useful, because you simply will not be able to communicate properly. Often, medication is the first step in getting you back on your feet. It is then followed by talk therapy. What you need to know about medication for depression is discussed in the next chapter.

Understanding Your Mental Health-Care Rights

Legislation on mental health laws varies from state to state. As of this writing, no document pertains to your rights as a mental health patient. The Department of Health and Human Rights is advocating federal legislation to create a patient's bill of rights. A fact sheet on the proposed bill can be accessed by calling the HHS Press Office at (202) 690-6343.

On page 149 you'll find the Mental Health Patient's Bill of Rights, compiled by the American Psychological Association, and which is used by various counseling and therapy organizations. On page 154 you'll find information on the Mental Health Parity Act, which pertains to coverage of mental health care.

You can also contact your state insurance commissioner or public information office for quality standards and conditions of participation for the private health (individual/group) insurance market. The National Association of Insurance Commissioners (NAIC) provides a list of state locations if you call the Help Desk, at (816) 374-7231.

MENTAL HEALTH PATIENT'S BILL OF RIGHTS

Principles for the Provision of Mental Health and Substance-Abuse Treatment Services

This list of rights is supported by the following participating organizations: American Association for Marriage and Family Therapy; American Counseling Association; American Family Therapy Academy; American Nurses Association; American Psychiatric Association; American Psychiatric Nurses Association; American Psychological Association; Clinical Social Work Federation; National Association of Social Workers; American Group Psychotherapy Association; American Psychoanalytic Association; National Association of Alcoholism and Drug Abuse Counselors; National Depressive and Manic-Depressive Association; National Mental Health Association; Therapeutic Communities of America.

You can also order a brochure or poster of the following by contacting the American Psychological Association, at 1-800-374-2721 or through E-mail at order@apa.org.

Right to Know

- *Benefits.* If you have not already received information about your health plan, ask your benefits manager for a copy of the benefits; you have a right to have one of your own to keep. Does this document describe what mental health care and substance-abuse treatment benefits you are entitled to? Does it explain how to get services and how to appeal coverage decisions you do not agree with? Does it explain your financial responsibilities? Is the coverage equal to that offered for other illnesses? Individuals have the right to be provided information from the purchasing entity (such as the employer, union, or public purchaser) and the insurance/third-party payer describing the nature and extent of their mental health and substance-abuse treatment benefits. This information should include details on procedures to obtain access to services, utilization-management procedures, and appeal rights. The information should be presented clearly in writing with language that the individual can understand.

Continued on next page

- *Professional expertise.* Ask your benefits manager which mental health professionals your plan covers. Does it cover a full range of mental health professionals? Which is their training and experience? Are they licensed or certified? What kinds of treatments are available? Which treatments are excluded? Individuals have the right to receive full information from the potential treating professional about that professional's knowledge, skills, preparation, experience, and credentials. Individuals have the right to be informed about the options available for treatment interventions and the effectiveness of the recommended treatment.

- *Contractual limitations.* Ask if there are any financial agreements or arrangements that the professional has had to make with a third-party payer or insurer that could interfere with or influence her treatment decisions. Is the professional constrained from telling you about any treatment options, for example, those that are or are not covered in the plan? Is the professional in danger of being discharged from the plan for advocating for your optimal care? Does the plan pay the professional the same amount regardless of treatment prescribed? Does the plan reward the professional for limiting services? Individuals have the right to be informed by the treating professional of any arrangements, restrictions, and/or covenants established between the third-party payer and the treating professional that could interfere with or influence treatment recommendations. Individuals have the right to be informed of the nature of information that may be disclosed for the purposes of paying benefits.

- *Appeals and grievances.* If you have concerns about the certification or authorization of treatment decisions made by the payer or insurance company, ask how you can appeal them to the payer, your employer, or the purchasing agent, or to outside regulatory agencies. Ask what methods you can use to complain if you don't agree with the care provided by the professional. You have the right to complain to regulatory boards and/or professional associations, which have grievance processes, and you have the right to air your complaints to your union, your state and federal legislators, and to the media. Individuals have the right to receive information about the methods they can use to submit complaints or grievances regarding provision of care by the treating professional to that profession's regulatory board and to the professional association. Individuals have the right to be provided information about the procedures they can use to appeal benefit-utilization decisions to the third-party payer systems, to the employer or purchasing entity, and to external regulatory entities.

Confidentiality

Find out if the information to be disclosed to the payer would be anything other than diagnosis, prognosis, type, time, and length of treatment, and cost. Will the organizations receiving this information keep it as confidential as the mental health professional? How will they protect it? Are there penalties for disclosing information improperly? If your information is transmitted, stored, or used for any purpose as data, will information that identifies you be removed in order to protect your privacy? Will the information be transferred to others or sold?

Individuals have the right to be guaranteed the protection of the confidentiality of their relationship with their mental health and substance-abuse professional, except when laws or ethics dictate otherwise. Any disclosure to another party will be time-limited and made with the full, written, and informed consent of the individuals. Individuals shall not be required to disclose confidential, privileged, or other information other than diagnosis, prognosis, type, time, and length of treatment, and cost. Entities receiving information for the purposes of benefits-determination, public agencies receiving information for health-care planning, or any other organization with a legitimate right to information will maintain clinical information in confidence with the same rigor and be subject to the same penalties for violation as is the direct provider of care.

Information technology will be used for transmission, storage, or data-management only with methodologies that remove individual identifying information and assure the protection of the individual's privacy. Information should not be transferred, sold, or otherwise utilized.

Continued on next page

Choice

Ask if you are able to choose any licensed/certified professional for your mental health-care services. Which professionals are covered, and what are their credentials? What if you choose a licensed professional not usually covered by the plan? Individuals have the right to choose any duly licensed/certified professional for mental health and substance-abuse services. Individuals have the right to receive full information regarding the education and training of professionals, treatment options (including risks and benefits), and cost implications in order to make an informed choice regarding the selection of care deemed appropriate by the individual and professional.

Determination of Treatment

Is anyone other than your professional involved in your treatment decisions? If so, do they have the same training and experience as your treating professional? Do they have a financial interest in their decisions? Recommendations regarding mental health and substance-abuse treatment shall be made only by a duly licensed/certified professional in conjunction with the individual and her family, as appropriate. Treatment decisions should not be made by third-party payers. The individual has the right to make final decisions regarding her treatment.

Parity

Individuals have the right to receive benefits for mental health and substance-abuse treatment on the same basis as they do for any other illnesses, with the same provisions, copayments, lifetime benefits, and catastrophic coverage in both insurance and self-funded/self-insured health plans.

Discrimination

Individuals who use mental health and substance-abuse benefits shall not be penalized when seeking other health insurance or disability, life, or any other insurance benefit. Quality mental health and substance-abuse services should be provided to all individuals without regard to race, color, religion, national origin, gender, age, sexual orientation, or disability.

Benefit of Usage

The individual is entitled to the entire scope of the benefits within the benefit plan that will address her clinical needs.

Benefit of Design

Whenever federal and state law and/or regulations are applicable, the professional and all payers shall use whichever affords the individual the greatest level of protection and access.

Treatment Review

To ensure that treatment-review processes are fair and valid, individuals have the right to be guaranteed that any review of their mental health and substance-abuse treatment shall involve a professional having the training, credentials, and licensure required to provide the treatment in the jurisdiction in which it will be provided. The reviewer should have no financial interest in the decision and is subject to the section on confidentiality.

Accountability

Treating professionals may be held accountable and liable to individuals for any injury caused by gross incompetence or negligence on the part of the professional. The treating professional has the obligation to advocate for and document necessity of care and to advise the individual of options if payment authorization is denied. Payers and other third parties may be held accountable and liable to individuals for any injury caused by gross incompetence or negligence or by their clinically unjustified decisions.

Source: The American Psychological Association, 1997. Copyright © 1997 by the American Psychological Association. Reprinted with permission.

· · · · · · · · · ·

MENTAL HEALTH PARITY ACT

The Mental Health Parity Act (MHPA), signed into law on September 26, 1996, requires that annual or lifetime limits on mental health benefits be no lower than that of the dollar limits for medical and surgical benefits offered by a group health plan.

MHPA applies to group health plans for plan years beginning on or after January 1, 1998, and contains a so-called "sunset" provision that provides that the parity requirements do not apply to benefits received on or after September 30, 2001.

The law:

- generally requires parity of mental health benefits with medical/surgical benefits with respect to the application of aggregate lifetime and annual dollar limits under a group health plan;
- provides that employers retain discretion regarding the extent and scope of mental health benefits offered to workers and their families (including cost sharing, limits on number of visits or days of coverage, and requirements relating to medical necessity).

The law also contains the following two exemptions:

1. small employer exemption. MHPA does not apply to any plan or coverage of any employer who employed two to fifty employees on business days during the preceding calendar year, and who employs at least two employees on the first day of the plan year.

2. increased cost exemption. MHPA does not apply to a group health plan or group health insurance coverage if the application of the parity provisions results in an increase in the cost under the plan or coverage of at least 1 percent.

The law, however, does not apply to benefits for substance abuse or chemical dependency.

Source: U.S. Department of Labor: publication hot line: 1-800-998-7542 or www.dol.gov/dol/pwba.

omen and Medication

Pharmaceutical companies *love* women. In the United States, women account for two-thirds of the forty-four million hospital procedures performed each year, 61 percent of the seventy million annual doctor visits, 75 percent of nursing home residents (due to women outliving men), and 59 percent of prescription-drug purchases. And, since on average women live seven years longer than men, they're around longer to purchase drugs. In fact, the best-selling drug in history is Premarin (estrogen derived from the urine of pregnant mares), which has been sold by Wyeth-Ayerst for more than fifty years.

Considering these statistics, it's odd that when it comes to drugs designed to treat disorders that occur in both men and women, we know little about how they interact in women's bodies. That's because until 1993, women were excluded from clinical trials that tested drug potency, side effects, and interactions. There's a reason for that exclusion. Women, the elderly, minorities, and other vulnerable populations had a long history of being *abused* in medical research—to such an extent that public outcry demanded stronger regulations to protect them.

In the mid-1970s, in response to the horrors of thalidomide and DES (diethylstilbestrol), legislation was passed to protect pregnant women and women of childbearing age. For example, U.S. Department of Health and Human Services regulations deliberately exclude pregnant women from research. Thalidomide (marketed in 1958) was a morning sickness drug that was not properly tested prior to its release. It caused severe limb deformities in the developing fetus. DES was administered from the 1940s until the early 1970s as a miscarriage-prevention drug, which was later revealed to cause a rare form of vaginal cancer in DES daughters, as well as reproductive problems in DES sons. Even amidst protective legislation, more DES-like disasters loom, as widespread use of fertility drugs, which may cause ovarian cancer in women who do not conceive, echo the same concerns raised by DES activists. Tamoxifen (an antiestrogen drug that can cause endometrial cancer, and which is being administered to healthy women considered at high risk of developing breast cancer) raises similar questions of abuse; most disturbing, the off-label prescribing of Fen/Phen, the antiobesity drug therapy discussed in chapter 4, was an example of just what happens when the public is not protected.

Drugs used to treat mental health disorders in women also have a shady history. Millions of women were prescribed tranquilizers for social problems that had more to do with oppression than medical disorders. The good news is that far fewer women are prescribed tranquilizers for "social ailments" today than ten years ago; the bad news is that they are instead being prescribed antidepressants for the *same* social ailments. Such prescriptions can have damaging side effects. This chapter discusses what you need to know about the drugs you're taking to relieve depression, manic-depression, or other disorders accompanying a diagnosis of depression. The message of this chapter is *informed consent*. Make sure you know what you're taking and that you are fully informed about the side effects of all drugs you're prescribed. This book discusses myriad approaches to depression, ranging from various forms of talk therapy to alternative systems of healing (chapter 8). You need to understand that medication is an option, not a requirement. Some women are not presented with choices when it comes to mental health treatment. My job is to see that you are. If you are currently taking antidepressants and are responding well, please don't think this chapter is suggesting that you go off your drug. It is simply telling you what you may *not* have known before you went on it.

(At the end of this chapter, you will find lists of the generic and brand names, as well as common side effects of commonly prescribed antidepressants.)

DRUGS FOR DEPRESSION

First, a primer on brain chemistry: When your brain wants to send your body a message, a brain cell releases a substance called serotonin, which is a neurotransmitter (a chemical that helps to send signals through the brain) that rules our moods. Serotonin then locks onto a receptor on a neighboring brain cell, which relays the message to the next brain cell. Normally, the transmitting brain cell—the cell the serotonin locks onto—will reabsorb serotonin, making less of it available. The problem is that less serotonin is initially released by a particular brain cell (the presynaptic cell) when you're depressed, creating *really* low levels when reabsorption time occurs. These low levels of serotonin are associated with darker moods and depression.

A simple analogy is to imagine that this system of brain-chemistry exchange is like a washing machine. Serotonin is the "water" that flows in at certain times and is flushed out. Normally, enough water flows in and out, and the machine functions properly. But depression is akin to low water pressure. It would be like setting your washing machine on high only to find that the water level doesn't go beyond low.

Prozac

Prozac (fluoxetine hydrochloride) *blocks* reabsorption, which keeps more serotonin (and other chemicals) available for optimal functioning of the brain-chemistry exchange. This brightens your mood. What makes Prozac so special is that it primarily blocks serotonin, which is why it is called a selective serotonin reuptake inhibitor (SSRI). To return to our washing machine analogy, opening the lid of your washer midcycle stops the machine, thus keeping what little water you *have* from flushing out into your laundry sink. Prozac and all other SSRIs are analogous to opening the washer lid.

Introduced in 1987, Prozac has been touted as either being a "wonder drug" or "happy pill"—depending on who you talk to. All seem to agree that Prozac is to antidepressants what penicillin was to antibiotics: a breakthrough. This is because it was the first antidepressant that was both well tolerated and successful for the majority of people taking it. In 1998, combined sales from prescriptions for antidepressants (some Prozac, some Prozac-like) in the United States totaled $3.9 billion.

Predecessors of Prozac were not as selective and blocked many other neurotransmitters in the process, causing a wide range of side effects, such as tremors, blurred vision, gastrointestinal problems (constipation and nausea, for example), weight gain, and sexual dysfunction. It's not that Prozac has no side effects, but for many, they're much milder than the older generation of antidepressants, known as tricyclic antidepressants and monoamine oxidase inhibitors (MAOIs), both of which were discovered accidentally in the 1950s while looking for a tuberculosis cure. MAOIs destroy an enzyme called monoamine oxidase and break down neurotransmitters, which leaves available more serotonin and norepinephrine (another neurotransmitter that affects mood).

Side effects of Prozac still include nausea, nervousness, insomnia, and a decreased desire for sex, which for most women, is *huge*.

Bad press and Prozac

More than twenty million people have used Prozac to date, but it has had some bad press. Reports have surfaced of Prozac users being driven into agitated states, violence, rage, suicide, and mania. Considering all the users of Prozac, these negative effects are said to occur in only a small minority of users. It's also difficult to determine whether these effects are strictly related to Prozac or to the disorders/depression/mindset of the individuals taking the drug. The current advice is to take note of your moods while on Prozac, and if you feel you're acting more aggressively or not "like yourself," request to be taken off this drug. If you are concerned about these negative effects, request an alternative SSRI.

A newer study indicates that 25 to 35 percent of the benefits a typical person on antidepressants experiences is simply the placebo effect: the belief that the drug is making her feel better. Although this study has been criticized, it makes the use of Prozac and Prozac-like drugs less appealing.

Side effects, including a decline in sex drive or an inability to achieve orgasm, can have serious consequences for women suffering from depression. Their self-esteem and feelings regarding body image are compromised at the best of times. Switching to another type of antidepressant or adjusting your dosage may help.

Then there is the ethical question: Should we be offering "cosmetic pharmacology"? That is, since Prozac is prescribed for less severe depression, such as dysthymia (a low-grade depression, which is characterized by bad-attitude traits), are we eliminating human angst and melancholy, which is often necessary for spiritual and emotional growth? Are we changing personality traits that ought not be changed? On the other hand, if you are truly informed about the risks and benefits of the drugs you're taking, shouldn't you have the right to alleviate your suffering and try for a better quality of life?

After Prozac

Other popular Prozac-like drugs, made by competing manufacturers, include Zoloft, Paxil, Luvox, Celexa, and Effexor (which blocks both serotonin and neurotransmitter norepinephrine, and is known therefore as an SNRI). These newer SSRIs are even more finely tuned than Prozac and are reported to have fewer side effects.

The problem with SSRIs, in particular, is that you can build up a tolerance to the initial dosage, which means that the antidepressant benefits may subside. In this case, the dosages must be increased. You'll start on the lowest effective dosage of your SSRI, and then it will be increased gradually. In pharmacyspeak, this is known as "start low, go slow." (You will find questions to ask your pharmacist at the end of this chapter.)

Antidepressants don't always work. Some brains are more resistant to antidepressants than others. Your doctor may start you on an SSRI and, if that doesn't work, switch you to another SSRI—or sometimes a third or fourth. If you're still not responding within three to five weeks, you may be offered an older antidepressant, such as a tricyclic antidepressant or an MAOI.

SSRIs and Hypomania

Perhaps the most serious problem with SSRIs is their tendency to induce mild mania (also known as hypomania), in women who have never had any prior episodes. In short, taking an SSRI could put you at risk for a more serious problem, known as manic-depression, or bipolar disorder. This can be a medication nightmare as you struggle to find balance. You may bounce from one therapy to another and struggle with severe depression in between states of hypomania. When more serotonin is available to you, you can get high on it, meaning that you have exchanged your depression for an even more difficult condition to treat. This is a risk all physicians should discuss with you prior to putting you on any antidepressant medication. If you have a personal or family history of bipolar disorders, you may not be a good candidate for antidepressant medication.

Some doctors believe that misdiagnosis, not antidepressants, may be more the culprit. You may have simply been misdiagnosed with depression instead of manic-depression. In this case, "normal" to you may have been your mild high. You sought help only when you were low, or depressed, and were diagnosed with unipolar depression. The magnification of the mania due to the antidepressants is simply revealing your true condition.

Regardless of what causes the mania, what *is* clear is that antidepressants can be truly disastrous for women already diagnosed with manic-depression, or bipolar disorder. First, they can increase the frequency of future depressive episodes, pushing you into a chronic depression instead of an episodic depression. Second, these next bouts of depression may become resistant to treatment with antidepressants and may be accompanied by other symptoms, such as irritability and anxiety.

Other antidepressants
The following antidepressants may be prescribed:

- *Wellbutrin* (Bupropion). This has a low incidence of side effects that impact sexual function and has less chance of triggering hypomania.
- *Serzone* (Nefazadone). This may be a less effective antidepressant, but it does not affect your sexual drive or sleep patterns as dramatically.

- *Remeron* (Mirtazapine). Rather than blocking serotonin absorption, this drug triggers nerve cells to release more serotonin and norepinephrine.
- *Desyrel* (Trazodone). Again, rather than blocking serotonin absorption, this drug increases levels of serotonin in the brain.
- *Celexa,* the newest SSRI, is said to be even more selective than Prozac in blocking serotonin.

Combination Therapy

A number of people taking antidepressants will be labeled with "treatment-resistant depression." This means that your depression is not responding to first-line drug treatments, such as SSRIs. In these cases, a combination of drugs may be used to treat your depression. It's important to be monitored closely when taking any antidepressant; it is especially important when the following drugs are added to your therapy:

- *Lithium.* As many as half of all treatment-resistant depressions respond well to lithium, which may be combined with other medications.
- *Tricyclic antidepressants.* In many cases, adding a tricyclic to an SSRI works well as a combination.
- *Psychostimulants.* These drugs may be added if you are diagnosed with attention-deficit hyperactivity disorder (ADHD), in which case treatment with stimulants in addition to the SSRI would clearly be indicated (stimulants are the treatment of choice for ADHD). But if you have a history of substance abuse, psychostimulants are not a good idea: They can become addictive. Psychostimulants are also used in the treatment of depressed, medically debilitated patients.

- *Estrogen.* Estrogen replacement may be prescribed along with your antidepressant if you are past menopause, because estrogen is by itself a weak antidepressant. In some women, high doses of estrogen alone have been shown to treat depression. However, high doses of estrogen must be balanced against other risks, such as breast cancer.
- *Thyroid hormone.* A type of thyroid hormone known as T3, available as Cytomel, is used to improve the effectiveness of antidepressants. (Studies have also shown that people normally taking thyroid replacement hormone, which is T4, available as thyroxine, often feel better when T3 is added to their regimen.)

DRUGS FOR MANIA

As discussed in chapter 1, there are several different patterns of manic-depression, also known as bipolar disorder. If you've been diagnosed with bipolar disorder, antimania drugs may be used to stabilize your moods. But the main problem with treating bipolar disorder, or mania, is the resistance to treatment. Women who experience euphoric mania or milder forms of mania do not usually want to give up their highs. After all, it is part of who they are. If you suffer—or, on the contrary, *don't* suffer—from your manic episodes, you should consider or discuss with your mental health-care provider what benefits you derive from your moods and whether the path of destruction typically laden with mania (i.e., destroyed relationships and debt) is worth the high.

Many women who experience episodes of mania have a hard time believing they have a disease. Euphoria is also addictive. Why give up something your body produces naturally, which seems so great? The problem with addiction is that everything else in your life takes second place to that short-lived, ecstatic feeling. Women addicted to their natural highs can suffer the same destructive lifestyle patterns as women addicted to artificial substances, including buying sprees (which often result in debt). Therefore, once you begin taking anti-mania drugs, you may be grieving the loss of your highs, because they were what made you who you were. Kay Redfield Jamison, in her book *An Unquiet Mind*, an autobiography of manic-depressive illness, writes:

> If you have had stars at your feet and the rings of planets through your hands, are used to sleeping only four or five hours a night and now sleep eight, are used to staying up all night for days and weeks in a row and now cannot, it is a very real adjustment to blend into a three-piece-suit schedule, which, while comfortable to many, is new, restrictive, seemingly less productive, and maddeningly less intoxicating. People say, when I complain of being less lively, less energetic, less high-spirited, "Well, now you're just like the rest of us," meaning, among other things, to be reassuring. But I compare myself with my former self, not with others. Not only that, I tend to compare my current self with the best I have been, which is when I have been mildly manic. In short, for myself, I am a hard act to follow.

Lithium

If you opt for drug therapy, the most common antimania drug is lithium, a natural compound in our bodies that goes awry in people who suffer from mania. When lithium levels are increased, moods can be stabilized. But lithium can also prevent the lows in people with bipolar disorder.

Lithium is an element similar to sodium and potassium. In the 1940s, it was discovered to have a calming effect, which was especially helpful in people who were manic. Lithium was approved by the U.S. Food and Drug Administration in 1970 and has been the "gold standard" in treating manic-depression. It prevents the highs and lows, helps to clear your mind, slows you down, calms you down a bit, and helps you to "maintain an even strain."

In lithium's early days, there were problems with people becoming toxic from too high a dosage. Today, this shouldn't happen if your blood-concentration level of lithium is carefully monitored. When lithium is first started, you may need to have blood tests to check lithium levels every twelve hours. However, once the drug is stabilized, blood tests can drop down to one-to-three-month intervals. You should also have your thyroid levels checked at regular intervals, since lithium can cause hypothyroidism, a condition in which you're not producing enough thyroid hormone. This causes fatigue and a "slowing down" of your metabolism.

Lithium carbonate is the most common form of lithium and is sold under the following brand names: Eskalith, Lithane, Lithotabs, and Lithnobid. Lithium citrate is another form of lithium and is sold as Cibalith-S.

Side effects

Roughly 40 percent of people on lithium report gastrointestinal problems (nausea, vomiting, diarrhea), which usually taper off after a week or so. Side effects that may not disappear are tremors in the hand, thirst, and frequent urination (a sign that your kidneys are working to eliminate the lithium), as well as fatigue and muscle weakness (which may also be a sign of hypothyroidism—have this checked). Depending on the tremor's severity and how problematic the thirst and urination are, other drugs (such as diuretics) may be prescribed to offset these side effects. Weight gain and hypothyroidism may also be side effects (often weight gain is also a feature of hypothyroidism).

If you experience the following while on lithium, you may be on too high a dosage:

- fatigue/sleepiness
- confusion
- muscle weakness or twitches, and a feeling of heaviness in your limbs

- slurred speech
- tremors in the hand or lower jaw
- unsteady walk
- nausea that does not subside
- ringing in the ears (tinnitus)

Lithium can also interact with a variety of over-the-counter and prescription drugs, which can cause lithium levels in your blood to become unstable. For more information, see the section on drug dosing and monitoring on pages 167 to 173.

Pregnancy and lithium

I'll keep this short: Do not plan a pregnancy while on lithium unless you have a thorough discussion with your doctor about all the risks, complications, and possible harms this drug can pose to your pregnant health and that of your developing baby's. In many cases, you may be able to go off lithium in order to conceive and have a baby; in other cases, your dosages may need to be closely monitored, but it may be too risky to take you off lithium.

Other Mood-Stabilizing Drugs

Some physicians are now prescribing anticonvulsants (which have also been shown to stabilize moods), such as carbamazepine and valproate, and which in some cases may be combined. And then there are drugs used to help with insomnia, which can include the benzodiazepines clonazepam and lorazepam.

The usual route is to combine a short course of antidepressants with either lithium or an anticonvulsant; sometimes all three are prescribed. Antidepressants, as discussed above, can exacerbate bipolar disorder. Most experts now agree that any antidepressant used in conjunction with lithium or other antimania drugs should be used only for short spurts of time. If you don't respond to medication, you may be prescribed a newer anticonvulsant drug, or a new antipsychotic drug, such as risperidone.

Before you agree to take any mood-stabilizing drug, it's crucial to chart your moods. This will help to establish what kind of pattern you have. Using the PMS charts in chapter 4 works fine.

A Final Word About Mania

Most women who suffer from manic episodes have other areas of their lives—aside from brain chemistry—that need "regulating." Manic-depression is known as the relationship-destroyer because euphoria will exhaust most partners and family members physically and emotionally. It will exhaust your bank account if you go on spending sprees, and it will probably interfere with your ability to interact with employers or coworkers. If you're on medication for bipolar disorder, or mania, it's important to talk to a therapist about putting your life back in order. In this case, therapy without medication probably won't do much good; you may be too high to hear anything.

WHAT TO ASK ABOUT YOUR DRUGS

All of the drugs discussed in this chapter are powerful, and only a few have been mentioned by name. Without exception, the drugs currently being prescribed for depression or manic-depression have a long list of mostly unpleasant and sometimes debilitating side effects.

So the first question you must always ask before you take any drug prescribed is: What are its side effects? Many doctors have ethical problems with disclosing all potential side effects because you might panic if you knew about all *potential* side effects. It's akin to an airline passenger reading about all the things that could go wrong with a plane before she flies. Do you *really* want to know? I can't answer that question for you. (You know your information threshold better than I do.) But, in general, when you ask your doctor about side effects, she'll disclose those that are *common.* The drug's manufacturer will also have patient information available toll-free or on an advertised Web site. If you insist on being told about rare and unlikely side effects, your doctor or pharmacist cannot legally withhold this information from you. If she does, and you're willing to risk unnecessary anxiety in exchange for probably *way* too much information about your drug, then you can always look up the drug in the *Compendium of Pharmaceuticals and Specialties (CPS)*, available in your local library. (If you have questions, take a photocopy to your doctor or pharmacist so she can provide more information and probably alleviate some fears.)

For the record, most psychiatrists are in the practice of withholding anything but the most common and serious of side effects. There is a belief that full disclosure could actually put certain patients at risk for increased anxiety or a worsening of the symptoms the drugs are meant to alleviate. This is certainly a valid point, but you have the right to be fully informed.

It's also crucial to ask how diet, certain activities, and exercise can affect your medications. For example, dehydration can dramatically affect lithium levels in the blood, which can cause serious problems.

A Dozen More Questions

1. *How do these drugs affect my fertility, a pregnancy, or breast-feeding?* If your drugs should not be taken during pregnancy or breast-feeding, ask for safe alternatives. For example, many drugs pass through the placenta or can be excreted through breast milk.
2. *What are the alternative therapies?* Even if you're not pregnant or breast-feeding, it's worth investigating alternatives, such as St. John's wort.
3. *What other therapies will be combined with this drug?* Anything from estrogen and thyroid hormone to anticonvulsants could be combined with your drug. Therefore, you may need to repeat questions about side

effects, as well as the effects on fertility for each drug added to your "main course" drug.

4. *How long does it take before I begin to feel better?* You should be charting your moods after you begin medication to help gauge this.

5. *What drugs or substances should not be combined with this drug?* Can you have wine? Cough medicine? Caffeine?

6. *How does this drug interact with other prescription drugs I'm taking or over-the-counter medications?* Whether you're taking oral contraceptives or drinking herbal tea, find out.

7. *How does my medical history affect the potency or toxicity of this drug?* Have you had any major surgeries? Do you have diabetes? Do you have a history of seizures? The tricyclics can affect heart rhythm, for example, which would be a problem if you have heart disease. All kinds of problems can turn up if you don't ask this question.

8. *How long does it stay in my system after I stop taking the drug?* For example, do you plan to get pregnant in three months and worry that it will take longer than that for the drug to leave your body?

9. *Can I stop the medication as soon as I feel better?* Great question, and usually the answer is "no." That's because you may experience a recurrence, or even a worsening of your symptoms, shortly after going off your medication.

10. *How long do I have to take this drug?* Often the answer is "for the rest of your life," because it's believed that you will suffer from repeated relapses unless you're on medication permanently. If you don't want to be on lifelong medication, you don't have to be. You should discuss a regimen that works for you, and weigh that against the risk of recurrence or relapse. Ultimately, the decision is always yours.

11. *How often do I have to take the drug, and when is the best time?* Some drugs must be taken three times a day, some once a day. Some drugs need to be taken at bedtime, some

with meals. Make sure you have *all* this information. It could make a difference between good and bad side effects, potency, or how long the drug stays in your system.

12. *What if I miss a dose?* Sometimes the answer is to double up; other times you're told to skip it and carry on. This depends entirely on your medication, manufacturer, and dosage.

A Word About Dosages

Every brain has different chemistry and therefore requires different dosages. What works for Jane's brain may not work for Joan's. Therefore, as discussed earlier, the "start low, go slow" philosophy is always the rule, but if Jane is on a higher dosage than Joan for the same diagnosis, it doesn't mean that Jane is in worse shape than Joan. It simply means that it takes more drug to work in Jane than in Joan. It's like alcohol. Some people take longer to get drunk than others, which is based on their tolerance for alcohol and their ability to metabolize it.

The importance of being monitored

You need to be closely monitored while taking antidepressants (particularly lithium). This involves a simple blood test at regular intervals (the routine to be set by your health-care provider). Dosages of many of these drugs frequently need to be adjusted to changing blood levels. If being monitored is not discussed, this is a bad sign. In this case, raise the issue yourself. If you're told that being monitored isn't necessary, seek a second opinion.

Drug Studies

Obviously, what's needed in drug treatment for depression are effective drugs with fewer side effects. Therefore, the impetus to create new and improved drugs always exists. But that also means it's necessary to test the drugs on real people to see if they work better than the standard therapy. Thus, it's not at all unusual for you to be approached to participate in a drug study (also known as a clinical trial). But some studies are more ethical than others. It's perfectly reasonable, for example, to test the standard therapy against a new therapy. That's the only way to see whether the new therapy will be better than standard therapy, which is the only way of *raising* the standard for future patients.

But when you're suffering from an illness for which there is good, safe, and effective medication, it's not reasonable to ask you to participate in what is known as a "placebo-controlled" trial. Here, some people receive standard therapy in the form of real medication, while other people receive "dummy therapy" in the form of a fake pill that is made of a sugar solution. The purpose of a placebo-controlled trial is to test whether the real medication is better than nothing. In order to do this, what are known as double-blinded studies are done. Here, people are told that they may receive either a fake pill or a real pill, but you won't know what you've been given until the trial is over. Often, it becomes obvious who's getting the real pills. In these cases, the trials are stopped (or, at least, ought to be). But many studies have found that the placebo effect (the belief that the medication is working) can often be enough to cure an ailment or illness, proving that sometimes the drug really isn't better than nothing. Depression is different. We already *know* that without medication, a lot of people suffer needlessly. So when a good, effective, standard therapy exists to relieve your suffering, many bioethicists consider it unethical to give you nothing. That doesn't mean that placebo-controlled trials in psychiatry don't exist. It simply means that you ought to question whether they are fair to *you*.

Informed Consent and Medication

The term *informed consent* sounds nice, but most ethicists agree that it is misleading with respect to the health-care provider/patient relationship. Legal scholars and ethicists have noted that the term can be misunderstood by health-care providers to mean:

1. If you decline treatment, you're not informed.
2. Information is provided solely to obtain your consent.
3. Your refusing treatment does not have to be as informed as *consenting* to treatment.

Legally, if you are subjected to a treatment without your consent, that constitutes battery. If you are treated without *adequate* informed consent, that constitutes negligence. This applies to consenting to medication, drug trials, or any other form of therapy. To make sure you are being adequately informed, the following three things must occur:

- *Disclosure.* Have you been given relevant and comprehensive information by your health-care provider? According to medical ethicists, disclosure means that a description of the treatment; its expected effects (e.g., duration of hospital stay, expected time to recover, restrictions on daily activities, scars); information about relevant alternative options and their expected benefits and relevant risks; and an explanation of the consequences of declining or delaying treatment must be provided. You should also be given an opportunity to ask questions, while your health-care providers should be available to answer them.
- *Capacity to consent.* Do you *understand* information relevant to a treatment decision, and do you appreciate the reasonably foreseeable consequences of a decision or lack of a decision? Do you understand what's being disclosed, and can you decide on your treatment based on this information?
- *Voluntariness.* Are you being allowed to make your health-care choice free of any undue influences? Is information being distorted or omitted? Is someone (even a family member) forcing, manipulating, or coercing you into a decision that goes against your gut?

If you use the above as a checklist, you'll be able to make as informed a choice as anyone can expect from a layperson.

ELECTROCONVULSIVE THERAPY (ECT)

ECT, also known as shock therapy, involves a brief, electrical impulse to the brain, which results in a seizure that has an antidepressant effect. It is considered to be an effective treatment for severe depression, particularly psychotic depression.

When I initially researched this book, I had grave reservations about including information about ECT. For many, it evokes disturbing images of a patient being tied down against her will and going into violent seizures. But that's because we have an outdated vision of ECT, aided in part by old films depicting abuse in mental institutions. Another problem is that ECT is often confused with truly outdated treatments, such as insulin shock or hydrotherapy, which were not helpful in treating depression. Without exception, mental health-care experts from a wide variety of disciplines felt strongly that ECT is effective in some situations and pointed out that, in certain patients, it is often safer than medication.

The Early Years of ECT

When we think about ECT, most of us are thinking about the ECT of yesteryear. Introduced in the 1930s, it was, at that time, the only treatment available for depression. The ECT of the 1930s is not the same therapy used today. In the past, the patient was awake for the treatment and was subjected to a high-intensity electrical stimulus, which she received through electrodes placed on both sides of her head. She then went into a seizure characterized by violent muscle contractions, which required her to be restrained. After the treatment, she experienced memory loss and a host of other side effects. Obviously, this wasn't an optimal therapy for most cases of depression, particularly when you consider the stress it places on the patient. So when effective medications and new forms of therapy became available, ECT began to vanish as a standard form of therapy for depression.

Twenty-first Century ECT

The trouble with standard medications used in depression is that medication is not always effective, or recommended, for certain individuals. In these cases, ECT may be a reasonable alternative to antidepressant medication. ECT today involves a general anesthetic, as well as muscle relaxants to avoid the violent muscle contractions. The electrical charge is delivered through one or two electrodes, producing a seizure lasting twenty to forty seconds. Within a minute after the electrical charge, you wake up. The antidepressant effect of ECT is unfortunately short term and can last about four to six weeks. At that point, you would revisit your treatment options or be placed on antidepressant medication, or you may have additional ECT.

Side Effects

Short-term memory loss is still a problem with ECT. For instance, you may not remember the events occurring around your ECT therapy. Three months after your treatment, you may have trouble remembering your address or phone number. But once you look at your address again, or look up your phone number, your memory resets, and you shouldn't expect any more problems. Memory lapses six months after ECT are unusual.

It's only natural to wonder what other systems of healing are available if you suffer from depression or manic-depression. Alternative and self-healing strategies are discussed next. But keep in mind that you can combine alternative therapies with conventional Western medicine, also known as complementary medicine.

MEET YOUR ANTIDEPRESSANT

Monoamine oxidase inhibitors (MAOIs)

Common Side Effects: High/low blood pressure (this may cause dizziness), drowsiness, dry mouth, constipation. These drugs should not be used with over-the-counter cold and allergy medications, antidiabetic drugs, narcotic painkillers, tricyclic antidepressants (unless the person was already on the tricyclic when starting this drug), or any SSRI.

Generic Name	Brand Name
phenelzine sulfate	Nardil
tranylcypromine	Parnate

Tricyclic antidepressants (TCAs)

Common Side Effects: These vary between sedation or agitation, depending on the brand. Other common side effects include weight gain, dry mouth, blurry vision, low blood pressure, and sexual dysfunction (decreased interest in sex, problems with erection, and lack of orgasm in both women and men). Tricyclics should not be taken with narcotic painkillers or MAOIs (unless you are already on the MAOI when you begin the tricyclic) and should only be combined with SSRIs with careful monitoring.

Generic Name	Brand Name
desipramine hydrochloride	Norpramin, Pertofrane
imipramine hydrochloride	Tofranil/Norfranil
amitryptyline hydrochloride	Elavil
nortriptyline hydrochloride	Aventyl/Pamelor
doxepin	Sinequan/Triadapin
trimipramine	Surmontil
clomipramine	Anafranil
maprotiline	Ludiomil
protriptyline hydrochloride	Triptil/Vivatil
amoxapine	Asendin
trazadene	Desyrel

Continued on next page

Selective serotonin reuptake inhibitors (SSRIs)
Common Side Effects: Sexual dysfunction, such as the inability to achieve orgasm (Luvox excepted), nausea, and other gastrointestinal discomfort, diarrhea, sleepiness or insomnia, short-term memory loss, tremors, restlessness, muscle spasms and twitches, involuntary movements of the face, limbs, and trunk.

Generic Name	Brand Name
fluoxetine hydrochloride	Prozac
sertraline	Zoloft
paroxetine	Paxil
fluvoxamine	Luvox

Serotonin-norepinephrine reuptake inhibitors (SNRIs)
Common Side Effects: SSRI-like side effects, including agitation, nausea, headache, and gastrointestinal problems. Can cause high blood pressure.

Generic Name	Brand Name
venlafaxine	Effexor
nefazodone	Serzone

Reversible inhibitors of monoamine oxidase A (RIMAs)
Common Side Effects: Headaches, sleep disturbances, dizziness, tremors, increased agitation or anxiety, gastrointestinal problems, heart palpitations, low blood pressure, dry mouth. Not to be combined with other tricyclic antidepressants.

Generic Name	Brand Name
moclobemide	Manerix

· · · · · · · · ·

$\mathcal{S}$elf-Healing
Strategies

Can you heal depression without taking antidepressant medications or seeking counseling? When you're suffering from a mild to moderate depression, the answer in many cases is "yes." When you're struggling with severe depression or bipolar disorder, antidepressant medication or medication to treat mania may be the only way for you to get better. That said, regardless of whether you're seeking medical treatment and/or psychotherapy, the information in this chapter can complement your therapy.

HOW *ARE* YOU?

If you're suffering from depression, the first self-healing strategy is to ask yourself how you *are*. You can start to heal yourself by *caring* for yourself. Sleeping well, eating well, and exercising regularly are crucial to maintaining good health and well-being—which includes *mental* health and well-being.

Diet and Depression

We now know a variety of daily nutrients help to regulate our moods. Tryptophan, for example, which is found in milk and other dairy products, helps our bodies to build neurotransmitters, such as serotonin. Tryptophan is sometimes used separately as an "augmenter" to boost the effect of antidepressant medication.

The B vitamins are also important for our mental health. Vitamin B_{12} is crucial for good general health, while other B-complex vitamins (thiamine, riboflavin, niacin, pyridoxine, pantothenic acid, and biotin) are essential for brain function, enabling you to be cognizant and alert. You'll find the B vitamins in lean meats, whole grains, liver, seeds, nuts, wheat germ, and dairy products. Folate (a.k.a. folic acid) is particularly important for a healthy mood. It is found in liver, eggs, leafy greens, yeast, legumes, whole grains, nuts, fruits (bananas, orange juice, grapefruit juice), and vegetables (broccoli, spinach, asparagus, brussels sprouts). When you don't have enough "brain foods," you can become more prone to depression.

Calcium and magnesium are also linked to mood. Both of these nutrients aid your brain to properly transmit nerve impulses. Calcium is found in dairy products, leafy greens, eggs, and fish (particularly salmon and sardines); soy, nuts, whole grains, milk, meat, and fish contain magnesium.

Carbohydrates and Moods

One of the most important factors in diet and moods is your blood-sugar level. Many women, for example, find that they suffer from repeated episodes of low blood sugar, known as hypoglycemia. This is usually caused by consuming too many carbohydrates, which produces an initial rush of energy, followed by a tremendous crash, which is sometimes known as postprandial depression (or postmeal depression). In fact, during episodes of depression, it's not unusual to crave simple carbohydrates, such as sugars and sweets. The simpler the carbohydrate, the faster it breaks down into glucose and the faster the drop in blood sugar. This leads to a drop in mood. People with seasonal affective disorder (SAD) are known to especially crave sugars, such as chocolate and candy. The cravings for sweets are so powerful in SAD (80 percent of those with SAD have these cravings) that many doctors consider it a symptom of SAD.

If you think you suffer from low blood sugar, schedule an appointment with a nutritionist through your primary-care physician and plan a diet that is based on a variety of foods rather than one that is mostly carbohydrates. By increasing your intake of protein and fiber, you can help to delay the breakdown of your food into glucose, which will keep your blood-sugar levels more stable throughout the day.

Exercise and Depression

Aerobic exercise produces endorphins, "feel-good" hormones that have been shown to decrease the incidence of depression. If you can't find the time or don't have the inclination to exercise, try to incorporate some activity into your day. Inactivity and sedentary living breed depression. When you get up and do something, or see people, you feel more alive and part of this world.

Another important reason to exercise is to combat weight gain, which often occurs with depression. You may turn to food for comfort, but the more weight you gain, the more depressed you can feel, which fuels more comfort eating and worsens your depression.

The benefits of aerobic exercise

All that jumping around and fast movement are done to create faster breathing, so we can take in more oxygen into our bodies. How do we do this? The blood contains oxygen. The faster your blood flows, the more oxygen that flows to your organs. When more oxygen is in our bodies, we burn fat, our blood pressure is lower, and our hearts work more efficiently. More oxygen also makes our brains work better, so we feel better. Studies show that depression is decreased when we increase oxygen flow into our bodies. Ancient techniques such as yoga, which specifically improves mental and spiritual well-being, achieve this in a different way by combining deep breathing and stretching. This improves oxygen and blood flow to specific parts of the body.

You can increase the flow of oxygen into your bloodstream without exercising your heart muscle by learning how to breathe deeply through your diaphragm. There are many yogalike programs and videos available that can teach you this technique, which does not require you to jump around. The benefit is that you are increasing the oxygen flow into your bloodstream, which is better than doing nothing at all to improve your health. It also has many health benefits, according to myriad wellness practitioners.

Active living

If you don't exercise regularly, by simply leading a more active lifestyle you can improve your health and well-being. Here are some suggestions:

- If you drive everywhere, pick the parking space farther away from your destination so you can work some daily walking into your life.
- If you take public transit everywhere, get off one or two stops early so you can walk the rest of the way to your destination.
- Take the stairs more often than the escalator or elevator.
- Park on one side of the mall, and then walk to the other.
- After dinner, take a stroll around your neighborhood.
- Volunteer to walk the dog.
- On weekends, go to the zoo, the park, or out to flea markets.

Common Sense

An excellent way to care for yourself is to avoid people who make you feel bad or sad in your personal life. (Workplace issues are a different matter, because you often can't control who you come into contact with. Review chapter 2 for more details.) If a personal relationship does not bring you happiness, ask yourself why you're in it. If it's family, practice avoidance or "evasive maneuvers." Screen phone calls, if need be; gracefully decline family dinners, when possible. It's easy to do: "I have my X class that night; I already accepted at Y's; I'm ill" (which isn't necessarily a lie, if the family member you need to avoid upsets you). When a relationship does not bring you happiness, it can consume your time and energy and, ultimately, consume *you*.

There is also an important self-healing that can come from routine. Maintaining regular work and play hours helps to establish normal sleeping patterns. Oversleeping can exacerbate depression; missing sleep can make you irritable and anxious.

Herbs

One native North American tribe believes that disease was given to man by the animals in an effort to even out the odds for survival. The plant kingdom had a meeting about this and decided that it would do its best to cure disease, making itself available to man for preventive and curative remedies.

Every culture in the world has relied on plants and herbs to treat illness—Western medicine, too, taps into this tradition. Herbal therapies were taken as early as 4000 B.C. by the Sumerians, one thousand years before Chinese herbs were first used. By 3000 B.C., the Chinese were using more than one thousand medicinal herbs.

Much like today's pharmaceutical drugs, herbal therapies became established through trial and error. The herbs available today in your health-food stores and pharmacies are considered not only effective but powerful enough to do harm if not taken properly. And 25 percent of all prescription drugs in North America are derived from plants. Herbal medicine has become so popular because people are realizing that over-the-counter or prescription drugs are often no more or less potent. So why not go more natural?

North America is divided at the U.S. and Canadian border over how to classify herbs. Alternative-medicine practitioners argue that pharmaceutical companies won't fund research into herbal therapies because these remedies are natural and, hence, cannot be patented.

Since 1993, the United States has been selling more than $880 million of herbs and vitamins each year. Plant drugs are classified as "food" or "food additives" in the United States, and therefore many herbs are sold in groceries, health-food stores, or pharmacies. A variety of "nerve herbs" has been exploding onto the marketplace over the last decade. These have been effective in treating mild to moderate depression or are known to augment mood or antidepressant therapies.

St. John's wort

Also known as hypericum, St. John's wort has been used as a sort of "nerve tonic" in folk medicine for centuries. It's been shown to successfully treat mild to moderate depression and anxiety. It's been used in Germany for years as a first-line treatment for depression and is endorsed by the American Psychiatric Association. In Germany and other parts of Europe, it outsells Prozac. Since it was introduced in North America in the early 1990s, millions of North Americans have been successfully treated for depression with St. John's wort; in the United States, its sales and those of other botanical products reached an estimated $4.3 billion in 1998, according to the *Nutrition Business Journal.*

The benefits of St. John's wort are its minimal side effects. It can be mixed with alcohol, is nonaddictive, and you don't need to increase your dose as you do with antidepressants. You can go on and off of St. John's wort as you wish, without problems; it helps you to sleep and dream; it doesn't have any sedative effect; and, in fact, enhances your alertness. And finally, it doesn't put you at risk for agitation or hypomania.

The downside of St. John's wort is that, compared to prescription antidepressants, there is a longer lag time before you feel its effects, which means that it may not work well in severe depression. It can also make you overly sensitive to sunlight and may have some gastrointestinal side effects, such as nausea, loss of appetite, or abdominal pains. Experts advise that simply taking the herb with meals will alleviate the problem. Some people are also allergic to St. John's wort and can develop skin rashes.

Buyer Beware

Naturally, since St. John's wort is so popular, there are now many companies making it. But recent studies show that not all brands of the herb are equal, a hazard of a fast-growing herbal-therapy market that has yet to set standards. The *Los Angeles Times* conducted a consumer study which revealed that three out of ten brands of St. John's wort had no more than about half the potency listed on the label, while four other brands had less than 90 percent of the potency listed. If you're considering taking St. John's wort, ask health-food store owners and pharmacists about recommended brands, and call the manufacturers of various brands for more information about processing and quality control. For now, there are no other ways to ensure quality other than using your consumer power to ask questions.

Generally, out of the roughly 600 herbs available in the United States, fewer than 12 have been tested in a scientifically controlled trial, which is the process that usually determines whether an herb is safe and works better than a placebo. About 50 of those herbs have been tested under more lax conditions.

As of this writing, the American Herbal Products Association, a trade group of herbal manufactures, was compiling a reference manual on 600 herbal ingredients, including directions for safe use. Some experts suggest comparing most of the herbs sold to coffee when weighing "dosage"; two cups of coffee per day are considered safe; five cups may cause headaches and nervousness; fifteen cups can cause serious side effects. In other words, don't overconsume the herb. *More* isn't necessarily more effective.

Kava root

From the black pepper family, another popular herb is kava *(Piper methysticum)*, which has been a popular herbal drink in the South Pacific for centuries. Kava grows on the islands of Polynesia and is known to calm nerves and ease stress, fatigue, and anxiety. This results in an antidepressant effect. Kava can also help to alleviate migraine headaches and menstrual cramps. Placebo-controlled studies conducted by the National Institute of Mental Health showed that kava significantly relieved anxiety and stress, without the problem of dependency or addiction to the herb.

Kava should not be combined with alcohol, because it can make the effects of alcohol more potent. You should also check with your doctor before you combine kava with any prescription medications.

SAM-e

Pronounced "Sammy," this is another natural compound shown to help alleviate depression in mild to moderate cases. Since it was introduced in the United States in March 1999, more people have purchased Sam-e than St. John's wort. One reason could be because Sam-e has been shown to help relieve joint pain and also improve liver function, which makes it popular for people suffering from arthritis, as well as depression. Sam-e stands for S-adenosylmethionine, a compound made by your body's cells.

Studies done in Italy during the 1970s documented Sam-e's effectiveness as an antidepressant; recent U.S. studies confirm the same results. Psychiatrists are endorsing the use of Sam-e in cases of mild to moderate depression. But, like the effects of antidepressants, some Sam-e users experience mild mania. Some people have also reported hot, itchy ears as a side effect. Although Sam-e is available over-the-counter in the United States, it is still only available by prescription in Europe. If you're interested in trying Sam-e, discuss its availability with your family doctor.

Other natural compounds

A variety of other compounds has been linked to combating depression, or some of its features, such as sleeplessness or stress. These include:

- *Gamma-aminobutyric acid* (GABA). This amino acid is supposedly an antianxiety agent that may also help you to fall asleep if you suffer from sleeplessness.
- *Inositol.* This is a naturally occurring antidepressant present in many foods, such as vegetables, whole grains, milk, and meat, and should be available over-the-counter.
- *Dehydroepiandrosterone* (DHEA). This hormone is produced by the adrenal glands; production declines as we age. It has been shown to improve moods and memory in certain studies but is not yet available in Canada.
- *Melatonin.* This hormone improves sleep and helps to reset the body's natural clock. It is not yet available in Canada.
- *Phosphatidylserine* (PS). This phospholipid, a substance that feeds brain-cell membranes, has been shown in some studies to have natural antidepressant qualities.
- *Tetrahydrobiopterin* (BH4). This substance activates enzymes that control serotonin, noradrenaline, and dopamine levels, which are all important for stable moods. Some studies show BH4 is an effective natural treatment for depression.
- *Phenylethylamine* (PEA). This nitrogen-containing compound is found in small quantities in the brain. Studies show it works as a natural antidepressant.

- *Rubidium.* This chemical, which occurs natually in our bodies, belongs to the same family as lithium, potassium, and sodium. Studies show that it can work as an antidepressant.
- *Ginkgo.* This plant is used to treat a variety of ailments and is a common herb in Chinese medicine. It can improve memory, and some studies show that it can boost the effectiveness of antidepressant medications.
- *Valerian root.* This is similar to kava root in that it works as an antianxiety agent, as well as combats insomnia.

THE A–Z OF COMPLEMENTARY MEDICINE

A host of alternative or complementary systems of healing aid in general health and well-being or can be combined with other therapies, such as medication or counseling. The following offers you a quick glance at the types of complementary healing available, discussed in alphabetical order. (We would need to devote a separate book to this topic, but this will introduce you to the basics.)

Acupuncture

This ancient Chinese healing art aims to restore the smooth flow of life energy or *qi* in your body. Acupuncturists believe that your *qi* can be accessed from various points on your body, such as your ear, for example. And each point is also associated with a specific organ. So, depending on your physical health, an acupuncturist will use a fine needle on a specific point to restore *qi* to various organs. Each of the roughly two thousand points on your body has a specific therapeutic effect when stimulated. The National Institutes of Health (NIH) is funding research that studies the effects of acupuncture on depression, attention-deficit disorder, hypersensitivity disorder, osteoarthritis, and postoperative dental pain. In one large study, acupuncture offered short-term relief to 50 to 80 percent of patients with acute or chronic pain. It's now believed that acupuncture stimulates the release of endorphins, which is why it's effective for reducing pain.

Aromatherapy

Essential oils, extracted from plants (mostly herbs and flowers), can do wonders to relieve stress naturally; many essential oils are known for their calming and antidepressant effects. The easiest way to use essential oils is in a warm bath. Simply put a few drops of the oil into the water, and sit and relax in it for about ten minutes. The oils can also be inhaled (put a few drops in a bowl of hot water, lean over it with a towel over your head, and breathe); diffused (using a lamp ring or a ceramic diffuser—it looks like a fondue pot); or sprayed into the air as a mist. The following essential oils are known to have calming, sedative, and/or antidepressant effects: ylang-ylang, neroli, jasmine, cedarwood, lavender (a few drops on your pillow will also help you to sleep), chamomile, marjoram, geranium, patchouli, rose, sage, clary sage, and sandalwood.

Ayurvedic Medicine

The ayurveda, an ancient Indian approach to health and wellness, has been practiced for nearly three thousand years. Essentially, it divides the universe into three basic constitutions, or "energies" known as *doshas*. The three doshas are based on wind *(vata)*, fire *(pitta)*, and earth *(kapha)*. These doshas also govern our bodies, personalities, and activities. One person may be predominantly kapha—thicker in build, often overweight, and more lethargic; another may be predominantly vata—thinner in build, usually with a more finicky appetite and a more hyper personality. When our doshas are balanced, all functions well, but when they are not, a state of disease (dis-ease as in "not at ease") can set in. Finding the balance involves changing your diet to suit your predominant dosha (foods are classified as kapha, vata, or pitta, and we eat more or less of whatever we need for balance); doing certain yoga exercises; meditation; and avoiding or incorporating certain lifestyle habits.

An ayurvedic doctor determines your constitution by your appearance, lifestyle habits, and overall personality traits. In addition, the tongue is considered a map to the organs and can tell a doctor what part of the body is unbalanced.

Chinese Medicine

In the same way that ayurvedic medicine bases the universe on three constitutions, the three-thousand-year-old tradition of Chinese medicine bases the entire universe on two: yin and yang. Temperaments, organs, foods, activities, and individual personalities are yin or yang. Yang is considered a male constitution, and yin is female. But in all individuals, yin and yang coexist. In addition to yin and yang, there are five elements (similar to doshas in ayurvedic medicine) that are based on fire, earth, wood, metal, and water. Different organs in our bodies correspond to different elements. As in ayurvedic practice, when everything is balanced, all is healthy and the life force flows (*qi*—pronounced "chi") uninterrupted; when all is not balanced, *qi* can be disturbed, and disease can set in. Finding balance is the goal of Chinese medicine. To restore it, diet is either adjusted or supplemented with herbs, massage, or via pressure points in your body, which are stimulated through acupuncture (part of Chinese medicine). Your lifestyle habits may require change as well.

Chiropractic Medicine

This is becoming much more acceptable to Western practice, but your health insurer technically, considers it an alternative therapy.

The word *chiropractic* comes from the Greek *chir* and *praktikos,* which means "done by hand." This is a tradition that was perfected in the late 1800s by Daniel David Palmer of Port Perry, Ontario. He was a self-taught healer who eventually founded a practice in Iowa. He believed that all drugs were harmful and theorized that disease is caused by vertebrae impinging on spinal nerves.

Chiropractors believe that the brain sends energy to every organ along the nerves that run through the spinal cord. When the vertebrae of the spinal column are displaced through stress or poor posture, for instance, this can block or interfere with normal nerve transmission. These interferences are known as subluxations. To cure disease in the body, the chiropractor must remove blockages via adjustments—quick thrusts, massages, and pressures along your spinal column—which move the spinal vertebrae back to normal positions.

Sometimes adjustments involve manipulating the head and extremities (elbows, ankles, knees). This is mostly done by hand, but there are special devices that chiropractors use to aid them in treatment. A chiropractor takes your medical history, does a general physical exam, and may X-ray your spine to look for malalignments.

Environmental Medicine

This is still considered an alternative medicine, although, in light of what I've revealed in chapter 3, it probably should be incorporated into a conventional practice. Nevertheless, environmental medicine is a subspecialty of the allergy and immunology field, which is sometimes called clinical ecology. An environmental medicine practitioner looks at the impact of environmental factors on your individual health, focusing particularly on the foods, chemicals, and water pesticides, as well as indoor and outdoor air quality surrounding your life. Treatment usually involves a cleanup of whatever is affecting you: diet, air quality (by moving often, or getting air filters, and so on). Sometimes drugs are used to treat specific allergies, but only minimal doses of drugs are prescribed.

Holistic Medicine

Holistic medicine was begun as a reaction to the rather narrow, body-focused approach of more Western medicine. A holistic doctor looks at the whole person—body, mind, and spirit—and uses a variety of Western or non-Western techniques for treatment, based on the individual. Essentially, a holistic doctor enters into partnerships with patients, encouraging them to learn how to reduce risks of illness and how to choose the best therapies they're comfortable with. It is an approach to health that emphasizes self-care and personal responsibility for wellness.

Homeopathy

This began in the early nineteenth century as a reaction to heroic measures commonly used to treat disease at that time, such as bloodletting, induced vomiting, and the application of massive doses of drugs. Dr. Samuel Hahnemann, a German physician who was trained in conventional medicine and chemistry, founded homeopathy because he was disillusioned with conventional approaches to disease.

Homeopathy is based on the theory that "like cures like," or what Hahnemann called the Law of Similars. Essentially, a substance that produces certain symptoms in a healthy person can cure a sick person who shows the same symptoms. He coined the term *homeopathy* from the Greek *homoios* and *pathos* (similar sickness).

To treat disease, a homeopath uses minute doses of substances instead of large amounts. Hahnemann found he could preserve the healing properties and eliminate the side effects of a medication through a pharmacological process he called *potentization,* a process where substances are diluted with distilled water. The more diluted a substance, the more potent it was found to be. As a result of this discovery, Hahnemann created the Law of Infinitesimals, which basically means that good things come in small quantities. In fact, to prove the theory, Hahnemann constantly referred to the minute amounts of hormones our bodies produce, which are nonetheless so potent, they govern our bodies.

Homeopathy was particularly popular in the nineteenth century to treat infectious diseases—particular epidemics. Homeopathy is often confused with holistic, but it's actually a different discipline. Homeopaths call their approach holistic because they believe they're not just treating one organ but the entire patient. They see symptoms as positive signs that the body is trying to defend itself against an underlying disease. In fact, homeopathic drugs might even aggravate symptoms. A homeopath says that a worsening of symptoms is really a sign that the body is stimulating its own self-healing mechanism.

Homeopathy involves long medical history–taking sessions. There are more than two thousand remedies used by a homeopath, all derived from various plant, mineral, animal, and chemical sources. Some examples include marigold flowers, onions, graphite snake venom, honeybee extract, and other wild concoctions. These treatments may sound dangerous, but since the doses are so diluted, they are widely recognized as at worst harmless to the general population.

Iridology

No healer believes that the eyes are "windows to the soul" more than an iridologist, who "reads" the iris. Iridology is not really a therapy but a diagnostic tool used by a wide variety of non-Western healers. Iridology observes the iris's changes in texture and color and correlates them with your physical and mental state of health. An iridologist may not only tell you about an unsuspected thyroid problem but also reveal to you that you have an unhealthy relationship with your spouse. Many people have found the experience accurate and helpful.

Iridology is also used to identify dietary deficiencies and an accumulation of toxic chemicals in the body. In fact, in the same way that a Western doctor may send you for a blood test, a natural-medicine doctor may send you to an iridologist to expand a diagnosis.

Originally developed by Ignatz von Peczely, a Hungarian physician in the nineteenth century, iridology was adapted for modern practice in the 1950s by Bernard Jensen, an American chiropractor. Jensen based his practice on detailed diagrams of the left and right irises. He then assigned every organ, many body parts, and bodily functions to a specific location on one or both irises.

Iridologists believe that the degrees of light and darkness in the iris offer enormous clues to the body's general health. They also examine textures of fibers in the iris. Of course, ayurvedic or Chinese practitioners also examine the eyes not just for nearsightedness but for clues to the body's general health. Iridologists counsel you about nutrition or life habits but, for the most part, send you elsewhere for treatment.

Massage Therapy

Massage therapy can be beneficial whether you're receiving the massage from your spouse or a massage therapist trained in any one of dozens of techniques from shiatsu to Swedish massage.

In the East, massage was extensively written about in *The Yellow Emperor's Classic of Internal Medicine,* published in 2700 B.C. (the text that frames the entire Chinese medical tradition). In Chinese medicine, massage is recommended as a treatment for a variety of illnesses.

Swedish massage, the method Westerners are used to, was developed in the nineteenth century by a Swedish doctor and poet Per Henrik, who borrowed techniques from ancient Egypt, China, and Rome.

It is from shiatsu in the East and Swedish massage in the West that all the forms of massage were developed. While the philosophies and styles differ in each tradition, there is a common element: to mobilize the natural healing properties of the body, which will help it to maintain or restore optimal health. Shiatsu-inspired massage focuses on balancing the life force (*qi*).

Swedish-inspired massage works on physiological principles: relaxing muscles to improve blood flow throughout connective tissues, which ultimately strengthens the cardiovascular system.

No matter the type of massage you choose, there are numerous gliding and kneading techniques used, as well as deep, circular movements and vibrations that relax muscles, improve circulation, and increase mobility. This is known to help relieve stress and, often, muscle and joint pain. In fact, a number of employers cover massage therapy on their health plans.

Mind/Body Medicine

This is a discipline where physicians, therapists, or other health-care providers draw upon the East to heal their Western clients. They use a variety of techniques, such as meditation, relaxation training, imagery, biofeedback, and breath therapy to help you to heal yourself. These techniques are designed for you to take away and practice on your own, so that you're not dependent on going to the practitioner every time you need a fix. An excellent book on mind/body medicine is *Healing Mind, Healthy Woman,* by Alice Domar, Ph.D.

Naturopathy

Naturopathy encompasses a broad spectrum of natural therapies. In fact, it's now a recognized graduate degree in North America, at two colleges in the United States and one in Canada, which grant the degree of Naturopathic Doctor (ND).

Naturopathy is not any one tradition of healing but instead is an umbrella term that refers to an entire array of healing approaches, all based on the body's intrinsic healing powers. This tends to appeal to people who distrust prescription medications or are interested in preventive therapies.

NDs aim to educate their patients about proper lifestyles, which can help them avoid degenerative diseases, such as osteoporosis. In many ways, advice from an ND probably won't differ much from that given by conventional doctors regarding low-fat, high-fiber diets, stress reductions, and so on. What they may do, however, is instead of prescribing an antidepressant, aim to treat through nutritional means. They instill the belief that prescription drugs are costly. They encourage reliance on natural medicine, including acupuncture, herbs, hydrotherapy, homeopathy, and vitamin and mineral supplements.

Reflexology

This is a twentieth-century version of an ancient healing and relaxation technique that's probably as old or older than acupuncture. Western reflexology was developed by Dr. William Fitzgerald, an American ear, nose, and throat specialist, who talked about reflexology as "zone therapy." In fact, reflexology is practiced in several countries, including Egypt, India, Africa, China, and Japan. In the same way that the ears are a map to the organs, with valuable pressure points that stimulate the life force, here, the feet play the same role.

In a nutshell, the "sole is *qi* (i.e., life force) to the soul." By applying pressure to certain parts of the feet, reflexologists can ease pain and tension and restore the body's life force—be it *qi* in China or *prana* in India.

Reflexologists don't limit themselves to the feet, however. They also work on hands and ears, although the feet are the most common site. Like most Eastern healing arts, reflexology aims to release the flow of energy through the body along its various pathways. When this energy is trapped for some reason, illness can result. When the energy is released, the body can begin to heal itself.

A reflexologist views the foot as a microcosm of the entire body. Individual reference points or reflex areas on the foot correspond to all major organs, glands, and parts of the body. Applying pressure to a specific area of the foot stimulates the movement of energy to the corresponding body part.

ARE THERE RISKS?

It's important to keep in mind that when it comes to investigating alternative therapies, most Western researchers don't know enough about them to design proper studies. And many of these ancient disciplines just don't lend themselves well to Western-style research, such as double-blind-controlled studies. There are other risks with non-Western medicine that you should be aware of:

1. There is no scientific proof to support most of the treatments you'll be offered, or claims of the therapies.
2. Since there is no advisory board or guidelines that govern non-Western practitioners, the alternative "industry" attracts quacks and charlatans; there can also be prohibitive costs for some therapies.
3. Academic credentials are all over the map in this industry. Again, beware.
4. Certain preparations are boiled down in clay or metal pots, leaving residues of lead, mercury, arsenic, gold, or cadmium. And it's been reported that sometimes Chinese herbal preparations are laced with prescription drugs. You have to be careful to purchase from reputable places.
5. Dosages too are all over the map. For example, the active ingredient in many herbs may not be accurately measured. One reason modern medicine moved away from herbal preparations is that manufactured drugs were easier to purify and standardize. When you buy ten 325-milligram tablets of an antidepressant, that's what you get. But when you buy ten capsules of an herb, the dosages may vary from capsule to capsule.

6. Some non-Western healers may coerce you into dropping out of Western therapy even if you're clearly responding to it. If you're doing well on antidepressants, for example, you shouldn't be coerced into going off them.
7. You may prefer to abandon clearly curative Western therapies in favor of your non-Western therapy. This can have unfortunate consequences. For example, you may decide to go off antidepressant medication, when, in fact, you are doing very well with it.

If you're not taking care of yourself, your health will suffer in all areas. This requires looking after the most basic human needs: eating, sleeping, and *using* our bodies—in the form of exercise and activity. Otherwise, you will suffer physical as well as emotional consequences. By making your body stronger, you will also give yourself better tools with which to cope with your feelings. But ultimately the best way to heal yourself is to learn to *trust* yourself. Listen to that voice in your head. (But don't tell your doctor you "hear voices.")

Appendix

Where to Go for More Information

Note: This list was compiled from dozens of sources. Because of the volatile nature of many health and nonprofit organizations, some of the addresses and phone numbers below may have changed since this list was compiled. Some of these organizations did not have E-mail addresses or Web sites available at press time. Many more resources can be found on the Internet; see Useful Web sites and Useful Newsgroups at the end of this list.

General Information (listed alphabetically)

The Alliance for the Mentally Ill/Friends and Advocates of the Mentally Ill (AMI/FAMI)
432 Park Avenue S., #710
New York, NY 10016-8013
Help line (212) 684-FAMI
Office (212) 684-3365
Events line (212) 684-4237

American Association of Marriage and Family Therapy
    1133 15th St., N.W., Ste. 300
    Washington, DC 20005-2710
    (202) 452-0109
    Web site www.aamft.org

American Counseling Association
    5999 Stevenson Ave.
    Alexandia, VA 22304
    (703) 823-9800
    Web site www.counseling.org

American Psychological Association
    Office of Public Affairs
    750 First St., N.E.
    Washington, DC 20002-4242
    (202) 336-5700
    Web site www.apa.org

Center for Cognitive Therapy
    3600 Market St., 8th Floor
    Philadelphia, PA 19104-2649
    (215) 898-4100

Depression Awareness, Recognition and Treatment
(DART) Program
    National Institute of Mental Health
    1-800-421-4211 or (301) 443-4140

Depressives Anonymous: Recovery from Depression
    329 E. 62nd St.
    New York, NY 10021
    (212) 689-2600

Foundation for Depression and Manic-Depression
    24 E. 81st St.
    New York, NY 10028
    (212) 772-3400

Freedom from Fear
    308 Seaview Ave.
    Staten Island, NY 10305
    (718) 351-1717
    Fax (718) 667-8893
    (Freedom from Fear is a not-for-profit organization acting as advocate for those suffering from anxiety and depressive disorders.)

Jonathan O. Cole Mental Health Consumer Resource Center
    McLean Hospital
    115 Mill St., Rehab. 113
    Belmont, MA 02178
    (617) 855-3298 or 2795
    Fax (617) 855-3666

Justice in Mental Health Organization United States of America
    421 Seymour St.
    Lansing, MI 48933
    (517) 371-2266

National Alliance for the Mentally Ill (NAMI)
    200 N. Glebe Rd., #1015
    Arlington, VA 22201-3754
    Help line 1-800-950-NAMI
    Office (703) 524-7600
    Fax (703) 524-9094

The National Association of Social Workers (NASW)
    750 First St., N.E., Ste. 700
    Washington, DC 20002-4241
    (202) 408-8600
    Fax (202) 336-8311
    TTD (202) 408-8396

For a list of chapter offices, see pages 219 to 232.

National Depressive and Manic-Depressive Association
　　730 N. Franklin St., Ste. 501
　　Chicago, IL 60610
　　1-800-82-NDMDA or (312) 642-0049
　　Fax (312) 642-7243

National Foundation for Depressive Illness
　　1-800-248-4344

NIMH (National Institute of Mental Health)
　　Public Inquiries
　　6001 Executive Blvd., Rm. 8184, MSC 9663
　　Bethesda, MD 20892-9663
　　(301) 443-4513
　　Fax (301) 443-4279
　　E-mail nimhinfo@nih.gov
　　Web site www.nimh.nig.gov

National Institute of Mental Health Panic Disorder Division
　　National Institute of Mental Health,
　　Panic Disorder Education Program
　　Room 7C-02, Fishers Lane
　　Rockville, MD 20857
　　1-800-64-PANIC

National Mental Health Association
　　1021 Prince St.
　　Alexandria, VA 22314-2971
　　1-800-969-6642 or (703) 684-7722

World Federation for Mental Health
　　1021 Prince St.
　　Alexandria, VA 22314-2971
　　(703) 684-7722

Psychiatric Services Listed by State

Alabama Psychiatric Society
Judy Lovelady, Executive Director
Alabama Psychiatric Society
P.O. Box 1900
Montgomery, AL 36102
(334) 263-6441 or 1-800-239-6272 (AL only)
Fax (334) 269-5200
E-mail alapsych@aol.com

Alaska District Branch
Stephanie Gisseman, Executive Secretary
P.O. Box 143147
Anchorage, AK 99514-3147
(907) 566-7800 A.M.
(907) 337-7311 P.M.
E-mail apa@pobox.alaska.net

Arizona Psychiatric Society
Jacquelyn Hyde, Executive Director
4730 E. Indian School Rd., #120-101
Phoenix, AZ 85018
(602) 808-9558
Fax (602) 912-0455
E-mail jhazpsy@msn.com
Web site www.azpsych.org

Arkansas Psychiatric Society
Barbara Stockton, Executive Director
P.O. Box 250910
Little Rock, AR 72225
Voice/Fax (501) 663-6182

California Psychiatric Association (Area VI Council)
Barbara Gard, Executive Director
1400 K St., Ste. 302
Sacramento, CA 95814
(916) 442-5196
Fax (916) 442-6515
Web site http://www.calpsych.org/

Central California Psychiatric Society
Patricia Howell, Executive Director
P.O. Box 1071
Fresno, CA 93714-1071
(559) 228-6156
Toll-free 1-888-234-1613 or 1-800-835-3924
Fax 559-227-1463
E-mail phowell@pesc.com

Northern California Psychiatric Society
Janice Clark Targart, Executive Director
1631 Ocean Ave.
San Francisco, CA 94112
(415) 334-2418
Fax (415) 239-2533
E-mail ncps@slip.net

Orange County Psychiatric Society
Holly Appelbaum, Executive Secretary
300 S. Flower St.
Orange, CA 92868
(714) 978-1160 or 3016
Fax (714) 978-6039
E-mail happelbaum@ocps.org

San Diego Psychiatric Society
   Lori Petrowski, Executive Administrator
   3702 Ruffin Rd., Ste. 202
   San Diego, CA 92123-3581
   (619) 279-4586
   Fax (619) 279-4587
   E-mail sdpsych@znet.com
   Web site http://www.psychsd.org

Southern California Psychiatric Society
   Mindy Thelen, Administrative Director
   2999 Overland Ave., Ste. 116
   Los Angeles, CA 90064
   (310) 815-3650
   Fax (310) 815-3653
   E-mail scps2999@loop.com

Colorado Psychiatric Society
   Laura Michaels, Executive Director
   4596 E. Iliff Ave., Ste. B
   Denver, CO 80222
   (303) 692-8783
   Fax (303) 692-8823
   E-mail cps@nilenet.com
   Membership Contact: Barbar Dygert,
   Membership Coordinator

Connecticut Psychiatric Society
   Jacquelyn Coleman, Executive Director
   One Regency Dr., P.O. Box 30
   Bloomfield, CT 06002
   (860) 243-3977
   Fax (860) 286-0787
   E-mail execoff@aol.com
   Web site http://206.102.254.34/CTPS/index.html
   E-mail jcoleman_cps@ssmilligramst.com

Psychiatric Society of Delaware
Medical Society of Delaware
    1925 Lovering Ave.
    Wilmington, DE 19806-2166
    Attn: Mary LaJudice
    (302) 658-7596
    Fax (302) 658-9669
    E-mail mml@medsocdel.org

Florida Psychiatric Society
    Margo S. Adams, Executive Director
    521 E. Park Ave.
    Tallahassee, FL 32301-2524
    (850) 222-8404
    Fax (850) 224-8406
    E-mail fpse@aol.com

South Florida Psychiatric Society, Inc.
    Doris J. Shellow, Executive Director
    P.O. Box 331266
    Miami, FL 33233-1266
    (305) 665-0130
    Fax (305) 665-0390

Georgia Psychiatric Association
    Tara Morrison, Executive Director
    1330 W. Peachtree St., N.W., Ste. 500
    Atlanta, GA 30309-2904
    (404) 881-5090, ext. 5091
    Fax (404) 249-9503
    (404) 881-5091 (Stephanie Bower, Secretary)
    E-mail sbower@mag.org

Hawaii Psychiatric Medical Association
Lydia Hardie, Executive Director
5090 Likini St., #1601
Honolulu, HI 96818
(808) 839-3070
Fax (808) 833-8165
E-mail lydiahpma@aol.com

Idaho District Branch
Michele Han, Executive Director
2683 Peregrine Pl.
Boise, ID 83702
(208) 342-4840
Fax (208) 342-0636
E-mail idpsych@micron.net
Membership Contact: Dave Kent, M.D.
(208) 323-1125

Illinois Psychiatric Society
Laura Leeper
20 N. Michigan Ave., Ste. 700
Chicago, IL 60602
(312) 263-7391
Fax (312) 782-0553
Membership Contact: Dorthy Freeston
(312) 263-7391

Indiana Psychiatric Society
Donna Fahrner, Secretary
322 Canal Walk
Indianapolis, IN 46202-3268
(317) 261-2060, ext. 256
Fax (317) 261-2076
E-mail dfahrner@ismanet.org

Iowa Psychiatric Society
Karen Loihl, Executive Director
PMB 338
2643 Beaver Ave.
Des Moines, IA 50310-3909
(515) 633-0341
Fax (515) 279-5206
E-mail iowapsych@aol.com

Kansas Psychiatric Society
Charles (Chip) Wheelen, Executive Director
623 S.W. 10th Ave.
Topeka, KS 66612-1627
(785) 266-7173
Fax (785) 235-5114
E-mail kps@cjnetworks.com

Kentucky Psychiatric Association
Theresa N. Walton, Executive Secretary
P.O. Box 198
Frankfort, KY 40602
(502) 695-4843
Fax (502) 695-4441
E-mail waltonkpa@aol.com

Louisiana Psychiatric Medical Association
Charlene Smith, Executive Director
P.O. Box 15765
New Orleans, LA 70175
(504) 891-1030
Fax (504) 891-1077
E-mail csmith@lpma.net

Maine Psychiatric Association
    Warene Eldridge
    P.O. Box 190
    Manchester, ME 04351-0190
    (207) 622-7743
    Fax (207) 549-5786
    E-mail weldridge@ctel.net

Maryland Psychiatric Society, Inc.
    Heidi E. Bunes, Executive Director
    1101 St. Paul St., Ste. 305
    Baltimore, MD 21202
    (410) 625-0232
    Fax (410) 625-0277
    E-mail hbunes@mdpsych.org
    Membership Contact: Aileen Fuss,
    Membership Coordinator

Massachusetts Psychiatric Society
    Dorothy Mooney, Executive Director
    40 Washington St.
    Wellesley Hills, MA 02481
    (781) 237-8100
    Fax (718) 237-7625
    E-mail mps2@tiac.net

Michigan Psychiatric Society
    Kathleen Williams, Executive Director
    15920 W. 12 Mile Rd.
    Southfield, MI 48076
    (248) 552-9300
    Fax (248) 552-8790
    E-mail kwilliams@msms.org
    Membership Contact: Margaret Cole
    E-mail Mbcole@voyager.net

Minnesota Psychiatric Society
  Linda Vukelich, Executive Director
  2738 Evergreen Circle
  St. Paul, MN 55110-5768
  (615) 406-1873
  Fax (615) 407-1754
  E-mail vukelich@winternet.com

Mississippi Psychiatric Association
  Donna Emidy, Executive Secretary
  2500 N. State St.
  Jackson, MS 39216
  (601) 984-5888
  Fax (601) 984-5842
  E-mail jan@fiona.umsmed.edu
  E-mail demidy@psychiatry.umsmed.edu

Central Missouri Psychiatric Society
  Lee Gibson, Executive Secretary
  1122 11th St.
  Boonville, MO 65233
  (660) 882-9449
  E-mail cmps@mid-mo.net

Eastern Missouri Psychiatric Society
  Gordon Garrett, Ed.D., Executive Secretary
  3839 Lindell Blvd.
  St. Louis, MO 63108
  (314) 371-5225
  Fax (314) 533-8601
  E-mail rongarratt@sprintmail.com

Western Missouri Psychiatric Society
  Ron Cosens, Executive Director
  3036 Gillham Rd.
  Kansas City, MO 64108
  (816) 531-8432
  Fax (816) 531-8438
  E-mail rcosens@sprintmail.com
  Membership Contact: Marlena Hickerson
  E-mail Marlena@sprintmail.com

Montana Psychiatric Association
  Virginia Hill, M.D., Executive Secretary
  Drawer N
  Warm Springs, MT 59756-0227
  (406) 693-7000
  E-mail ghill@imine.net

Nebraska Psychiatric Society
  Sheila Rosenberg, Executive Secretary
  985575 Nebraska Medical Center
  Omaha, NE 68198-5575
  (402) 559-6669
  Fax (402) 559-9002
  E-mail srosenbe@unmc.edu

Nevada Association of Psychiatric Physicians
  William Stone, M.D., Secretary/Treasurer
  P.O. Box 12477
  Las Vegas, NV 89112
  (702) 877-6000
  E-mail nvapa@aol.com
  Web site http://members.aol.com/NVAPA/index.html

New Hampshire Psychiatric Society
    Mary Pyne, Executive Secretary
    c/o New Hampshire Medical Society
    7 N. State St.
    Concord, NH 03301
    (603) 224-7083
    Fax (603) 226-2432
    E-mail mpyne@juno.com

New Jersey Psychiatric Association
    Carla A. Ross, Administrator
    P.O. Box 8008
    Bridgewater, NJ 08807-8008
    (908) 685-0650
    Fax (908) 725-8610
    E-mail njpa@mail.idt.net

Psychiatric Medical Association of New Mexico
    Marsha VerPloegh, Executive Secretary
    801 Encino Pl., N.E., Ste. F-21
    Albuquerque, NM 87102
    (505) 224-7720
    Fax (505) 224-7725
    E-mail pmanm@compuserve.com

New York State Psychiatric Association, Inc.
    Seth P. Stein, Esq., Executive Director and General Counsel
    100 Quentin Roosevelt Blvd., Ste. 509
    Garden City, NY 11530
    (516) 542-0077
    Fax (516) 542-0094
    E-mail nyspamd@idt.net

Bronx District Branch
Mary B. Cliffe, Executive Director
3801 Purchase St.
Purchase, NY 10577
(914) 946-3105
Fax (914) 946-3050
E-mail pswapadb@aol.com

Brooklyn Psychiatric Society, Inc.
Linda M. Majowka, Executive Director
Four Chimney Ct.
Brookhaven, NY 11719
Phone/Fax (516) 286-9193
E-mail lindabps@nais.com

Central New York District Branch
Noreen Lannon, Executive Secretary
c/o Department of Psychiatry
750 E. Adams St.
Syracuse, NY 13210
(315) 471-2716
Fax (315) 464-3163

Genesee Valley Psychiatric Association
Susan Shuryn, Executive Director
66 Hardison Rd.
Rochester, NY 14617-3852
Phone/Fax (716) 544-1257

Greater Long Island Psychiatric Society
Jackie Cast, Executive Director
P.O. Box 3468
Farmingdale, NY 11735
(516) 249-1117
Fax (516) 249-7202
E-mail jackie32@aol.com

Mid-Hudson Psychiatric Society
Annette Patterson, Executive Secretary
P.O. Box 3445
Poughkeepsie, NY 12603
(914) 452-5894
Fax (914) 452-5387
E-mail midhudson@msn.com

New York County District Branch
Rosalie Landy, Executive Director
150 E. 58th St., 31st Floor
New York, NY 10155-2396
(212) 421-4732/33/34
Fax (212) 754-4671
E-mail NYDBAPA@Mail.Idt.Net
Web site hudson.itp.net/~nydbapa

New York State Capital District Branch
Nancy Sykes, Executive Secretary
P.O. Box 5
New Baltimore, NY 12124
(518) 756-7030
E-mail psych4@aol.com

Northern New York District Branch
Carol Alsheimer, Executive Secretary
1400 Noyes at York
Utica, NY 13502
(315) 738-4405
Fax (315) 738-4414
E-mail nnydb@borg.com

Queens County Psychiatric Society
  Debbie Wessely, Executive Director
  7 Romary Ct.
  Glen Rock, NJ 07452
  (877) 612-7110 (toll free New York & New Jersey)
  (201) 612-7110
  Fax (201) 612-7126
  E-mail dawqcps@earthlinks.net

Westchester County District Branch
  Mary B. Cliffe, Executive Director
  3801 Purchase St.
  Purchase, NY 10577
  (914) 946-9008
  Fax (914) 946-3050
  E-mail pswapadb@aol.com

West Hudson District Branch
  Paul Ducker, M.D., Secretary
  Dr. R. L. Yeager Center
  24 Robin Hood Rd.
  Suffern, NY 10901
  (914) 357-6957
  Fax (914) 364-2214
  E-mail SWDABD@aol.com
  Web site http://www.rfmh.org/whps

Western New York Psychiatric Society
  Donna Ball, Executive Secretary
  Erie County Medical Center, Dept. of Psychiatry
  462 Grider St.
  Buffalo, NY 14215
  (716) 898-5941
  Fax (716) 898-4538
  E-mail dmball@acsu.buffalo.edu

North Carolina Psychiatric Association
  Katherine P. Hux, Executive Director
  4917 Waters Edge, Ste. 250
  Raleigh, NC 27606
  (919) 859-3370
  Fax (919) 851-0044
  E-mail ncpakph@msn.com or ncpalcp@msn.com
  Membership Contact: Lana Frame,
  Membership Coordinator

North Dakota Psychiatric Society
  David Peske, Executive Director
  P.O. Box 1198
  Bismarck, ND 58502-1198
  (701) 223-9475
  Fax (701) 223-9476
  E-mail dpske@ndmed.com

Ohio Psychiatric Association
  Philip Workman, Executive Director
  1480 W. Lane Ave., Ste. F
  Columbus, OH 43221
  (614) 481-7555
  Fax (614) 481-7559
  E-mail paworkman@aol.com
  Web site http://www.ohiopsych.org

Oklahoma Psychiatric Association
  Claudene Channell, Executive Secretary
  P.O. Box 1328
  Norman, OK 73070
  (405) 360-5066
  Fax (405) 447-1053
  E-mail opa@telepath.com
  Web site http://www.okpsych.com

Oregon Psychiatric Association
    John H. McCulley, Executive Secretary
    Oregon Psychiatric Association
    P.O. Box 2042
    Salem, OR 97308
    (503) 587-8063
    Fax (503) 399-8082
    E-mail mcculley@compuserve.com
    Membership Contact: Julie McCulley,
    Membership Coordinator

Pennsylvania Psychiatric Society
    Gwen Lehman, Executive Director
    Charlene Miller Wandsilak, Assistant, Executive Director
    777 E. Park Dr.
    P.O. Box 8820
    Harrisburg, PA 17105-8820
    (717) 558-7750
    1-800-422-2900 (within Pennsylvania)
    Fax (717) 558-7841
    E-mail glehman@pamedsoc.org
    Membership Contact: Sue Ann Timco,
    Membership Secretary
    Web site http://www.papsych.org

Puerto Rico Psychiatric Society
    Nestor J. Galarza, M.D., President
    33113 Veterans Plaza
    San Juan, PR 00933
    (787) 758-7575, ext. 5407
    Fax (787) 766-6194
    E-mail nesile@caribe.net
    Web site members.tripod.com/~nesile/PRPShome.html

The Rhode Island Psychiatric Society
Edwina Rego, Membership Secretary
106 Francis St.
Providence, RI 02903
(401) 331-1450
Fax (401) 751-8050
E-mail RIMS@ids.net
Web site http://www.butler.org/~psy/RIPS/

South Carolina Psychiatric Association
Debbie Shealy, Executive Director
P.O. Box 11188
Columbia, SC 29211
(803) 798-6207
Fax (803) 772-6783
E-mail tara@scmanet.org
Membership Contact: Tara Smith, Membership Coordinator

South Dakota Psychiatric Association
Kate Bedi
1400 W. 22nd St.
Sioux Falls, SD 57105
(605) 357-1585
Fax (605) 357-1460
E-mail knaylor@sunflowr.usd.edu

Tennessee Psychiatric Association
Kimberly Settle, Executive Director
209 10th Ave. S., Ste. 506
Nashville, TN 37203
(615) 255-3102
Fax (615) 254-1186
E-mail TPAMD@mindspring.com

Texas Society of Psychiatric Physicians
John Bush, Executive Director
401 W. 15th, Ste. 675
Austin, TX 78701
(512) 478-0605
Fax (512) 478-5223
E-mail tsppofc@aol.com

Utah Psychiatric Association
Paige De Mille, Executive Director
540 E. 500 S.
Salt Lake City, UT 84102
(801) 355-7477
Fax (801) 532-1550
E-mail paige@utahmed.org

Vermont Psychiatric Association
Stephanie Lane, Acting Executive Secretary
c/o Vermont State Medical Society
P.O. Box 1457
Montpelier, VT 05601
(802) 223-7898
Fax (802) 223-1201
E-mail slane@vtmd.org

Psychiatric Society of Virginia, Inc.
Sandra Peterson, Executive Director
8606 Oakcroft Dr.
Richmond, VA 23229
(804) 754-1200
Fax (804) 754-2321
E-mail spetersonpsv@erols.net

Washington Psychiatric Society
    Walter Hill, Executive Director
    1400 K St., N.W.
    Washington, DC 20005
    (202) 682-6159
    Fax (202) 682-6369
    Membership Contact: Rosemary Polley, Executive Secretary
    E-mail WPSdesk@psych.org
    (202) 682-6192

Washington State Psychiatric Association
    James Goche, Executive Director
    110 5th Ave. S.E., Ste. 207
    Olympia, WA 98501
    (360) 357-4648
    Fax (360) 357-3468
    E-mail wspa@halcyon.com
    Membership Contact: Beverly McCoy, Office Manager

West Virginia Psychiatric Association
    Susan Engle, Executive Secretary
    Chestnut Ridge Hospital
    930 Chestnut Ridge Rd.
    Morgantown, WV 26505
    (304) 293-5312
    Fax (304) 293-8724

Wisconsin Psychiatric Association
    Edward Levin, Executive Secretary
    P.O. Box 1109
    Madison, WI 53701
    (414) 223-4455
    (608) 283-5424
    E-mail wpa@smswi.org
    Membership Contact: Kathy Monelnitzky
    1-800-762-8967

Wyoming Psychiatric Society
    Jean Davis, Executive Secretary
    2521 E. 15th St.
    Casper, WY 82609
    (307) 237-7444
    Fax (307) 473-7144
    E-mail cwd@coffey.com

Society of Uniformed Services Psychiatrists
    Barbara Ross, Executive Secretary
    1730 N.W. 113th Dr.
    Gainesville, FL 32606
    (352) 332-9578
    E-mail susp1@aol.com

The National Association of Social Workers (NASW), Chapter Offices

Alabama Chapter
    Governors Park II
    2921 Marti Lane, #G
    Montgomery, AL 36116
    (334) 288-2633
    Fax (334) 288-1398
    E-mail naswal@the-link.net

Alaska Chapter
    318 4th St.
    Juneau, AK 99801
    (907) 586-4438
    Fax (907) 586-4439
    E-mail naswak@alaska.net
    Web site www.naswak.org

Arizona Chapter
    610 W. Broadway, #116
    Tempe, AZ 85282
    (480) 968-4595
    Fax (480) 894-9726
    E-mail nasw-az@primenet.com
    Web site http://www.naswaz.com

Arkansas Chapter
    1123 S. University 1010
    Little Rock, AR 72204
    (501) 663-0658
    1-800-797-6279
    Fax (501) 663-6406
    E-mail naswar@cei.net
    Web site http://alumni.uark.edu/~hmcfadin/naswar/

California Chapter
    1016 23rd St.
    Sacramento, CA 95816
    (916) 442-4565
    1-800-538-2565
    Fax (916) 442-2075
    E-mail naswca@naswca.org
    Web site //naswca.org/

California Chapter
    Los Angeles Office
    6030 Wilshire Blvd., Ste. 202
    Los Angeles, CA 90036-3617
    (213) 935-2050
    Fax (213) 934-7393
    E-mail naswla@aol.com

Colorado Chapter
  6000 E. Evans, Bldg #1, Ste. 121
  Denver, CO 80222
  (303) 753-8890/91
  1-800-595-NASW
  Fax (303) 753-8891
  E-mail naswco@aol.com

Connecticut Chapter
  2139 Silas Deane Hwy., Ste. 205
  Rocky Hill, CT 06067
  (860) 257-8066
  Fax (860) 257-8074
  E-mail naswct@worldnet.att.net

Metro D.C. Chapter
  P.O. Box 75236
  Washington, DC 20013
  (202) 371-8282
  Fax (202) 371-6578
  E-mail office@naswmetro.org
  Web site www.naswmetro.org

Delaware Chapter
  3301 Green St.
  Claymont, DE 19703
  (302) 792-0646
  Fax (302) 792-0678
  E-mail naswde@diamond.net.udel.edu

Florida Chapter
345 S. Magnolia Dr., Ste. 14-B
Tallahassee, FL 32301
(850) 224-2400
1-800-352-6279
Fax (850) 561-6279
E-mail naswfl@unr.net
Web site www.naswfl.org

Georgia Chapter
3070 Presidential Dr., Ste. 226
Atlanta, GA 30340
(770) 234-0567
Fax (770) 234-0565
E-mail naswga@mindspring.com

Hawaii Chapter
200 N. Vineyard Blvd., Ste. 415
Honolulu, HI 96817
(808) 521-1787
Fax (808) 521-3299
E-mail naswhi@aloha.net

Idaho Chapter
200 N. 4th St., Ste. 20
Boise, ID 83702
(208) 343-2752
Fax (208) 385-0166
E-mail nasw-id@rmci.net

Illinois Chapter
   180 N. Michigan Ave., Ste. 400
   Chicago, IL 60601
   (312) 236-8308
   Fax (312) 236-6627 or 8410
   E-mail office@naswil.org
   Government Affairs
   E-mail smills@naswil.org
   Web site www.mtco.com/~rlongmsw/ilsw.htm

Indiana Chapter
   1100 W. 42nd St., Ste. 375
   Indianapolis, IN 46208
   (317) 923-9878
   Fax (317) 925-9364
   E-mail naswind@aol.com

Iowa Chapter
   4211 Grand Ave., Level 3
   Des Moines, IA 50312
   (515) 277-1117
   Fax (515) 277-2277
   E-mail naswiowa@aol.com

Kansas Chapter
   Jayhawk Towers
   700 S.W. Jackson St., Ste. 801
   Topeka, KS 66603-3740
   (785) 354-4804
   Fax (785) 354-1456
   E-mail naswks@mail.cjnetworks.com

Kentucky Chapter
310 St. Clair, Ste. 104
Frankfort, KY 40601
(502) 223-0245
Fax (502) 223-0525
E-mail naswky@aol.com
Web site members.aol.com/NASWKY/index.html

Louisiana Chapter
700 N. 10th St., Ste. 200
Baton Rouge, LA 70802
(504) 346-1234
1-800-899-1984
Fax (504) 346-5035
E-mail naswla@intersurf.com
Web site http://www.intersurf.com/~naswla

Maine Chapter
222 Water St.
Hallowell, ME 04347-1397
(207) 622-7592
Fax (207) 623-4860
E-mail nasw99me@aol.com

Maryland Chapter
5710 Executive Dr., #105
Baltimore, MD 21228
(410) 788-1066
Fax (410) 747-0635
E-mail chapter@nasw-md.org
Web site www.nasw-md.org

Massachusetts Chapter
   14 Beacon St., #409
   Boston, MA 02108
   (617) 227-9635
   Fax (617) 227-9877
   E-mail chapter@naswma.org
   E-mail cbrill@naswma.org

Michigan Chapter
   741 N. Cedar St., Ste. 100
   Lansing, MI 48906
   (517) 487-1548
   Fax (517) 487-0675
   E-mail nasw-michigan@usa.net

Minnesota Chapter
   1885 University Ave. W.
   St. Paul, MN 55104
   (612) 293-1935
   Fax (612) 293-0952
   E-mail ingra002@tc.umn.edu

Mississippi Chapter
   P.O. Box 4228
   Jackson, MS 39216
   (601) 981-8359
   1-800-543-7098
   Fax (601) 981-6922
   E-mail naswms@aol.com
   Web site http://members.aol.com/naswms

Missouri Chapter
    Parkade Ctr., Ste. 138
    601 Business Loop, 70 W.
    Columbia, MO 65203
    (573) 874-6140
    1-800-333-6279
    Fax (573) 874-8738
    E-mail nasw-mo@usi.com

Montana Chapter
    25 S. Ewing, Ste. 406
    Helena, MT 59601
    (406) 449-6208
    Fax (406) 449-2533
    E-mail naswmt@mt.net
    Web site www.mt.net/~naswmt

Nebraska Chapter
    P.O. Box 83732
    Lincoln, NE 68501
    (402) 477-7344
    1-800-737-6279
    Fax (402) 476-6547
    E-mail assoc@navix.net
    Web site www.homestead.com/naswne

Nevada Chapter
    1651 E. Flamingo Rd.
    Las Vegas, NV 89119
    (702) 791-5872
    Fax (702) 791-5873
    E-mail naswnv@worldnet.att.net
    Web site www.angelfire.com/nv/nasw

New Hampshire Chapter
 c/o NH Association for the Blind
 25 Walker St.
 Concord, NH 03301
 (603) 226-7135
 Fax (603) 228-3836
 E-mail naswnh@worldpath.net

New Jersey Chapter
 2 Quarterbridge Plaza
 Hamilton, NJ 08619
 (609) 584-5686
 Fax (609) 584-5681
 E-mail naswnj@aol.com
 Web site www.stockton.edu/~falkd/nasw.htm

New Mexico Chapter
 1503 University Blvd., N.E.
 Albuquerque, NM 87102
 (505) 247-2336
 Fax (505) 243-0446 (attn: Dolores)
 E-mail nasw@thuntek.net
 Web site www.naswnm.org/

New York City Chapter
 50 Broadway, 10th Floor
 New York, NY 10004
 (212) 668-0050
 Fax (212) 668-0305
 E-mail schachter@naswnyc.org
 Web site www.naswnyc.org/

New York State Chapter
    188 Washington Ave.
    Albany, NY 12210
    (518) 463-4741
    1-800-724-6279 (in state)
    Fax (518) 463-6446
    E-mail naswnys@aol.com
    Web site www.naswnys.org

North Carolina Chapter
    P.O. Box 27582
    Raleigh, NC 27611-7581
    (919) 828-9650
    1-800-280-6207
    Fax (919) 828-1341
    E-mail naswnc@aol.com
    Web site http://members.aol.com/naswnc

North Dakota Chapter
    P.O. Box 1775
    Bismarck, ND 58502-1775
    (701) 223-4161
    Fax (701) 224-9824
    E-mail nasw@aptnd.com
    Web site http://www.aptnd.com/NASW

Ohio Chapter
    118 E. Main St., Ste. 3 W.
    Columbus, OH 43215
    (614) 461-4484
    Fax (614) 461-9793
    E-mail ohnasw@aol.com

Oklahoma Chapter
116 E. Sheridan, #210
Oklahoma City, OK 73104
(405) 239-7017
Fax (405) 236-3638
E-mail naswok@ionet.net
Web site www.ionet.net/~naswok/

Oregon Chapter
7688 S.W. Capitol Hwy.
Portland, OR 97219
(503) 452-8420
Fax (503) 452-8506
E-mail nasw@earthlink.net
Web site www.nasworegon.com

Pennsylvania Chapter
1337 N. Front St.
Harrisburg, PA 17102
(717) 232-4125
Fax (717) 232-4140
E-mail exec@nasw-pa.org
Web site www.nasw-pa.org

Puerto Rico Chapter
P.O. Box 192051
San Juan, PR 00919-2051
(787) 758-3588
Fax (787) 281-8433

Rhode Island Chapter
260 W. Exchange St.
Providence, RI 02903
(401) 274-4940
Fax (401) 274-4941
E-mail rinasw@aol.com

South Carolina Chapter
P.O. Box 5008
Columbia, SC 29250
(803) 256-8406
Fax (803) 254-4116
E-mail scnasw@earthlink.net
Web site www.scnasw.org

South Dakota Chapter
830 State St.
Spearfish, SD 57783
(605) 339-9104
Fax (605) 339-9104
E-mail sdnasw@ideasign.com

Tennessee Chapter
1808 W. End Ave., Ste. 805
Nashville, TN 37203
(615) 321-5095
Fax (615) 327-2676
E-mail tnnasw@aol.com
Web site www.bcity.com/tnnasw

Texas Chapter
810 W. 11th St.
Austin, TX 78701
(512) 474-1454
1-800-888-6279
Fax (512) 474-1317
E-mail naswtx@realtime.net
Web site www.naswtx.org/

Utah Chapter
University of Utah GSSW #229
395 S. 1500 E.
Salt Lake City, UT 84106
(801) 583-8855
Fax (801) 583-6218
E-mail utnasw@aros.net
Web site www.utnasw.org

Vermont Chapter
P.O. Box 1348
Montpelier, VT 05601
(802) 223-1713
Fax (802) 457-3645
E-mail naswvt@madriver.com

Virginia Chapter
1506 Staples Mill Rd.
Richmond, VA 23230
(804) 204-1339
Fax (804) 204-1539
E-mail naswva@earthlink.net

Virgin Islands
Havensight Secretarial Services
2 Buccaneer Mall
St. Thomas, VI 00802
(340) 776-3424
Fax (340) 777-8108

Washington Chapter
    2366 Eastlake Ave. E., Rm. 302
    Seattle, WA 98102
    (206) 322-4344
    1-800-864-2078 (in-state only)
    Fax (206) 322-4303
    E-mail nasw@jetcity.com

West Virginia Chapter
    1608 Virginia St. E.
    Charleston, WV 25311
    (304) 343-6141
    Fax (304) 343-3295
    E-mail naswwv@aol.com
    Web site www.naswwv.org/

Wisconsin Chapter
    16 N. Carroll St., Ste. 220
    Madison, WI 53703
    (608) 257-6334
    Fax (608) 257-8233
    E-mail naswwi@aol.com

Wyoming Chapter
    2601 Central Ave.
    Cheyenne, WY 82001
    (307) 634-2118
    Fax (307) 634-7512
    E-mail wynasw@worldnet.att.net

Chronic Fatigue

The CFIDS Association of America, Inc.
P.O. Box 220398
Charlotte, NC 28222-0398
1-800-442-3437 (44-CFIDS) or (704) 362-2343
Fax (704) 365-9755
E-mail info@cfids.org

Allergy Asthma Information Center & Hot line
P.O. Box 1766
Rochester, NY 14603
1-800-727-5400

American Academy of Allergy and Immunology
611 E. Wells St.
Milwaukee, WI 53202
1-800-822-2762

American Chronic Pain Association
P.O. Box 850
Rocklin, CA 95677
(916) 632-0922

American College of Allergy and Immunology
800 E. Northwest Hwy., Ste. 1080
Palatine, IL 60067-6516
1-800-842-7777

Candida Research Foundation
Elizabeth Naugle, Director
P.O. Drawer J-F
College Station, TX 77840

Center for Fatigue Sciences
Dr. Ruby Simpkins, Director
28240 Agoura Rd., Ste. 201
Agoura Hills, CA 91301

CFIDS Activation Network (CAN)
P.O. Box 345
Larchmont, NY 10538
(212) 627-5631

CFS Crisis Center
27 W. 20th St., Ste. 703
New York, NY 10011
(212) 691-4800
Fax (212) 691-5113

Chemical Injury Information Network
P.O. Box 301
White Sulphur Springs, MT 59645-0301
(406) 547-2255

The Cheney Clinic, P.A.
10620 Park Rd.
Charlotte, NC 28210
(704) 542-7444

Chicago CFS Association
818 Wenonah Ave.
Oak Park, IL 60304
(708) 524-9322

Compuserve CFIDS Support Area
CFS/CFIDS/FMS Section (16)
Health & Fitness Forum (GOODHEALTH)
CFIDS Info (505) 898-4635
Compuserve Info 1-800-898-8199

The Connecticut CFIDS Association
 P.O. Box 9582
 Forestville, CT 06011
 (203) 582-3437; (582-CFIDS)

Sensitive To a Toxic Environment (STATE)
 (For people with multiple chemical sensitivities
 The STATE Foundation
 P.O. Box 834
 Orchard Park, NY 14127
 (716) 675-1164

National CFIDS Foundation
 103 Aletha Rd.
 Needham, MA 02492
 (781) 449-3535
 Fax (781) 449-8606 or (781) 925-3393

National CFS & Fibromyalgia Association
 P.O. Box 18426
 Kansas City, MO 64133
 (816) 313-2000

Fibromyalgia Network
 5700 Stockdale Hwy., Ste. 100
 Bakersfield, CA 93309
 Info (805) 631-1950 from 10 A.M. to 2 P.M. Pacific

American Academy of Environmental Medicine
 P.O. Box 16106
 Denver, CO 80216
 (303) 622-9755

Useful Web sites

American Counseling Association
   www.counsling.org

American Psychoanalytic Association
   www.apsa.org

American Psychological Association
   www.apa.org

The National Mental Health Services
Knowledge Exchange Network
   www.mentalhealth.org

Mental Health Net
   www.chmc.com

RXList, The Internet Drug Index
   www.rxlist.com
   www.pharmweb.net

Useful Newsgroups

alt.support.depression

alt.support.depression.manic

alt.support.depression.seasonal

soc.support.depression.crisis

soc.support.depression.manic

soc.support.depression.family

soc.support.depression.seasonal

soc.suppport.depression.treatment

Glossary

Adrenaline. A hormone produced by the body when we are under stress; adrenaline increases our heart rate, blood flow, and blood pressure.

Agitated depression. Occurs when you're anxious and depressed. You have many of the symptoms of major depression, but you have the added symptoms of anxiety disorders.

Anorexia nervosa. An eating disorder characterized by food refusal and self-starvation.

Atypical depression. You're depressed but have some of the symptoms in "reverse." Anxiety and phobias are also not unusual nor are temporary "remissions." Here, you may feel fine when "good things" happen, but as soon as a small disappointment hits, you crash back down again.

Bacterial cystitis. A urinary tract infection.

Binge eating disorder. Compulsive overeating.

Bioethicist. A professional who is trained to facilitate ethical and moral practices and decision making in health-care settings.

Biologically informed psychotherapy. This is "biopsychiatry," where your therapist believes depression is a medical problem triggered by some life pressure or stressor. Medication combined with talk therapy is the preferred approach.

Bipolar I disorder. A mood disorder characterized by two moods, which fluctuate between highs and lows.

Bipolar II disorder. A less severe form of manic-depression.

Bulimia nervosa. An eating disorder characterized by bingeing followed by purging.

Chronic fatigue syndrome (CFS). Symptoms of fibromyalgia (chronic muscle and joint aches and pains), accompanied by flulike symptoms and extreme fatigue. Also known as myalgic encephalomyelitis and postviral fatigue syndrome.

Cognitive-behavioral therapy. A form of therapy based on the premise "what you think can affect how you feel." It focuses on changing and shifting your perspective in order to bring happiness into your life.

Cortisol. The hormone released by the adrenal gland in response to stress.

Cyclothymia. Barely recognizable manic-depression, characterized by a subtle manifestation of manic features.

Depression with catatonic features. A severe state, where the sufferer is immobile or in a trance of sorts.

Dysthymia. A chronic low mood that manifests as a bad attitude to life and is considered a mild depression.

Endometriosis. A condition occurring when parts of the uterine lining grow outside of the uterus and into the abdominal cavity.

Euphoric mania. This occurs in less than 40 percent of all people with bipolar I, and is characterized by an inflated sense of self-esteem. Hallucinations and delusions at this stage are not uncommon.

Fibromyalgia. A soft-tissue disorder that causes you to hurt all over—all the time. Appears to be triggered and/or aggravated by stress.

Hyperthyroidism. Overactive thyroid gland.

Hypomania. A mild mania.

Hypothyroidism. An underactive thyroid gland.

Interpersonal therapy. A form of therapy based on the premise that your interpersonal relationships interfere with your quality of life.

Interstitial cystitis (IC). An inflammation of the interstitium, the space between the bladder lining and the bladder muscle.

Irritable bowel syndrome (IBS). Unusual bowel patterns that alternate between diarrhea and constipation, and everything in between. Also called *functional bowel disorder.*

Melancholic depression. Similar to major depression but more severe than a severe episode of major depression.

Mixed states. Symptoms of both mania and depression at once.

Postpartum depression (PPD). A depression that occurs after childbirth, which affects 10 to 15 percent of the postpartum population.

Postpartum psychosis. When a psychosis develops after the birth of the baby. Here, the new mother has lost touch with reality.

Postpartum thyroiditis. Occurs when the thyroid becomes inflamed after delivery and is either overactive or underactive.

Premenstrual dysphoric disorder (PDD). A new term introduced to replace PT; it does not rule out premenstrual symptoms that occur outside of the luteal phase of the menstrual cycle.

Psychiatrist. A medical doctor who specializes in the medical treatment of mental illness, who can prescribe drugs.

Psychoanalysis. A style of psychotherapy that involves journeying back into your childhood.

Psychologist. A person who is licensed to practice therapy with either a master's degree or a doctoral degree.

Psychotic depression. You're depressed—and you've lost touch with reality. This is a bad combination and is characterized by hallucinations, delusions, and hearing voices.

Rapid cycler. A person who experiences four or more episodes of mania or mixed states per year.

Recurrent depression. You're depressed, or have been depressed, but despite treatment with antidepressants, your episodes of depression recur. This suggests bipolar depression of some form.

Seasonal affective disorder (SAD). A mood disorder triggered by changes in seasons. The typical sufferer notices symptoms of depression during the winter.

Unipolar disorder. A mood disorder characterized by one low or blue mood, such as major depression.

Bibliography

Allardice, Pamela. *Essential Oils: The Fragrant Art of Aromatherapy.* Vancouver: Raincoast Books, 1999.

"Antidepressants' Impact Mainly from Boost of Getting Treated, Study Suggests." *The Associated Press,* 20 July 1998.

Bellafante, Ginia. "Who Put the 'Me' in Feminism?" *Time,* 29 June 1998.

Boston Globe Magazine 8, 19:99.

Breen, Mary J. "Poverty and Ill Health." In *The Healthsharing Book: Resources for Canadian Women.* Toronto: The Women's Press, 1985.

Breggin, Peter R. *Toxic Psychiatry.* New York: St. Martin's Press, 1991.

Breggin, Peter R., and Ginger Ross Breggin. *Talking Back to Prozac.* New York: St. Martin's Press, 1994.

Burstow, Bonnie. "Women and Therapy." In *The Healthsharing Book: Resources for Canadian Women.* Toronto: The Women's Press, 1985.

Burstow, Bonnie, and Don Weitz. *Shrink Resistant: The Struggle against Psychiatry in Canada.* Vancouver: New Star Books, 1998.

Bursztajn, Harold J., and Archie Brodsky. "Authenticity and Autonomy in the Managed-Care Era: Forensic Psychiatric Perspectives." *The Journal of Clinical Ethics* 5, no. 3 (fall 1994): 237.

Caplan, Paula J. *They Say You're Crazy: How the World's Most Powerful Psychiatrists Decide Who's Normal.* New York: Addison-Wesley Publishing Co., 1995.

Carroll, Rory. "Recovered Memory Techniques Are Bogus, Report Says." *The Guardian*, 13 January 1998.

Cass, Hyla. *St. John's Wort: Nature's Blues Buster.* New York: Avery Publishing Group, 1998.

Costin, Carolyn. *The Eating Disorder Sourcebook*, 2d ed. Los Angeles: Lowell House, 1999.

Dadd, Debra Lynn. *The Nontoxic Home and Office.* Los Angeles: Jeremy P. Tarcher, 1992.

"Depression Medicines Can Kill Women's Sex Drive." *The Vancouver Sun,* 5 May 1997.

Dreher, Henry, and Alice D. Domar. *Healing Mind, Healthy Woman.* New York: Henry Holt and Co., 1996.

Environmental Research Foundation. "Major Causes of Ill Health." *Rachel's Environment & Health Weekly #584.* http://www.rachel.org/bulletin/index.cfm?St=3 (2 February 1998).

"FDA Approves Sibutramine to Treat Obesity." FDA Talk Paper, Food and Drug Administration U.S. Department of Health and Human Services, 24 November 1997.

"Food Alone Can't Always Provide Requisite Nutrition." *The Globe and Mail,* 28 September 1998.

Frances, Allen, and Michael B. First. *Your Mental Health: A Layman's Guide to The Psychiatrist's Bible.* New York: Scribner, 1998.

Fransen, Jenny, and I. Jon Russell. *The Fibromyalgia Help Book.* New York: Smith House Press, 1996.

Friedan, Betty. *The Feminine Mystique*. New York: Dell Publishing Co., 1963.

Greenberg, Brigitte. "Stress Hormone Linked to High-Fat Snacking in Women." The Associated Press, 4 April 1998.

Greenspan, Miriam. *A New Approach to Women and Therapy*, 2d ed. Blue Ridge Summit, Pa: Tab Books, 1993.

Guidelines for Conducting Assessments of Capacity. Office of the Public Guardian and Trustee, Ontario Ministry of the Attorney General. The Queen's Printer for Ontario, 7 June 1996.

Healthy Weight Journal 12, 5 (1998): 66.

Hendren, John, "Popular Herbal Remedy Reportedly Fails Potency Tests." *The Associated Press*, 31 August 1998.

"Investing in Pride." *The Toronto Star*, 10 October 1998.

Jacobson, James L., and Alan M. Jacobson. *Psychiatric Secrets: Questions You Will Be Asked on Rounds, in the Clinic, and on Oral Exams*. Philadelphia: Hanley and Belfus, 1996.

Jamison, Kay Redfield. *An Unquiet Mind: A Memoir of Moods and Madness*. New York: Vintage Books, 1995.

Joffe, Russell, and Anthony Levitt. *Conquering Depression*. Hamilton: Empowering Press, 1998.

Johnson, Catherine. *When to Say Goodbye to Your Therapist*. New York: Simon and Schuster, 1988.

"Keeping Women in Line." News segment. Appeared on *ABC-NEWS 20/20*, originally air date 21 July 1995.

Kotulak, Ronald. "Researchers: Lack of Sleep May Cause Aging, Stress, Flab." *Chicago Tribune*, 5 April 1998.

Kramer, Peter D. *Listening to Prozac*. New York: Penguin Books, 1993.

Laidlaw, Toni Ann, and Cheryl Malmo. *Healing Voices: Feminist Approaches to Therapy with Women*. San Francisco: Jossey-Bass Publishers, 1990.

Lark, Susan M. *Chronic Fatigue and Tiredness*. Los Altos, Calif.: Westchester Publishing Co., 1993.

Leibenluft, Ellen. "Why Are So Many Women Depressed?" *Women's Health* 9, 2 (summer 1998).

Leutwyler, Kristin. "Dying to Be Thin." *Women's Health* 9, 2 (summer 1998).

Linton, Marilyn. *Taking Charge by Taking Care.* Toronto: Macmillan Canada, 1996.

McConnell, Kathleen, and Mariana Valverde, eds. *The Health-sharing Book: Resources for Canadian Women.* Toronto: The Women's Press, 1985.

Mattila, Antti. "Life at The Crossroads: Depression—Philosophical Perspectives." Paper presented at The Fourth International Conference on Philosophical Practice, Bergisch Gladbach, Germany, August 3–7, 1998.

Morin, Benoit. "Suffering: A Philosophical Pathology." Paper delivered at the Canadian Bioethics Society Conference, Toronto, Ontario, October 16, 1998.

Myers, Michael. "SIBUTRAMINE—A Medication to Assist with Weight Management." http://www.weight.com/sibutramine.html (18 July 1999).

"National Eating Disorders Screening Program." American Anorexia Bulimia Association Inc. http://www.nmisp.org/eat.htm.

Nelson, Philip K. "Defining Chronic Fatigue Syndrome." *The Manasota Palmetto,* January 1995.

Nichols, Mark. "Questioning Prozac." *Maclean's,* 23 May 1994.

"Numerous Roadblocks Keeping Botanicals Across Border." *The Globe and Mail,* 28 September 1998.

Orbach, Susie. *Fat Is a Feminist Issue.* New York: Berkley Books, 1990.

Papolos, Dimitri, and Janice Papolos. *Overcoming Depression,* 3d ed. New York: HarperCollins, 1997.

Pepper-Smith, Robert, William R.C. Harvey, and M. Silberfeld. "Competency and Practical Judgment." *Theoretical Medicine* 17, 2 (June 1996).

"Placebo or Pharmacological Effect with Antidepressant." *The Associated Press,* 20 July 1998.

"Prozac: Help or Hype?" *Health for Women* 7, 2 (spring/summer 1998).

Quinn, Brian P. *The Depression Sourcebook.* Los Angeles: Lowell House, 1997.

Recer, Paul. "Women Hurt More, in More Places, but Cope Better, Studies Say." *The Associated Press,* 7 April 1998.

Roberts, Francine M. *The Therapy Sourcebook.* Los Angeles: Lowell House, 1998.

Rosenthal, M. Sara. *The Breast Sourcebook,* 2d ed. Los Angeles: Lowell House, 1999.

———. *The Breastfeeding Sourcebook,* 2d ed. Los Angeles: Lowell House, 1999.

———. *The Gynecological Sourcebook,* 3d ed. Los Angeles: Lowell House, 1999.

———. *The Pregnancy Sourcebook,* 3d ed. Los Angeles: Lowell House, 1999.

Roth, Loren H., Alan Meisel, and Charles W. Lidz. "Tests of Competency to Consent to Treatment." *The American Journal of Psychiatry* 134, 4 (1977).

"Sibutramine: Replacement for 'Fen/Phen'?" *Medical Sciences Bulletin* no. 239. http://pharminfo.com/pubs/msb/sibutramine 239.html (7 September 1997).

Statistics on domestic violence. Senate Judiciary Committee, University of Maryland Women's Studies Database. http://www.inform.umd.edu/Ed/Res/topics/Women's/Studies.

Statistics on female employment. Fair Pay Clearinghouse, Women's Bureau, U.S. Department of Labor. http://www.dol.gov/dol/wb/public/programs/fpc.htm.

Steward, Donna E., and Gail Erlick Robinson. "Violence Against Women." In *Advances in Psychiatry.* London: J.C. Oldham, 1995.

"Study Further Links Smoking to Depression." *Reuters News Service,* 10 February 1998.

Sturdivant, Susan. *Therapy with Women: A Feminist Philosophy of Treatment.* New York: Springer Publishing Co., 1980.

Szasz, Thomas S. *The Myth of Mental Illness: Foundations of a Theory of Personal Conduct.* New York: Harper & Row Publishers, 1974.

Szasz, Thomas. *Cruel Compassion: Psychiatric Control of Society's Unwanted.* New York: John Wiley & Sons, Inc., 1994.

Wenger, Neil S., and Jodi Halpern. "Can a Patient Refuse a Psychiatric Consultation to Evaluate Decision-Making Capacity?" *The Journal of Clinical Ethics* 5, 3 (fall 1994): 230.

"Women Find Themselves Courted by Pharmaceutical Firms." *The Associated Press,* 20 July 1998.

"Your Medical Test Guide." *Health for Women* 7, 2 (spring/-summer 1998).

Zellerbach, Merla. *The Allergy Sourcebook.* Los Angeles: Lowell House, 1996.

Index

A

acupuncture, 186–87
alcohol, 47–48
alternative therapies, investigating risks, 195–96
alternative therapies and CFS, 58–59
anhedonia (nothing gives pleasure)
described, 8, 9
different ways of expressing, 8
Overcoming Depression (Papolos and Papolos), 9
sex, loss of interest in, 9
suicidal thoughts, help for, 9
weight gain, 8, 9
weight loss, 8
antidepressants
and CFS, 58

Monoamine oxidase inhibitors (MAOIs), 175
Reversible inhibitors of monoamine oxidase A (RIMAs), 176
Selective serotonin reuptake inhibitors (SSRIs), 176
Serotonin-norepinephrine reuptake inhibitors (SNRIs), 176
Tricyclic antidepressants (TCAs), 175
antiobesity pills
Fenfluramine and Phentermine (Fen/Phen), 85–86
Orlistat (Xenical), 85
sibutramine (Meridia), 86
aromatherapy, 72
asylum life, 114
ayurvedic medicine, 187–88

B

bath, taking, 73
bathroom, hazards of not being able to go
bathroom liberties, 65
   diapers, being forced to wear, 65
   "holding it" in workplace, 64
   restraining bowel movements, 64–65
bathroom blues and stress
   about, 63
   bladder problems, 70–71
   hazards of not be able to go, 64–65
   irritable bowels, 65–70
beauty standards and depression, 15
biopsychiatry, 134–35
bipolar disorder, signs of
   about, 30–31
   An Unquiet Mind (Redfield Jamison), 31–32, 33–34, 164
   shades of moods, 32–33
bipolar disorders
   about, 28
   crashes, 33–34
   cyclothymia, 37–38
   dramatic mood swings, 28–29

episodes of mania, characteristics of, 28
   initial appearance of, 29
   manic-depression, about, 28
   myth of mania, 29–30
   signs of, 30–33
   types of, 34–36
   your mood cycle, 36–37
bipolar disorders, types of, 34–36
bipolar I, types of manias and mood states
   bipolar I euphoric mania, 35
   mixed states, 35
bipolar I disorder
   about, 34
   depressive episodes, 34–35
   manic episodes, 34
   types of manias and mood states in, 35
bipolar II disorder
   about, 35–36
   hypomania, about, 36
bladder problems
   causes, 71
   explained, 70
   symptoms, 70–71
body image
   about, 75–76
   body as object in culture, 76
   body-image problem, 87
   body sculpting, 77
   compulsive eating, 83–84

depression, stress, and weight, 86–87
drug treatment for obesity, 84–86
fat, perception of, 81–83
low self-esteem and, 77
New York Times, 76
relationship with body, 76
signs of body-image or eating problem, 78
thinness, perception of, 79–81
too much focus on body, 77
body image, hormones and psychological issues
body image, 75–87
depression and menopause, 105–7
hard time after having baby, 99–105
your time of month, 88–99
body-image problem
professional help, when to seek, 87
reasonable weight, questions for establishing, 87
British Journal Nutrition, 86

C

caffeine, 47
carbohydrates and moods, 178–79
caring for yourself
carbohydrates and moods, 178–79
common sense, 181
diet and depression, 178
exercise and depression, 179–80
herbs, 181–86
CFS (chronic fatigue syndrome), symptoms of
Annals of Internal Medicine, 54
causes of, 56–57
defined, 53–54
exercise tolerance, 54–55
fibromyalgia *vs.* CFS, 56
listing of, 54
treatments for, 57–59
what doctor should rule out, 55–56
chemical reactions
exposure to workplace chemicals, 48
Journal of the American Medical Association (JAMA), 48
materials hazardous to health/well-being, 49–50
multiple chemical sensitivity (MCS), 50–51
occupational asthma, causes, 49
reproductive concerns, 51–52

Chesler, Phyllis, 111, 114
chick-flick, 73
Chinese medicine, 188
chiropractic medicine, 188–89
chronic fatigue syndrome
    (CFS)
    about, 52–53
    causes of, 56–57
    defined, 53
    fibromyalgia *vs.* CFS, 56
    other names for, 53
    symptoms of, 53–55
    treatments, 57–59
    what doctor should rule out,
        55–56
cognitive-behavioral therapy,
    135–36
combination therapy
    monitoring needed for
        certain drugs, 162–63
    "treatment-resistant
        depression," 162
common sense, 181
*Compendium of Pharmaceuti-
    cals and Specialties (CPS),*
    168
complementary medicine
    acupuncture, 186–87
    aromatherapy, 187
    ayurvedic medicine, 187–88
    Chinese medicine, 188
    chiropractic medicine,
        188–89
    environmental medicine,

        189
    holistic medicine, 190
    homeopathy, 190–91
    iridology, 191–92
    massage therapy, 192–93
    mind/body medicine, 193
    naturopathy, 193–94
    reflexology, 194–95
compulsive eating
    bingeing and purging, 83
    desire to get fat, 83–84
    typical profile of, 84
concentration (trouble with)
    and depression, 7–8
Conquering Depression (Joffe
    and Levitt), 2
crashes, 33–34
cyclothymia
    about, 37
    symptoms of, 37–38

D

DeFoe, Daniel, 112
depressed or "just sad"
    depression, 6–21
    sadness, 1–6
depression
    causes of, 11–16
    described, 6
    genetic link, 18–19
    psychotic, 27
    reasons for, 19–21
    recurrent, 27

sunlight, lack of, 16. *See also*
    seasonal affective disorder
    (SAD)
as symptom of physical
    ailment, 16–18
symptoms of, 2, 6–10
those affected by, 10–11
depression, all types of
bipolar disorders, 28–38
*DSM IV (Diagnositc and
    Statistical Manual of
    Mental Disorders)*, 23
labeling, 23–24
treating, 38–42
unipolar disorders, 24–27
depression, causes of
depressing circumstances,
    12–16
diagnosis on rise, 11
*Diagnostic and Statistical
    Manual of Mental
    Disorders,* 4th edition
    (DSM IV), American
    Psychiatric Association,
    11
environmental triggers of,
    11–12
depression, circumstances
    causing
about, 12
beauty standards, 15
divorce, 16
hormonal factors, 15. *See
    also* period, having your

illness, 15–16
infertility, 16
menopause, 15. *See also*
    menopause and depres-
    sion
poverty, 14–15
pregnancy. *See* postpartum
    blues
pregnancy loss, 16
sleep deprivation, 45–46
violence, 12–13
violence and pregnancy,
    13–14
workplace stress and/or
    harassment, 15. *See also*
    chemical reactions
depression, masked, 27
depression, reasons for
coping mechanism, 19–20
escaping indecision, 20
larger purpose of, 20–21
depression, signs of
anhedonia: when nothing
    gives pleasure, 8–10
concentration, trouble with,
    7–8
Conquering Depression (Joffe
    and Levitt), 2
insomnia, 7
symptoms of, 2, 7
depression, stress, and weight
British Journal of Nutrition,
    86
cortisol, 86

low-fat eating, 86–87
negative body image and
    resulting depression, 86
stress and weight gain, 86
depression, symptoms, 3–4, 10
depression, those affected by
    statistics on, 10–11
    women, reasons for, 10
depression, treating different
    types of
    about, 38–40
    family support, 41–42
    long-term solutions, 41
    short-term treatment
        strategies, 40–41
depression agitated, 27
depression and menopause
    emotional symptoms, causes
        of, 105
    estrogen loss and mood
        swings, 105–6
    menopause blues, 106–7
    mother/daughter "hormone
        clash," 106
    physical symptoms, 105
depression as symptom of
        physical ailment
    abnormal fatigue: chronic
        fatigue syndrome, 52–59
    about, 43–44
    bathroom blues, 63–71
    chemical reactions, 48–52
    examples of organic or
        physical causes, 16–17

managing stress, 18
seasonal affective disorder
    (SAD): light-deprived,
    61–63
stress and fatigue, normal,
    44–48
stress reduction, 71–73
thyroid disorders, 59–61
working in "sick building,"
    17
depression *vs.* sadness, 3–4
depression with catatonic
    features, 26
*Diagnostic and Statistical
    Manual of Mental Disor-
    ders,* American Psychiatric
    Association, 11
diet, 48
diet and depression, 178
diet modification and CFS, 58
divorce and depression, 16
Domar, Alice, 16, 193
dosages
    about, 170
    monitoring, 170
double depression, 26
downshifting and CFS, 58
drugs, what to ask
    *Compendium of Pharmaceu-
        tical and Specialties
        (CPS),* 168
    dosages, 170
    drug information, finding,
        168

drug studies, 170–71
informed consent and
    medication, 171–73
more questions, 168–70
side effects, 167–68
drugs for depression
combination therapy,
    162–63
Prozac, 158–60
serotonin, 157–58
SSRIs and hypomania,
    160–62
drugs for mania (bipolar
    disorder)
about, 163–64
lithium, 164–66
mania, other effects of, 167
other mood-stabilizing
    drugs, 166–67
problem with treating,
    163–64
drug studies
about, 170–71
"placebo-controlled" trial,
    171
DSM IV (Diagnostic and Statis-
    tical Manual of Mental
    Disorders, 4th edition),
    23
dysthymia
early onset dysthymia, 26
genetic predisposition for,
    25–26
symptoms of, 25, 26

E

electroconvulsive therapy
    (ECT)
about, 173
early years of, 173–74
side effects, 174
twenty-first century and,
    174
environmental medicine, 189
exercise and depression
active living, 180
benefits of aerobic exercise,
    179–80

F

fat, perception of
as excuse for success, 82
as expression of anger, 83
feeling powerless, 81–82
as a protection, 82
when fat means "mother,"
    82–83
fatigue, abnormal. See chronic
    fatigue syndrome
fees for therapist, 130–31
Feminine Mystique, The
    (Friedan), 118
feminism as cure
about, 118–19
liberated women and de-
    pression, 120–22

"Mary Tyler Moore Show, The," 118–19
sexual abuse, stigma of, 119–20
feminist therapy
about, 136
contacting, 138
goals for, 137–38
Fitzgerald, William, 194
Friedan, Betty, 118

G

genetic predisposition to depression
about, 18
critics of genetic linking, 18–19
grieving *vs.* depression
grief, symptoms of progression into depression, 5
grief as cause of sadness, 4
Men Don't Leave (film), 5–6
people more susceptible to depression after loss, 4
pet, grieving loss of, 5
relationship or friendship, grieving loss of, 4

H

Hahnemann, Samuel, 190
Healing Mind, Healthy Woman (Domar), 193

help, finding
family support, 41–42
support groups, 144–48
talk therapy, 140–44
therapist, in search of, 123–34
therapy, styles of, 134–40
Henrik, Per, 192
herbs
classifying, 182
ensuring quality, 183–84
herbal therapies, 181–82
kava root, 184
"nerve herbs," 182
other natural compounds, 185–86
SAM-e, 184–85
St. John's wort, 182–83
herbs, ensuring quality, 183–84
Hite, Shere, 110
holistic medicine, 190
homeopathy, 190–91
hormonal factors and depression, 15
hyperthyroidism, 59
hypomania, 36
hypothyroidism, 59

I

idiopathic fatigue, 56
illness and depression, 15-16.
See also self-healing strategies

infertility and depression, 16
informed consent and
    medication
    adequate informed consent,
        checklist, 172–73
    informed consent, misun-
        derstandings with,
        171–72
insomnia and depression, 7
insurance, health, 131
interpersonal therapy, 139
iridology, 191–192
irritable bowel syndrome (IBS)
    explained, 66
    functional bowel disorder,
        66
    labeling, 65–66
    stress and IBS, 69
    symptoms of, 67–68
    what to rule out, 68–69
    women and IBS, 69–70
irritable bowel syndrome (IBS),
    symptoms of
    about, 67–68
    constipation and diarrhea,
        timing of, 68
    distinguishing from infec-
        tious diarrhea or inflam-
        matory bowel diseases, 68

J

Jensen, Bernard, 192
Joffe, Russell, 2

*Journal of the American Med-
    ical Association (AMA),*
    13, 48

K

kava root, 184
Kinsey, Alfred, 110

L

Lange, Jessica, 5
Levitt, Anthony, 2
lifestyle factors, stress and
    fatigue
    alcohol, 47–48
    caffeine, 47
    diet, 48
    smoking, 47
lithium
    about, 164
    early problems with, 165
    pregnancy and, 166
    side effects of, 165–66
Los Angeles Times, 183

M

Maines, Rachel P., 110
major depression, 24–25
mania, myth of
    highs of manic episodes,
        about, 29–30
    myth of productivity, 29

mania, other effects of, 167
massage therapy
    benefits of, 192, 193
    origins of, 192–93
    *Yellow Emperor's Classic of
    Internal Medicine, The,*
    192
maternal blues
    causes of, 100–1
    symptoms of, 100
    treating, 101
Mattila, Antti, 20
McCartney, James L., 116–17
meditation, modern, 73
melancholic depression, 26
memories: repressed *vs.* false
    about, 141–42
    false memory syndrome,
    142
    recovered memory
    techniques, 142
Men Don't Leave (film), 5–6
menopause
    about, 15
    depression, 105–7
    hormone replacement ther-
    apy (HRT), 106–7
mental health-care rights,
    understanding
    about, 148
    Mental Health Parity Act,
    154
    Mental Health Patient's Bill
    of Rights, 149–53

Mental Health Parity Act, 154
Mental Health Patient's Bill of
    Rights
    accountability, 153
    benefit of design, 153
    benefit of usage, 153
    choice, 152
    confidentiality, 151
    determination of treatment,
    152
    discrimination, 152
    parity, 152
    right to know, 149–51
    treatment review, 153
mind/body medicine, 193
mood cycle
    about, 36–37
    rapid cycling, 36–37
mood-stabilizing drugs, other,
    166–67
multiple chemical sensitivity
    (MCS)
    symptoms, 50
    those at risk for, 50–51

N

names (of therapists), locating
    community family services
    or women's health clinics,
    124–25
    community services listings,
    125
    crisis lines, 125

employee assistance program, 124
friends, 125–26
hospitals, 125
phone book, 126
referrals, 124
natural compounds for combating depression, 185–86
naturopathy, 193–94

O

obesity, drug treatment for
antiobesity pills, 85–86
thyroxine, 84
Overcoming Depression (Papolos and Papolos), 9

P

Packard, Elizabeth, 112
Palmer, Daniel David, 189
Papolos, Dimitri F., 9
Papolos, Janice, 9
period, having your
emotional changes, 91
physical changes, 90–91
positive side, 91
premenstrual dysphoric disorder (PDD), 88
premenstrual signs, experiencing, 89–90

pleasures for unwinding, 72–73
postpartum blues
depression and pregnancy, 99–100
maternal blues, 100–1
postpartum psychosis, 104
postpartum thyroiditis, 104–5
postpartum depression (PPD)
causes of, 102–3
symptoms of, 102
treating, 103–4
poverty
and depression, 14–15
"hidden homeless," 14–15
making ends meet, 14
pregnancy loss and depression, 16
premenstrual changes
about, 96
confusion and negative myths about, 96–97
premenstrual changes, treating
alleviating with drugs, 98–99
natural remedies, 97–98
validation, 97
premenstrual disorder
changes: emotional behavioral, and physical, 92
charting examples, 94, 95
charting premenstrual changes, 92, 93, 95

psychiatric illness and, 92–93

premenstrual signs, 88–89

professionals and corresponding credentials

counselor, 129–30

marriage and family counselor, 130

psychiatric nurse, 129

psychiatrist, 127

psychologist and psychological associate, 127–28

social worker, 128–29

Prozac

bad press about, 159–60

explained, 158

other Prozac-like drugs, 160

predecessors of, 158–59

side effects of, 159

psychiatric patient, long-term, 113–14

psychoanalysis, 139

psychodynamic therapy, 140

psychotherapy, biologically informed, 134–35

R

Redfield Jamison, Kay, 31–32, 33–34, 164

reflexology, 194–95

reproductive concerns

resources for chemical identification and toxins, 51

secondhand smoke, 52

Robinson, Gail Erlick, 13

S

sadness

causes of, 2–3

defined, 1, 2

grieving *vs.* depression, 4–6

sadness *vs.* depression

symptoms of depression, 3–4

symptoms of sadness, 3–4

SAM-e, 184–85

seasonal affective disorder (SAD)

about, 61–62

treating, 62–63

self-healing strategies

complementary medicine, 186–95

how are you, 177–86

risks, 195–96

sex, 73

sexual abuse, stigma of

about, 119

DSM IV (Diagnostic Statistical Manual), 120

post-traumatic label, 120

"recovery movement," 120

sleep deprivation

cortisol, about, 45–46

phases of sleep, 46

repercussions of, 45

"workout time," 46
smoking, 47
solutions, long-term, 41
SSRIs (Selective serotonin re-
    uptake inhibitors) and
    hypomania
    about, 160–61
    other antidepressants,
        161–62
St. John's wort
    benefits of, 182–83
    downside of, 183
    Nutrition Business Journal,
        182
Steinem, Gloria, 77
Steward, Donna E., 13
stress and fatigue, normal
    fatigue, 44–45
    lifestyle factors, 47–48
    raising a family, 46–47
    sleep deprivation, 45–46
stress reduction
    pleasures for unwinding,
        72–73
    sources of stress, suggestions
        for reducing, 71–72
stroll, going for, 73
suicidal thoughts, help for, 9
sunlight, lack of. *See* seasonal
    affective disorder (SAD)
support, family
    about, 41
    how to help, guidance, 42
support, where to look

community-based programs,
    146
things women talk about,
    146–48
support groups
    factors for finding right, 145
    mental health-care rights,
        understanding, 148–54
    value of, 144–45
    where to look, 145–48

T

talk therapy
    about, 140
    hallmarks of good thera-
        pists, 140–41
    memories: repressed *vs.*
        false, 141–42
    rent-a-friend problem, 144
    talking *vs.* drugs, 142–43
    therapy, finishing, 143
    when not to use, 148
Technology of Orgasm: Hysteria,
    the Vibrator, and Women's
    Sexual Satisfaction
    (Maines), 110
therapist, fees
    health insurance, 131
    resources about, 130
therapist, gauging feelings
    about
    age and lifestyle issues,
        133–34

precautions, 132–33
questions to ask yourself,
   131–32
therapist, in search of
about, 123–24
credentials, looking for,
   126–31
feelings about therapist,
   questions to ask yourself,
   131–34
names, locating, 124–26
therapist, looking for credentials
about, 126
credential confusion,
   126–27
fees, 130–31
health insurance, 131
professionals and corre-
   sponding credentials,
   127–30
therapist, relationship with,
   144
therapy, finishing, 143
therapy, styles of
biologically informed
   psychotherapy, 134–35
cognitive-behavioral therapy,
   135–36
feminist therapy, 136–38
interpersonal therapy, 139
psychoanalysis, 139
psychodynamic therapy, 140
therapy, women in male

about, 114–15
Feminine Mystique, The
   (Friedan), 118
male therapists and female
   patients, 117
penis-envy plot, 116
psychological development,
   distorted version of,
   115–16
psychotherapy, critics of,
   118
socioeconomics, 117–18
thinness, achieving
about, 79–80
anorectics, 81
anorexia and bulimia,
   80–81
overexercising, 80
thinness, perception of, 79–81
thyroid disorders
autoimmune thyroid dis-
   eases, 59–60
hyperthyroidism and hy-
   pothyroidism, 59
symptoms, 60–61
thyroid function test, 60
thyroid gland, 59
treatment, 61
thyroid disorders, symptoms
if you're hyperthyroid, 60
if you're hypothyroid, 61
*Thyroid Sourcebook for Women,
   The* (Rosenthal), 105
treatment strategies, short-
   term, 40–41

U

unipolar disorders
  agitated depression, 27
  common characteristic of,
    27
  depression with catatonic
    features, 26
  double depression, 26
  dysthymia, 25–26
  early onset dysthymia, 26
  major depression, 24–25
  masked depression, 27
  melancholic depression, 26
  psychotic depression, 27
  recurrent depression, 27
Unquiet Mind, An (Redfield
  Jamison), 31–32, 33–34,
  164

V

violence and depression
  domestic violence, cycles of,
    12–13
  results of, 13
violence and pregnancy
  about, 13
  *Journal of the American
    Medical Association,* 13
  studies on, 13–14
von Peczely, Ignatz, 192

W

women and depression, liberated
  about, 120–21
  advances in workplace,
    121–22
  psychotherapy, dramatic
    changes in, 122
  Superwoman and Super-
    model, 121
  women's liberation, 121
Women and Madness (Chesler),
  111
women and "madness,"
  history of
  asylum life, 114
  career psych patient,
    113–14
  involuntary confinement,
    112
  madhouses, 111–12
  mental asylums, 112
  mental hospitals, 112–13
  psychiatric services, 113
  women in male therapy,
    114–18
women and medication
  about, 155–56
  antidepressants, 175–76
  drugs for depression,
    157–63
  drugs for mania, 163–67

drugs for mental health disorders, misuse of, 156
drug testing and protective legislation, 156
electroconvulsive therapy (ECT), 173–74
informed consent, about, 156–57
what to ask about drugs, 167–73
women and psychotherapy, history of
about, 109–11
feminism as cure, 118–22
hysteria as diagnosis for depression, 109–10
women and "madness," 111–18
workplace stress and/or harassment, 15. *See also* sleep deprivation and chemical reactions